To Juan, in appreciation! + Remi

Even Greater Things

Hope and Challenge After Vatican II

Bernard Daly,

Mae Daly

and

Bishop Remi J. De Roo

+ Remi J. De Roo

NOVALIS

© 1999 Novalis, Saint Paul University, Ottawa, Canada

Cover: Blair Turner Communications
Layout: Chris Humphrey

Novalis Business Offices
49 Front St. East, Second Floor
Toronto, Ontario
M5E 1B3

1-800-387-7164 or (416) 363-3303

The epigraph quotation of Scripture on page 4 is from the Holy Bible: New International Version, Zondervan Bible Publishers, Grand Raphids, Michigan, © 1978 by the New York International Bible Society. All other Scripture quotations are from the New Revised Standard Version Bible, © 1989 by the Division of Christian Education of the National Council of the Churches of Christ in the U.S.A. Used by permission.

Canadian Cataloguing-in-Publication Data

Daly, Bernard M. (Bernard Michael), 1925-
Even greater things: hope and challenge after Vatican II
Includes bibliographical references.
ISBN 2-89507-002-4
1. Vatican Council (2nd: 1962-1965) I. De Roo, Remi. J.
II. Daly, Mae, 1928-   III. Title.
BX830 1962.D24 1999   262'.52   C98-901417-7

Printed in Canada

To Tom, Pat, Mary Anne, Michael,
Teresa and Timothy

– Mae & Bernard Daly

To all believers
who have shared their stories with me,
especially the people of the diocese of Victoria

– Remi J. De Roo

Believe me when I say that I am in the Father and the Father is in me; or at least believe on the evidence of the miracles themselves. I tell you the truth, anyone who has faith in me will do what I have been doing. He [/she] will do even greater things than these, because I am going to the Father. And I will do whatever you ask in my name, so that the Son may bring glory to the Father. You may ask me for anything in my name, and I will do it.

John 14:11-14
(New International Version)

Contents

Introduction

We begin this book with hope. Our aim is to share that hope. We firmly believe that God is invisibly active in this world, bringing about the divine reign.

Seventy-plus years of life; half a century together in Christian marriage; 48 years as priest and 36 as bishop – our experiences as a couple and as a bishop fill us with hope, despite the suffering and evil we know exist. We talked about our experiences during ten days together in and around Victoria, BC, early in December 1997, with the understanding that our conversations would be the basis for a book Bernard would draft, with Mae and Remi as co-authors and full partners in the project. The format of an exchange of letters evolved after that, as the most flexible way to present both personal and shared opinions.

Since our baptisms as infants, our faith in God has been shaped in the Roman Catholic church. In the light of our faith, we look upon the world around us as both a marvel and a mess. We believe our church has been called by Vatican II to undergo a surge of renewal and reform of which only the first few possibilities have yet been realized. We are called to renewal, in the sense of constantly adapting to meet the new needs of humanity, of which we Christians, God's pilgrim people, are a part. Human discovery (science) and human inventiveness (technology) give rise to unending challenges. New minds in each generation also probe and see deeper into the mystery of God. All this marvel of change calls us as church to renew and update ourselves, in the sense of the *aggiornamento* called for by Pope John XXIII. At the same time, we recognize the mess, in the world at large and in our own lives, caused by our sins and the sins of others. As church members, we are involved in the struggle of good and evil in both the church and the world. The church is therefore called to reform, in the sense of conversion, both as individual members and as an institution, as we also carry on our mission to call all humanity, all the world, to turn to God and be faithful to God's will.

Some people, including some in Vatican offices, are trying to reverse the thrust of Vatican II. Emphasizing the church's divinity, they resist the call to renewal and reform. Many more Catholics simply have not understood the council or taken it seriously enough. Renewal and reform will go on, however, because that is God's will.

We believe that Christ, in and through us, the church, continues in mysterious ways God's work in the world. To our timeless God, that work is all one action; but with our limitations we speak of a series of events: creation; Christ's birth, life, death and resurrection; the sending of the Holy Spirit; our life as the church; our final judgment. We believe we will be judged by how we love God and our neighbours and care for all creation.

We can't get a print-out of how God rates our fidelity and love. However, if we are failing God as much as we are neglecting our neighbours and destroying the rest of creation, we are in big trouble.

The sense, indeed the fear, that humanity is in difficulty is widespread. Some people just give up, as shown by the rise in the number of suicides everywhere. Some lash out in violence against others. Many try to blot out reality in orgies of pleasure-seeking. Many more turn their full attention to piling up personal wealth as a defence against an uncertain future. The result of their efforts is that less than 20 percent of all people control and consume more than 86 percent of all wealth and resources. These United Nations figures reveal two classes of people around the world: the greedy and the needy. Other accounts show widespread and increasing destruction of the natural world which, at creation, God judged to be good and intended for the needs of all.

In the letters which make up this book, we look back at Vatican II (chapters 1 and 2). We highlight some aspects of the renewal and reform to which the Holy Spirit calls us, to make us more faithful to Christ's ways of loving our neighbours and serving the world. Then we look at the world around us, to see both the marvels and the mess we produce by the way we treat nature (Chapter 3) and our neighbours (Chapter 4). The backdrop of this review is God's two-fold primordial commission to us: to cultivate and tend creation for the good of all; and to love our neighbours as ourselves.

God created us female and male, as equals in the divine image, directed to multiply and fill the earth through our enduring, faithful and fruitful love. We look at how we are handling equality (Chapter 5) and fruitfulness (Chapter 6).

What kind of Christians can do God's work in the midst of human weaknesses, as shown by ecological disasters, rampant poverty, male abuse of women, and uncertainty about how to handle human fertility? Christians, we suggest, who really understand what it means to be transformed by the Holy Spirit through baptism and confirmation (Chapter 7). Who feel personally called to stand close to God always, seeking heroism in holiness (Chapter 8). Who, like God, dedicate each "seventh day" to contemplating their week's work and worshipping God by presenting their bodies as living sacrifices (Chapter 9). Who work to fill the visible church with the power of the Spirit and free it from human weaknesses and sins (Chapter 10). Who welcome the signs of "the seeds of the word" in all peoples, building unity among Christians and solidarity with peoples of all religions (Chapter 11).

In a brief epilogue, we try to sum up all our faith, hope and love. We are optimistic. We believe that the church *is* Christ, slain, yet worthy "to receive power and wealth and wisdom and might and honour and glory and blessing" (Revelation 5:12). We believe the church of Christ is still very near to the beginning of its mission. We are talking about a church that we know is possible, is necessary, and *is emerging*. We look forward to a church whose members respond actively to the gifts of the Spirit given to all; a church that welcomes both women and men as equal in God's image; a church in which authority is always exercised as gentle, loving care, especially for the weakest; a church open to the diversity that comes from recognizing that God's love is at work in all peoples; a church constantly renewing and purifying itself in order to bring about the reign of God in every human heart and throughout the universe. We, the church, are called to work at restoring all things in Christ, according to God's loving plan for creation, which God contemplated and found to be very good. We believe that we, as Christ in the world now, have been promised that we can do for our world even greater work than Christ did (John 14:12).

Bernard and Mae Daly
Remi J. De Roo

Acknowledgements

We acknowledge debts of gratitude to family and friends. The latter include members of the Novalis staff.

Our thanks to Cathy Bagnall, Teresa Bolton, Mary Anne Burke, Thomasina and Aaron Dumonceau, Patricia Grappolini, Rosalie Lahey, Alice van Lieshout, Darlene Southwell, Jack Sproule and Diane Tolomeo. They read an early version of the manuscript and gave us their reflections.

Pat Brady and Bill Ryan gave us extensive and detailed critiques of our next-to-last draft, pointed us to helpful background resources, and suggested important adjustments.

Pearl Gervais offered significant insights and challenges as the book was being planned. She also critiqued the entire manuscript and assisted with research on the bibliography.

At Novalis, Stephen Scharper welcomed our first offering and helped to shape the final text. Chris Humphrey handled the major editing tasks, Anne Louise Mahoney did detailed revisions, and Nancy Keyes carefully proof-read the text. Michael O'Hearn and Lauretta Santarossa smoothed the administrative path.

Abbreviations

Throughout our book, a standard abbreviation system is used for references to Vatican II texts, as follows: AA, decree on the lay apostolate; AG, decree on missionary activity; CD, decree on the office of bishops; DH, declaration on religious freedom; DV, constitution on revelation; GE, decree on Christian education; GS, constitution on the church in the modern world; IM, decree on the media of communication; LG, constitution on the church; NA, declaration on relations with non-Christian religions; OE, declaration on Catholic Eastern churches; OT, decree on the training of priests; PC, decree on the renewal of religious orders; PO, decree on the ministry and life of priests; SC, constitution on the liturgy; UR, decree on ecumenism. For example, (AA, 1) in our text would refer to Article 1 of the decree on the lay apostolate. We used the same abbreviation system for papal documents: UUS for John Paul's 1995 encyclical on Christian unity, *Ut Unum Sint;* CL for *Christifideles Laici,* his 1988 apostolic exhortation summing up the 1987 synod on the laity; EN for *Evangelii Nuntiandi,* Paul VI's summary of the 1974 synod on evangelization; and TMA for *Tertio Millennio, Adveniente,* John Paul's apostolic letter on the third millenium.

—— 1 ——

Why Remember
the Second Vatican Council?

This chapter introduces the Second Vatican Council, which was held in four ses-
sions in the autumns of 1962 to 1965. It recalls what the council was and what
it tried to do. Vatican II was a gathering of all the bishops of the Catholic
church, around Pope John XXIII for its first session, and around his successor,
Pope Paul VI, for the final three. The council's general aim, outlined by John
XXIII, was to update the church, to promote Christian unity, and to prepare the
church for greater service in a rapidly changing world. From the time he
announced it, John XXIII faced some opposition from those, including some
Vatican officials, who resisted change and thought a council unnecessary. That
resistance continued during the four sessions, and divided the bishops into a
Roman minority and the majority who supported John XXIII's vision. Public
opinion in the church since the council has been similarly divided. This chapter
begins with an overview of post-council public opinion. It goes on to sketch how
the council was organized and to explore the background of some of the issues
debated by the bishops. Some features of the pre-council church are recalled.

Dear Remi,

"Vatican II? Forget it! It's history." That's what some friends of ours said the
other day when we told them we were working with you on a book about the
council and the future of the church and of the world. They'd call themselves
"graduate Catholics." They say most things about the church are relics of a

past that won't return. They are even pessimistic about the future of humanity. They fear that the earth's resources will be depleted, that their own living standards will fall, and that violence will escalate.

Probably the main difference between them and us is that they tend to think that the church has had its moment in history. In their eyes, it is a failing, declining institution. We believe that the church – as God's people, and not necessarily with all of today's institutional form – is far from finished. In fact, it is much closer to the beginning of its mission than to the end of it. Look at all that still needs to be done, to restore all things in Christ, in the love of God! As for the human race, we know the risks involved in environmental degradation, the destruction of species and the threat of weapons of mass destruction. We also know God has promised that the Spirit will be with us always. And we know *the Spirit will prevail.*

Vatican II was a time of great excitement and hope, our friends agree. They recall the three main goals that John XXIII set for the council: to renew and update the church (*aggiornamento*); to promote the unity of Christians; to prepare the church to serve the modern world better. They call the council an opportunity wasted and lost over the years since it closed in 1965. They scoff at us a bit. The three of us – a bishop, a journalist who was at the council, and his wife – might be nostalgic and want to talk about Vatican II. Not they. It's history!

We agree to disagree. We disagree for two reasons. The main one is our faith that Vatican II was the work of the Holy Spirit, even though it was also highly political; and church politics are still going on, as they always will. Also, we see plenty of evidence that the church is better off today than if Vatican II had never happened.

"A storm-tossed ship"

We try to understand why many things in the Catholic church remained virtually unchanged in the 400 years from the close of the Council of Trent in 1563 until the opening of Vatican II in 1962. We know people thought differently then, and we don't judge them. But we cannot imagine what a mess we'd be in today if the church had continued to try to stand still, outside history, during the past five tumultuous decades. The late Cardinal Suenens of

2

Belgium, a leading advocate of change at Vatican II, said that if the post-council church is like a storm-tossed ship, this is in part the result of "the condition of the sea." The church exists in and for the world. It is profoundly affected by the extraordinary upheavals that are transforming the world. England's Cardinal Hume said more recently that the church in our day is undergoing the most profound, far-reaching and positive renewal since the time of the Counter-Reformation in the seventeenth century. "Some see only death. Others already discern resurrection," Hume observed. "To the new world being created around us, the renewed church, the Easter people, brings a message of life and hope."

We agree a new world is being created. It needs a message of life and hope and a sense of purpose and direction. To make that contribution to the world is our job as Christians. That is why we believe we have to continue and expand the renewal and reform of the church begun at Vatican II.

A workshop for adult religious development which we attended recently proved that Catholics can still get excited about Vatican II. In general, though, the story of that great council is not well known. It is not part of our religious culture, the way the exodus from Egypt is a story which the Jews have kept alive, and which we Christians share. Yet, the God who led the Israelites into the promised land is the same Spirit who inspired Vatican II and is leading Christians into the twenty-first century and beyond. And just as the Israelites had their leaders – Abraham and Sarah, Moses, Miriam, Aaron, and the long list of later prophets – so, too, Vatican II had Popes John XXIII and Paul VI and the many other visionary bishops who led it in renewing the church. Jewish families keep retelling the Passover story. Similarly, we must not let Vatican II slip into the category of "The Greatest Story Never Told." That was the theme of the workshop we attended, suggesting the extent to which the council risks being ignored.

Some people at that workshop were born after the council opened in October 1962, and so had no direct memories. Most had been in grade school or high school during the council, 36 years ago. They spoke of vague recollections of Pope John XXIII calling a meeting in Rome of more than 2,400 bishops from all parts of the Catholic world, western and eastern. Most workshop participants are active in their parishes. They brought to the discussion an awareness that Vatican II had launched major changes in the church. Mostly, they agreed with those changes, and they wanted change to continue. "I wasn't a Catholic before the council," one woman said, "and I probably wouldn't be one today if there'd been no council."

They had a varied list of issues they said the church would have to face if a Vatican III were convened: genetic engineering, the role of women in the church, deeper reflection on the church as people of God, sexuality, marriage and divorce, the priesthood and celibacy, simplification of vestments and church furnishings, responses to the culture of death, the fact that 90 percent of Canadians call themselves Christian but a much smaller percentage regularly go to church, more emphasis on John XXIII's understanding that power is for service, more decentralization of authority in the church, greater involvement of young people and more church participation in youth culture, evangelization, relations with Muslims and other world religions, social justice and poverty.

Things lost, things gained

Some spoke of things lost because of Vatican II changes, but even some of the losses were counted as gains. "We lost our fear of every damn thing," one man said. We lost our fear of Protestants and of non-Christian religions. Others added, but with regret: We also lost Latin and a musical heritage thousands of years old; we lost some popular devotions; we lost a sense of reverence and mystery; we lost a sense of certitude. But, said others, we gained a new sense of church as community instead of just hierarchy. We gained an understanding of Jesus as a friend, and greater personal responsibility for our faith, and increasing lay involvement, and new ministries, and the vernacular, and an emphasis on sacred Scripture.

The workshop rekindled interest in what John XXIII was like, and what he said and did. People chuckled at stories of his folksy wit. "I do not understand God," he once said. "He has known from all eternity that I would some day be pope; why didn't he make me more photogenic?" They applauded his success in launching Vatican II despite objections by his most powerful coworkers in the Vatican curial offices.

Indeed, most people would say Pope John XXIII launched Vatican II and gave it its openness. But isn't that only part of the truth? John XXIII himself always played down his own part and credited the Holy Spirit as the one who pushed him into it. He reportedly told his secretary, Mgr Loris Capovilla, "When we believe that an inspiration comes to us from the Holy Spirit, we must follow it: what happens after that is not our responsibility."

Council archives also show a third major factor in shaping Vatican II. It was the work of a group of cardinals outside Rome, led by Cardinal Suenens of Belgium and including Cardinal Montini of Milan (the future Pope Paul VI), other European cardinals (Alfrink of Holland; Doepfner and Frings of Germany; Koenig of Austria; Lienart of France), and Cardinal Léger of Montreal. These cardinals and their collaborators did important work with John XXIII before the first session began. Once the council was underway, they were joined by the majority of the bishops, including you, Remi.

If asked, then, whom to thank for Vatican II, we begin with the Holy Spirit and go on to an impressive list of people, starting with John XXIII and including Paul VI. We think of people who have received too little notice, such as Bishop Gerard-Marie Coderre of St. Jean, Quebec, who was the first at Vatican II to call for the declericalization of the church and the promotion of women. Indeed, we end up thanking all the bishops and specialists who helped to draft and refine the texts, and the majority of the 2,400 bishops at the council whose votes gave the texts their place in the history of the church and of the world. So, thank you!

Mae and Bernard

Dear Mae and Bernard,

I probably don't have to tell you that I share your positive assessment of Vatican II and your optimism for the future of the Christian church and of the entire world. As John Paul II has said, the best preparation for the new millennium is "a renewed commitment to apply, as faithfully as possible, the teachings of Vatican II to the life of every individual and of the whole church" (TMA, 20). However, we cannot therefore be complacent – as if everything is set on automatic pilot and we can just have a party at the back of the plane.

Yes, the Spirit will prevail; but we, too, have our responsibilities – for continuing Vatican II renewal, for the church, and for the universe.

We can't over-emphasize the importance of John XXIII's vision. It should be ours, too. I am happy to hear that you've met people who still get excited about him and what he did. I meet lots of them in my travels. Everyone should know that John XXIII's tomb in the crypt of St. Peter's in Rome is a place of pilgrimage. He is not being forgotten.

John XXIII shifted the very nature of the council. That's what made everything else possible. Before Vatican II the church held 20 ecumenical councils. The main thing to know about them is that each had a specific focus, and often a fairly narrow one. Most were called to deal with a particular problem. For example, the Council of Constance (1414-1418) had to settle which one of three claimants was really the pope!

A radical idea

Pope John surprised everyone when he announced early in 1959 that he was calling a council. Some people thought that, because Vatican I a century earlier had defined papal infallibility, there would never be another council. John XXIII said that even he was "surprised" by his own announcement – that the idea had come to him from the Holy Spirit, like a bolt from the blue. He repeatedly used the Italian word *aggiornamento* to describe the kind of renewal and updating he had in mind. He spoke of the council as a "new Pentecost."

Perhaps the greatest blessing of my life is that I was privileged to be named bishop by this great pope, and that I was able to attend all four sessions of the council, even if only for a few days of the first session.

The secrecy that was imposed on the preparatory work for Vatican II is now being stripped away. As you said, there are good new histories that tell who did what before it opened. The true genius of John XXIII, in the face of huge difficulties, is now well documented. In his original inspiration, he was clear that the council should have pastoral renewal of the church as its first aim. Unlike previous councils, he said, Vatican II should not be about defining doctrines and condemning errors. The church should update itself to be better prepared to evangelize the rapidly changing modern world. It should strive to overcome the divisions among Christians. It should be renewed and reformed – in the sense of coming closer to what Christ, its founder, intended – so that it would be better able to fulfill its mission to preach the Gospel to all nations and serve all peoples. That was John XXIII's vision; the church continues to need that kind of renewal and reform, and always will.

One can hardly imagine today that the pope's vision for the council could be seen by anyone as a radical idea! However, there never had been a council with such a purpose. As soon as it became clear that Pope John would not abandon his intention to call a council, various officials in Vatican offices began to try to shape it according to their ideas, along the lines of past councils.

In the background was the fact that Vatican I had been cut short by war in Europe in 1870, its agenda incomplete. Some thought that Vatican II should simply take up and polish off that old agenda. Some curia officials knew that both Pius XI and Pius XII had given some thought to a council, so their old files were dug up. In general, the people around John XXIII thought his council should be like those in the past, defining some doctrines and condemning some errors. For example, Vatican I defined papal infallibility. Vatican II might go on to define the role of bishops, and perhaps a new doctrine about Mary. And, of course, they thought communism was the main error to be condemned.

John XXIII asked that a document be prepared to inform the world's bishops about the council and to ask for their suggestions. The first draft he received included a sort of checklist, asking the bishops what doctrines they thought should be defined and which errors condemned. He set it aside, and directed Cardinal Tardini to send out instead a short letter that mentioned some likely topics but left each bishop free to suggest his own ideas. These may seem like little things now, but at the time they were important steps in assuring that Vatican II would be open and the bishops who attended would be free to speak openly.

Cloaked in secrecy

It is also hard to recapture the excitement that ran around the world after the news of Pope John's plan began to circulate. You'll remember all the speculation. Very few facts were available. The pope himself spoke only in general terms because he was starting with only a general idea. Officials around the Vatican didn't help clarify things.

Heavy secrecy was imposed. Canadian bishops did not reveal what topics they suggested. Only recently have we been getting a clear picture of the extent to which the preparations were bedevilled at all stages. First, the pope's call wasn't taken up very seriously. Then, when the heads of the various Vatican congregations finally got down to work, they proposed and defended their own agendas. Later, the various Roman universities got into these turf wars.

Bishops and specialists from outside Rome were invited to come to work behind firmly closed doors to help draft documents for discussion. Those named to 11 commissions and three secretariats included 15 Canadian bishops and 11 Canadian priests. Only one lay man, an Italian serving on the commission for studies and seminaries, was involved in all this work. No women (lay or religious) served on any preparatory commission. Even the commission on the apostolate of the laity had no lay participants! That is why Bishop Alex Carter of Sault Ste. Marie would later complain that the document this commission prepared on the lay apostolate "was conceived in sin – the sin of clericalism."

Because there was so much infighting and so little coordination around the pope's vision, most of the 70 documents prepared for discussion never made it to the floor of the council. Only one, the document on liturgical reform, was accepted as a basis for discussion, and eventually passed after many revisions.

A framework for the council

And behind the scenes, as you mentioned, Belgium's Cardinal Suenens and others were working with John XXIII to put his vision into a plan to guide the council's work. This plan finally became public at the end of the first session, proposed by Suenens and seconded the next day by Montini, who in a few months would be Paul VI. When we heard them speak, we knew their plan was the pope's. It gave us the framework for all the rest of the council's work in the three sessions under Paul VI.

It divided our work into two main parts. One, *ad intra,* looked inward at the church as mystery and sacrament. The main result of this study is Vatican II's *Constitution on the Church* and its *Constitution on Divine Revelation.* The other focus was *ad extra,* looked outward, and eventually produced *The Pastoral Constitution on the Church in the Modern World.*

Yes, it is important to keep telling ourselves these stories. They show that the Holy Spirit was with John XXIII and with Vatican II. They also show how the Spirit works through people. That's how the pope's inspiration from the Spirit became a reality. The plan that Suenens and Montini proposed near the end of the council's first session in December 1962 was drafted earlier by Suenens, in April that year, after long discussions with John XXIII. During the few months until the council opened in October, the plan was circulated at the pope's request among a few cardinals, mainly from outside Rome. This preliminary work was crucial for how the council later developed.

We also know that late in December 1962, after the first session, Pope John established a committee of a few cardinals to supervise preparations for a second session, and to give him advice about the documents being drafted. He entrusted Suenens with the main text on the church *ad intra* – which was to become *Lumen Gentium* (the church), and the final schema on the church *ad extra* – which was to become *Gaudium et Spes* (the church in the world).

The first draft of *Lumen Gentium* went quickly, Suenens has told us. It was done by a group of Belgian theologians headed by Mgr Gerard Philips. The text which eventually became *Gaudium et Spes* was more difficult. Suenens rejected three early drafts. He called a week-long meeting of a group of theologians: Gerard Philips; Yves Congar OP; A. Dondeyne; Roberto Tucci SJ; Karl Rahner SJ; and Philip Delhaye. They agreed on a text that, again, was drafted by Mgr Philips; but in the end, a different working plan was adopted. The first draft of *Gaudium et Spes* as we know it was the work of Mgr Pierre Haubtmann with the assistance of a special drafting committee, Suenens has recalled.

I think it is an important part of the Vatican II story to name bishops and their collaborators, when we can do so reliably. The Spirit worked through these people. Few are still with us as we write. Roberto Tucci, who worked on *Gaudium et Spes,* is one. He has long been head of the team that plans papal visits, including those to Canada in 1984 and 1987. I will write more later about our various collaborators. I hope this interests you, too.

+Remi

Dear Remi,

As you know, we joined the Christian Family Movement (CFM) just about the time John XXIII announced the council in January 1959. Looking back now, we can see that CFM involved us in several aspects of preparations for Vatican II that you did not mention in your letter. A lot of the church renewal that was formally voted during Vatican II did not start with the council debates.

You remember how five or six CFM couples used to meet in each other's homes every two weeks, with a chaplain like you. We knew we were part of the Catholic Action movement. We were following the idea of Mgr (later Cardinal) Joseph Cardijn of Belgium that lay Catholics should be more involved in the church and in the world. At each meeting, we read a passage from Scripture and then discussed how it applied in our lives, and what we should do about it as a group. Without thinking about it very much, we were giving life to the idea that Catholics should become more familiar with the Bible and apply its insights in daily life. Later, such ideas from leading Scripture scholars played a big part in Vatican II. In a sense, too, CFM was an early version of the basic Christian communities from which liberation theology arose.

Scriptural and liturgical renewal

In CFM we also heard at least echoes from the European pioneers of scriptural and liturgical renewal. In line with the experimental changes in a number of great monasteries, we CFMers championed dialogue masses, as well as modern music and new vernacular hymns. We were becoming active participants in the liturgy, instead of remaining mere silent spectators at an event performed by the priest.

Our point is that scholars and church leaders were working at scriptural and liturgical renewal, and other church members were beginning to respond, even before John XXIII was elected pope. Cardijn's "apostolate of like to like" was recognized by Pius XI and Pius XII. Ideas about greater involvement of laity in church and society were fermenting everywhere that Catholic Action was organized – throughout Quebec, for example, and in English Canada where we had CFM or Young Christian Workers and Young Christian Students. The "Dandelion Movement" centred in Calgary similarly aimed at greater lay involvement. And new kinds of clergy-lay relations were developing. You CFM chaplains, for example, were urging us couples to think and act on our own as Christians in the world. We had to wait until Vatican II passed *The Church in the Modern World* before we heard that as the official message that all priests should promote. We think most priests still are too slow to promote that teaching.

Living in Ottawa before the council, we had a rare opportunity to tell our bishop what we hoped might come from it. Archbishop Lemieux organized consultations, called "Council Days," at which large numbers of us discussed possibilities and expressed hopes. He told Bernard later in Rome that he always kept our ideas in mind as he listened to the debates and voted on council texts.

Apart from such indirect lay influence, the council was overwhelmingly a clergy affair. Some women and men "lay auditors" were eventually invited – about 50 in all by the end of the last session. Even if a few of them may have made important behind-the-scenes contributions to the development of ideas and the drafting of texts, their presence was always, as Bishop Alexander Carter said, "too little and too late."

Regarding the struggles that later developed in Vatican II, we recall that these were going on before it opened. You can fill in for yourself the names of Scripture scholars and other theologians who were put under a cloud by the Vatican's Holy Office in the years before the council for publishing ideas which Vatican II later endorsed. Many of those same formerly-condemned experts were invited to the council to work with the bishops. We journalists at the council saw some of these great priests enjoy this turn of fortune.

11

The replies sent by Canadian bishops to Pope John in reply to his request for suggestions can now be read and analyzed. As you say, most of them were limited to matters affecting mainly the bishops and priests, such as permission to wear black suits instead of cassocks in public, and to recite the breviary in the vernacular. It was not until the council actually began, therefore, that most Canadian bishops began to express their support for the council's efforts to renew the church. This "conversion" of the bishops themselves must be noted as one of the fruits of Vatican II.

Perhaps you as a priest saw a side of this that we did not. We look forward to hearing more from you.

Mae and Bernard

Dear Mae and Bernard,

Your letter stirred up a lot of memories. Let me start with the point you were making at the end, about the views of Canadian bishops as Vatican II began. In hindsight, it is probably unfortunate that Cardinal Tardini mentioned a few topics in his letter to the bishops. He wrote: "The subjects for the council can be points of doctrine, the discipline of the clergy and Christian people, the manifold activities of today's church, matters of greater importance with which the Church must deal nowadays, or, finally, anything else that Your Excellency thinks it would be good to discuss and clarify." Most Canadian replies, only a page or two in Latin, did not venture beyond the limited areas he mentioned. Tardini's letter said they could consult others, but their replies do not mention any consultations. The questions that most concerned them hardly needed an ecumenical council to settle them. Very little interest was shown in the question of Christian unity, although several expressed the hope that the council would lead to better ways of preaching the truth to Protestants. On this point, Quebec bishops were generally more positive about ecumenism than their English-speaking counterparts, who had more day-to-day experience with non-Catholics. The French looked more theoretically at the theology of baptism and so on, while the English were familiar with practical problems such as mixed marriages and local tensions, such as parades organized by the Loyal Orange Lodge.

The church in Canada before the council

The point is not to criticize these bishops but to try to understand the kind of church we were in Canada before the council. At that time, many bishops saw themselves only as delegates of the pope. Papal appointment was seen as the source of their sacramental power. It wasn't until the second and third sessions of Vatican II that we fully recovered the truth that his ordination to the fullness of the priesthood makes a bishop a member of the apostolic college. Head of a local church, he holds authority directly from Christ.

Before the council, it wasn't easy to think creatively about the future of the church. You thought the church had the truth, and your job as bishop was to follow established papal policies and teachings. I was somewhat of the same school when named bishop on October 31, 1962. The spirit of the age was so different! The culture was so different! There has been a massive shift from what I knew as a farm boy, a member of a community in rural Manitoba. Our pastor was a benign dictator who knew four languages. He used everything he knew for the benefit of everyone. I never saw him rage at anyone, but he was in control. He even advised the farmers when to sell their wheat, because he had a radio and could follow the grain futures market. He helped with wills, insurance policies, the whole bit. He knew which districts the banks and insurance companies had marginalized, where they wouldn't give loans or hail insurance coverage, because their maps showed too-high risks of hail.

I came out of the seminary ready to run my parish that way. I had all my books. The church had all the answers. I was comfortable. We just understood the way things were going to be. We had a basic security that if you did your work and said your prayers all would go well. Things began to change a bit after I came back from Rome with a traditional doctorate in theology. I had a year in a parish and then, in fairly quick succession, was named diocesan director of Catholic Action, secretary to Archbishop Baudoux, vice-chancellor of St. Boniface diocese, diocesan director of the Confraternity for Christian Doctrine, and secretary for the Manitoba bishops. That's how it was: everything had a priest in charge of it.

Some of the other priests thought I was somewhat unstable, with a job a year! Looking back, I see this as a time of being groomed for what was to come. But even when I was named bishop a couple of weeks after the start of the council, I had no idea what really was coming!

That brings me back to your point about CFM. You as a couple and I as a chaplain were benefiting from the beginnings of renewal in scriptural studies, liturgy and so on. Then, in just a few years, we bishops at the council were drawing on this great background of creative work in Scripture, liturgy, music, ecumenism – a lot of it done by creative lay people.

Listening to the Holy Spirit

Liturgical renewal, for example, was not something the bishops launched. The bishops at the council became conscious of needing to listen to the Holy Spirit. We heard the Spirit in the renewal efforts that had already begun. Then we built on these beginnings as the Spirit stirred us in turn. Vatican II would not have been what it is if we bishops had not recognized the Spirit in all that work that had gone on before it. One example is what England's Cardinal Newman said nearly a century ago about the need to consult the laity on matters of church teaching. Another example is our more positive outlook on democracy. The idea that the king must listen to the people was highlighted way back in Magna Carta. This great charter of English personal and political liberty was obtained from King John in 1215! However, up to the beginning of the twentieth century, the church feared democracy and preferred monarchy. Then at Vatican II the whole apparatus of democratic voting was seen to fit in with the work of the Spirit! It was accepted as a tool for the prayerful process of discernment which helped us make such significant decisions. Also, we began to rediscover and to appreciate the Eastern church's tradition of synodal church governance.

Vatican II didn't just pop out of the blue. We mentioned a number of charismatic leaders, starting with John XXIII. However, we must also acknowledge how many other streams of influence ran into the council. Some people complain that it was too sharp a break with the past. Actually, everything about it that seems new has deep, if hidden, roots in our history and tradition. And all of it can be celebrated as the work of the Spirit.

I am running out of time today, but I want to share some more of my council experiences. Until then,

+ *Remi*

For Discussion

1. What is the first thing you remember hearing about Vatican II? What is the main source of your information about it? Are you satisfied with what you know?
2. Discuss the council's three main aims – updating, unity, and service to the world. How are these linked and related? Have you seen progress in the church towards these goals? On which front is the greatest need for continuing renewal?
3. Discuss the signs you have seen of division in the church between those who resist change and those who welcome it. How do you account for these different views?
4. Do you think you and your friends take Vatican II seriously enough? Are you optimistic or pessimistic about the future of the church? Why?
5. At about the age of 2000 years, do you feel the Christian church is nearer to its beginning or to its end?

For Action

1. Look for books about Vatican II in your local public and school libraries. Borrow and read one.
2. Ask your parish priest and the president of your parish pastoral council what books or other sources they use in order to understand and interpret the teachings of Vatican II.
3. Interview someone known locally as a supporter of change in the church, and someone known to resist change. Compare their concerns and motives.

Further Reading

Alberigo, Guiseppe, and Joseph A. Komonchak, eds. *History of Vatican II.* Maryknoll, NY: Orbis; Leuven: Peeters, Volume 1, 1995; Volume 2, 1997.

Eagan, Joseph F. *Restoration and Renewal: The Church in the Third Millennium.* Kansas City: Sheed and Ward, 1995.

Routhier, Gilles, ed. *L'Eglise canadienne et Vatican II.* Montreal: Fides, 1997.

Suenens, Cardinal Leo-Joseph. *Memories and Hopes.* Dublin: Veritas, 1992.

Which Vatican II Change
Is Most Important?

The changes introduced into the Catholic church by Vatican II are outlined and discussed in this chapter. Its main focus is on how these changes affected the laity. It begins with a discussion of negative points. The positive changes are then introduced under 10 headings: updating, reform, Holy Scripture, collegiality, religious freedom, regional and local variety, ecumenism, dialogue with non-Christians, the church's mission in the world, and the role of the laity. Detailed discussion of the first nine of these points is left for later chapters. The focus here is on how Vatican II changed our understanding of the place in the church of those who are not ordained and not members of religious communities. The laity's call to holiness and their secular vocation are discussed, as well as some reasons why these Vatican II teachings are slow to catch on. The challenge to priests and faith educators is noted. This leads into a discussion of how Vatican II began the process of increasing awareness in the Western church of the work of the Holy Spirit, the third person of the Trinity.

Dear Mae and Bernard,

I have been asked to lead a retreat for diocesan priests and I would like to pick your brains a bit. I want to focus on how we might think about the church – an exercise in ecclesiology, if you will. Therefore I will be talking about Vatican II and the post-council church.

So, my question to you: As a couple, what would you like a group of priests to study and discuss about Vatican II? Bernard was there for all four sessions as a journalist; and Mae, you spent a few weeks in Rome during the third session, so you saw some of the action there, as well as following it from home in Ottawa. And, ever since, the two of you have been more involved in council follow-up than most people I know. What would you highlight as Vatican II's main achievements and failures? In what ways is the council succeeding or failing in the post-council church?

What Vatican II didn't do

I begin with some emphasis on difficulties or failures, for several reasons. First, it needs to be pointed out that some problems in the church today have nothing to do with Vatican II. Life goes on, new issues come up, new mistakes are made, and we can't blame the council if it didn't deal with later developments. This was also one of the conclusions of the 1985 Synod, which studied the 20 years after the close of the council. One of Vatican II's achievements was to situate the church in history. History keeps moving, and it's important to be able to sort out what is new since the council.

Second, people tend to forget that Vatican II deliberately left some questions open, or unresolved, or in a state of compromise. For example, it said some positive things about the role of women in the church but was silent on today's question about ordination of women. I was there, and that really didn't occur to us bishops then. Or, another example: We said that the pope acting alone has full authority, and also that the pope and all bishops have full authority; but we did not spell out just how authority will work both ways in practice.

Third, even after all these years since the council closed in 1965, some of its teachings have not really been brought to life in the local church. They lie dormant or half-used. There has been foot-dragging by some bishops, priests and people, and downright opposition by others.

Finally, some people, starting with some Vatican officials, have set out to try to rewrite or undo the council. They claim the Spirit really was with the tiny minority in council voting; and that majority votes – on use of the vernacular, for example – should not be taken as definitive. In thus trying to reconstruct Vatican II, they even ignore the solemn reconfirmation of the council by John Paul II and the bishops at the 1985 Synod, called especially to assess its effects after 20 years.

I start with these negative points because one way to clarify what Vatican II did is to be clear about what it did not do. Now, back to your reactions. Without dwelling on the negative, it would be helpful to hear some similar examples of post-council difficulties from your lay viewpoint. Mostly, however, I would like to see your list of positive council accomplishments, and your assessment of how these are working out in the church today.

Looking forward to hearing from you,

+ *Remi*

Dear Remi,

Thanks for the invitation. We have never directed a retreat, and participating in one through you and by e-mail is indeed a new experience.

Our experiences of Vatican II and what happened since are so vast that they are hard to sort out and put into order. The council's new teaching about us laity comes first, of course. Before Vatican II, we laity had a sense of being the church's second-class citizens. The council said, very clearly, that we are full and equal members, called to different service but not lesser dignity. This comes to mind first. But there is so much more that seems equally important. To get started, then, we would simply borrow the 10-point Vatican II check-list developed by the American Jesuit theologian Avery Dulles. He says that the council endorsed 10 basic principles, and that anyone who does not accept all of them cannot claim to have accepted the results of Vatican II.

Ten basic principles of Vatican II

The first is John XXIII's commitment to *aggiornamento* – church renewal and updating. Central to this kind of renewal is the idea that the church exists in human history. You touched this point in your letter. While basic elements of our faith are unchanging, some things can and should be updated as times change. Language is a prime example. Second, and related to this, is the

Vatican II teaching that the church is reformable. Today we have increased awareness that church members sinned in the past and still do so. We are more open to admitting our faults, including our part in the sin of Christian disunity. John Paul II has shown the way in this regard. He has called for a "dialogue of conversion" (UUS, 35), and invited all Christians to join him in "praying for that conversion which is indispensable for 'Peter' to be able to serve his brethren" (UUS, 4).

Third, we have renewed attention to the word of God. We accept the idea that the word keeps challenging us and so is a continual source of change in the church. Also central to Vatican II is the principle of collegiality – that all the bishops form the apostolic college with the pope. This teaching already has a deep impact on each local church or diocese, even though, as you noted, some problems arise from the ambiguity about how the pope alone and the pope with college both share full authority.

Dulles also listed what the council said on religious freedom, regional and local variety, ecumenism, dialogue with non-Christian religions, and on the mission of the church in the world. More on all these points later.

The tenth principle listed by Dulles – the active role of the laity – is the one we want to stress. It is hard to recapture the tremendous exhilaration we felt when Vatican II emphasized the concept of the people of God and taught that baptism gives each person a share in the triple priesthood of Christ as prophet, priest and sovereign, and full membership in the church. It was a bonus that the council went on to say so much that is entirely new about the vocation of the laity. John Paul II has emphasized that Vatican II was the first council *ever* to deal with the nature, dignity, spirituality, mission and responsibility of the laity. Then, after the 1987 Synod on the laity, in *Christifideles Laici*, he added new insights into the council teaching that the laity's special vocation is in temporal affairs. The church, a spiritual mystery, has a secular character through us laity – a council teaching that is still much neglected today.

What this means for the laity

We suppose most priests have not reflected much on what all this means for us laity. Younger priests probably can't even imagine how laity felt before

Vatican II. The church then was full of language which left us with the idea that we were somewhat second class. The term "church" meant the pope, bishops, priests and religious, with the laity somehow vaguely attached. Priests and bishops were "the teaching church." We laity "obeyed, prayed and paid," as the saying went. Religious men and women dedicated themselves to poverty, chastity and obedience, called the "evangelic counsels " or "the state of perfection." Priests and nuns chose a higher vocation than those who married "to avoid concupiscence." All this language implied that we laity settled for lesser goals. This way of speaking is ruled out now by the council teaching that we share in the priesthood of Christ through our baptism, and that all are called equally to holiness.

If you talk about this side of the pre-council church, some priests probably will say that we exaggerate, that most pre-council lay Catholics didn't complain about being repressed or put down. We agree. Most laity back then found ways to be happy and contented in the pre-council church. Attending mass on Sundays, abstaining from meat on Fridays, and following other disciplines or devotions made us feel that we were active church members. There were plenty of Catholic lay organizations to join. Our own pre-council experience of church was enriched by the Christian Family Movement. And, in the 1917 Code of Canon Law, if we asked someone to read the Latin, there were four lines about the rights of the laity – that we had the right to Christian burial, if we died well. Compare this with the 1983 Code which has many pages on the laity!

The laity's secular vocation

You mentioned that some council teachings have not been brought to life sufficiently. We think this is especially true regarding the laity's secular vocation. A couple of years ago in Toronto we were shocked by a Vocations' Sunday homily by a young American Jesuit. For him, vocations meant priests, religious, and "those laity involved in specialized church ministries." We asked him in a note: What about the council teaching that "by reason of their special vocation it belongs to the laity to seek the kingdom of God by engaging in temporal affairs and directing them according to God's will"? What about the pope saying in *Christifideles Laici* that services in the church can be a temptation that takes lay people away from their primary and particular secular vocation? He replied that we had a point, and that he had been stressing the traditional sense of vocations. Traditional, perhaps, but not up to date with the council.

In the past year or so, a number of lay friends have mentioned they've never heard anything in church which helped them see that holiness for them centred on striving to do their secular jobs "according to God's will." A woman who wrote editorials for years for Canada's largest daily newspaper, *The Toronto Star,* made this point. An accountant who retired from his own business to run as public auditor for a United States county with half a million residents had the same report. Another man, also an accountant, recently retired as an assistant deputy finance minister in Ontario, concurred. All regular churchgoers, they agreed they had never heard anything in church linking their secular jobs with the reign of God. Priests need to think about whether they neglect council teaching about the laity's secular vocation, as well as greater lay involvement in church affairs.

Many Sunday readings lend themselves to homilies touching on our secular vocations. Every baptism ceremony could be an occasion for saying something about the lay secular vocation. We are asked to renew our baptismal promises. We could be reminded at the same time of what Vatican II says about our baptismal responsibilities in the world and in the church.

How different the world might be if every one of the nearly one billion lay Catholics around the world really focused on seeking holiness by "engaging in temporal affairs and directing them according to God's will." Don't we mostly ignore the Gospel in our secular work? Aren't we mostly driven by self-interest and pragmatism, like anyone with no faith? Do many of us think about love of God and neighbour outside a few hours on Sundays?

Working with those who are ordained

Besides having a secular vocation, we laity are called to work, in our ways, with those who are ordained. The Holy Spirit calls us laity to serve in pastoral ministries along with our pastors. More than that, we have a right to demand of our pastors, including the bishop of Rome, the kinds of pastoral services that we think we need. Quite a bit of progress has been made in this regard, in Canada at least. Many dioceses and parishes have pastoral councils. They assess pastoral needs, plan services and organize church resources. At the same time, individual laity come forward to serve in many liturgical roles, as musicians, readers, altar servers, and eucharistic ministers who both serve in church and take communion to people who are shut in. Some laity are prayer group leaders. Prayer Companions in your diocese, you were telling us, have trained to help other people learn to use Holy Scripture for personal prayer and to deepen their spirituality. Others help children and adults preparing for the sacraments: baptism, confirmation, first reconciliation, first communion, and marriage. One result of Vatican II is that laity now are much more active in such ministries than we used to be.

You might ask the priests to reflect on what they do to promote the council's teaching on the secular vocation of the laity. Also, are they open and encouraging about lay coworkers, especially women, helping around their parishes? Or are they afraid? Do they feel their own ministerial priesthood is being devalued as laity become more active as a result of greater awareness of our common priesthood? A Vatican instruction late in 1997 warned that lay involvement in parishes might "devalue" the priesthood. How do your retreatants relate that warning to what the council taught?

You can say, then, that Vatican II tried to help us see that all the baptized are equal in dignity and capacity to serve, that all are called to holiness, and that the laity are as much "the church" as any members of the clergy or hierarchy. We should also see more clearly that Christ's reign in the world is carried forward in a special way by the laity: that our particular vocation gives the church its secular character.

Probably the key idea to sum up all that we want to say is that the Holy Spirit works in us laity. There is a challenge for all of us in Article 7 of the Vatican II *Constitution on the Liturgy*. It speaks of Christ being present in a fourfold way at our liturgies: as eucharist, and as word, and in the presiding priest, and *in the people,* members of Christ's body. This fourth "real presence," the real presence of the Spirit of Christ in each of us through baptism, is the one that is grasped and respected the least. You should stress this as a challenge to priests, as teachers.

Finally, for now, a few thoughts about the current decline in vocations to the priesthood and religious life in Canada and other Western countries. Where is the Spirit leading us? Towards greater openness to married men as priests and women priests? Towards acceptance of priests from other lands, as the world's white population continues to decline? Towards a church in which laity will have a much larger role in prayer life and spiritual guidance, especially as parents in the "little church" that is the family?

We have a few more ideas but they are not quite sorted out. More later.

Mae and Bernard

P.S. Ask the priests at that retreat especially about what they are doing to give women an equal place with men in their parishes. How do priests and other parish leaders respond when women claim their baptismal rights? And we don't mean just a few girls as altar servers and women as readers or eucharistic ministers, but equal places on committees, for example. Above all, do priests listen to what the women say, with as much attention, openness and positive feelings as they do to men? Do they go so far as teaching what Paul VI said, that people who have rights in the church also have responsibility for claiming them?

Mae

Dear Mae and Bernard,

I'm glad you reminded me of the list of 10 Vatican II principles outlined by Avery Dulles. I would add another one: Elements of a renewed theology of the Holy Spirit, or new pneumatology, to give it its technical name. Our rediscovery of the role of the Holy Spirit is basic to understanding the entire council. That ties in with the point you were making at the end of your letter. It is also the basis for all that you say about the laity.

Part of the genius of John Paul II was to invite us to prepare for the year 2000 by devoting the three preceding years, in turn, to Jesus, the Holy Spirit and God the Father. Notice the order: Jesus and the Spirit lead to the Father. Too often we leave the Spirit just tagging along, almost ignored, as when we bless ourselves, "In the name of the Father, and of the Son and of the Holy

Spirit." I am not questioning these traditional words, but I stress that the Spirit deserves much more than an afterthought. I always emphasize that at retreats.

It is very important to restore and deepen our understanding that the Holy Spirit, sent by the Risen Lord, is the source of all that mysterious reality we call church. The church is the bringing together in the Spirit of all the faithful, together with all people of good will who, perhaps unknown to us, are under the influence of the Holy Spirit. The other religions in varying degrees are also being moved by the Holy Spirit. Vatican II made an extremely important statement when it said that in some mysterious way the fullness of the reality of the reign of God "subsists" in (is present in) the Catholic church, and that other people share in the life of the Spirit in varying degrees.

Indeed, all of the council principles listed by Dulles have meaning and come to life only if we fully appreciate the work of the Spirit. This is true, as you wrote, for lay involvement as church in the world, and also for council teaching about church renewal and reform, regional and local cultural adaptations, ecumenism, dialogue with other religions, and religious freedom for everyone. And, of course, the Spirit also inspires our new appreciation for Holy Scripture and the Vatican II teaching on collegiality. There have been many shifts in our thinking and practice since Vatican II. To test which are valid we must start by asking which are truly the work of the Spirit.

The fourth eucharistic prayer and the Holy Spirit

When we start thinking about new appreciation of the work of the Holy Spirit, I suggest we look at the fourth eucharistic prayer. It is new since Vatican II. Before the council, the whole concept of the eucharist was focused on Jesus Christ and the priest seen as minister in the role of Christ, acting in the person of Christ. There was practically no reference to the Holy Spirit. I remember priests agonizing over whether they had pronounced the words of consecration properly. I have watched an older priest, recovering from a slight stroke, labour to repeat the words if they didn't come out right the first try. Many thought the validity of the mass depended on the priest doing it right. So we even watched for very little things, like whether the priest held his fingers correctly, and a lot of other details or rubrics.

Now, the fourth eucharistic prayer makes clear that the Holy Spirit brings about the eucharist. The Spirit does this by transforming the elements of bread and wine into the body and blood of Christ; by revealing the word of God in the scriptural readings; by empowering the priest to be a worthy minister; and by transforming all members of the church into the people of God. Church history shows that the faithful themselves were called "the body of Christ" before this term was used for the eucharistic species.

It is because the Spirit dwells in all members of the worshipping community that we are able to tell the story of the liturgy in an effective way. The fourth eucharistic prayer recognizes and picks up all of this. It recalls: "And that we might live no longer for ourselves but for him, he (Christ) sent the Holy Spirit from you, Father, as his first gift to those who believe, to complete his work on earth and bring us to the fullness of grace." This theological gem sums up our theology of the Holy Spirit. The prayer continues: "Father, may this Holy Spirit sanctify these offerings. Let them become the body and blood of Jesus Christ . . . and by your Holy Spirit, gather all who share this one bread and one cup into the body of Christ. . . ."

That same Spirit is behind the magisterium, the church's teaching authority, seen as operating not just through the pope but also the total people. The Spirit empowers those in authority — bishops and priests — and forms them into a kind of collegial consensus, to hear what the Spirit is saying to the whole people. The same Spirit empowers the people, through the charismatic movement and in other ways, including contemplation, prophetic gifts and inspired actions.

Christ and the Spirit at work in us

So there is an interpenetration, if you will, of Christ and the Spirit. It is fascinating how practically everything we say of Christ can be said of the Holy Spirit – the Spirit of Jesus, the Spirit that Jesus sent. Christ had to unite flesh with the divine to fulfill the work of the Incarnation, so that his flesh could come into our flesh, like a bridge, and as the gift of the Holy Spirit.

Lately, I have developed much more than ever before the idea that the Spirit of Jesus is at work in us. We are not reincarnations of some sort, as if Christ were somehow still living among us. Christ in terms of his humanity is in heaven, however you understand that. The humanity of Jesus, which is the bridge through which we receive divine life, is no longer present on earth. With us and in us now is the other Paraclete, as Jesus promised: "It is to your advantage that I go away, for if I do not go away, the Advocate will not come to you; but if I go, I will send him to you" (John 16: 7). So, now the Paraclete has been sent, at Pentecost. As a result it is now the gift of Jesus Christ that works in me. In that sense, it has been suggested that the person of the Holy Trinity closest to us is the Spirit – closer than Jesus is the Spirit of Jesus, but not Jesus as such.

The theology that a lot of people still have, of somehow walking hand in hand with Jesus, as if Jesus is carrying us, is unrealistic. Rather, we have the Spirit, not walking beside but dwelling within us, changing us into members of the body of Christ. The Spirit helps us to enter into that personal relationship with the Father that Jesus had (Romans 5); who prays in us even when we are unable to say *Abba*, which is Our Father. Like Jesus, we enter into a relationship with God which is that of members of the body of Christ. So the Spirit of Jesus is always working, just as Jesus works as the Father does. This is how he justifies his miracles on the Sabbath. And now you and I are called to continue his work and to do even greater work!

It is always the work of the Father that establishes the reign of God. The Spirit of Jesus, sent by Jesus from the Father after he had first received that Spirit, now continues that work, through us. That's why Jesus can say, you will be my members and you will do even greater things. This Spirit of Jesus dwells within us and inspires us to do the wonderful things that are to be done. That's the church, continuing in history the work of bringing about the reign of God.

There is a passage in Scripture that I want to put on record here: "The anointing that you received from him abides in you, and so you do not need anyone to teach you" (1 John 2:27). That doesn't mean we can just go it alone, so to speak. Rather, because of our faith and baptism we have been "taught by God" through the Holy Spirit, and so we don't run after false prophets. That's ultimately the teaching of the church. The mystery of salvation involves the divine power going out from the Godhead, creating all things; and then the return to the Godhead of all things recapitulated in Christ. This is fundamental.

The incarnation brings the divine into human flesh. Jesus then, through the mystery of the cross and the power of the Spirit, returns to the Father to be crowned as king of the universe. We share in the baptism that was bestowed on Jesus when he received the fullness of the Spirit at the resurrection. Through our flesh we receive the power of the Spirit from the glorified flesh of Jesus. We, in turn, as members of the extended body of Jesus, are called to do "even greater work" than Jesus did. John's gospel is as clear as it is dramatic: "Very truly, I tell you, the one who believes in me will also do the works that I do and, in fact, will do greater works than these, because I am going to the Father" (John 14:12). Our mission is ultimately to transform the whole universe. This is the role of every member and especially of the laity.

And, of course, as you said, the job of a priest is to help every church member to grasp this crucial Vatican II teaching: that the Spirit dwells in them and calls them to do "even greater work." I think a fundamental point for training priests and others in pastoral work is formation in the discernment of spirits. Not only for clergy but for all people in positions of responsibility in the church. We must learn how to be open to the gifts of the Holy Spirit, how to read the signs of the times, how to discern true gifts from false signs. I think this should be fundamental to all training.

The human side of Vatican II

With all this talk about the Spirit and the church as mystery, we might forget the human side of Vatican II. Even if John XXIII insisted that he was inspired by the Spirit to call the council, it was the man John XXIII who called it and shaped the pastoral vision with which it opened. After that, Paul VI and more than 2,400 bishops and other participants took up their responsibilities. I mention just one example for the moment.

To this day the radiant face of Yves Congar is etched in my memory. The insights of this outstanding Dominican theologian deeply influenced Vatican II. By naming him a cardinal not long before his death, John Paul II recognized Father Congar's pioneering achievements. One day he and I had an animated conversation in St. Peter's Basilica. He hurried over to my seat to share the good news that the drafting committee on which he served had finally accepted an important proposal. Quotations from Paul's Epistle to the Romans had been added to the *Dogmatic Constitution on the Church*. One passage added to Article 10 of the chapter on the People of God says that "all the disciples of Christ, persevering in prayer and praising God (cf. Acts 2:42-47), should present themselves as living sacrifice, holy and acceptable to God (cf. Romans 12:1)."

On this page, the idea may not look dramatic. However, what Paul says, that we should "present our bodies as living sacrifice," puts an end to a false division between life and worship. Temporal and spiritual are recognized as two facets of one graced reality. Our whole being and all of daily life relate to God. Our very life is what we bring to church on Sunday to offer "as living sacrifice, holy and acceptable to God." The idea is crucial for everyone – pope, bishop, priest, deacon, religious, and, in a special way, for all laity. This assures us that all our priestly, family and professional tasks – all daily work, proclaiming the gospel and ministering to people, car pools and diapers, memos and meetings – can and should be offered at week's end as "holy and acceptable to God." Each of us is to bring as offering the reality of all that our bodies have been doing. And that is now part of official church teaching because people like Congar argued and lobbied to have a drafting committee add this insight from Holy Scripture to a key council text. Hundreds of other such examples could be given. It was in this way, bit by bit, that Vatican II's magnificent body of teaching was built up, under the Spirit's inspiration and guidance.

The church is a mystery

This is how we arrived at the changes the council brought to our very concept of church. That's where the *Constitution on the Church* begins: the mystery of the church; the church as mystery. The church is truly a mystery. Reflecting about Christ, its founder and head, leads us into the mystery of the Holy Trinity. In the Creed, we proclaim our faith in Father, Son and Holy Spirit. We call the church the body of Christ, both divine and human. We are the church, so we are caught up in relationships with and within the Trinity. The church is a sacrament, a sign of Christ's presence, we also say. Centuries of teaching, countless books and a multitude of other media presentations have failed to examine all the church's inner riches. It can be approached from a great many perspectives. We need to reflect and pray over this constantly.

One problem is that when we talk about the divine mystery we must use symbols or images. We speak by way of analogy. Most of the images of the church found in the New Testament come from minding herds and cultivating land, from marriage and family life, and the art of building. We talk of the church as sheepfold, vineyard, bride, temple. There is a long list of these images gathered in Article 6 of the *Constitution on the Church*. Interesting reading, as you know, and everyone should take time to read it.

You will remember that not long ago, the church was often referred to as "the perfect society." This was to emphasize the view that the church had the truth, could stand alone, and had no need to change. For example, before Vatican II we used one canon of the mass – what we now call the eucharistic prayer – and that text had remained almost unchanged for centuries! Also, people thought of the church as a fortress, defending itself from an evil and hostile world, as well as from other Christian churches and other religions.

Vatican II helped us to see that the church is part of history. Part of its mystery is that, yes, the church is the body of Christ, but *in* history. We try to speak of this by saying that the reign of God is both "already" and "not yet." The church will reach its perfection only at the end of time, when Christ will return everything to the Father. Humanity, all of creation, the entire cosmos, will be made new. Then the church will be truly resplendent, as Holy Scripture says, like the bride adorned for her wedding. So, with this understanding emerging from the council, we no longer speak of the church as "perfect" society. It is the body of Christ "already," but we have "not yet" rid ourselves of all sin. We have not run the entire race toward perfection. Similarly, the council invites us to see the church not as the fortress on the hill but as a group of pilgrims journeying along in the valley, moving through history with all people of good will, and accompanied and animated always by the Holy Spirit.

We have less trouble after Vatican II admitting that truth exists outside the Catholic church, as well as in it. We have "the fullness of the means of salvation," the *Decree on Ecumenism* says (UR, 3). "The unity of the one and only church, which Christ bestowed on his church from the beginning, . . . subsists in the Catholic church as something she can never lose" (UR, 4). At the same time, we recognize that the Spirit of Christ uses other Christian churches as means of salvation. Even further, we say of all non-Christian religions that the Catholic church "rejects nothing of what is true and holy in these religions" (NA, 2). In varying ways, God's providence, evident goodness and saving designs extend to all of humanity (NA, 1). The bishops at the 1998 Synod for Asia noted this, stressing many important contributions to the church by Asian religions.

Seeds of the word

Catholic missionaries now are trained to watch and care for "those elements of truth and grace which are found among peoples, and which are, as it were, a secret presence of God" (AG, 9). In other words, other world religions are cautiously recognized as carrying within them *semina verbi,* seeds of the word. Missionaries try not simply to "bring Christ" to other peoples. They seek also to recognize signs of the Spirit already present in other cultures and religious expressions, even though they may have much to learn about the fullness of revelation entrusted to the Catholic church.

Karl Rahner, the great German theologian who worked with us at Vatican II but has since died, once said that one of the most significant shifts at Vatican II was the church's recognition of its true universality. Before the council, the Catholic church everywhere in the world had the mark of Europe. In fact, it was Mediterranean and Latin. The predominance of a Euro-centred culture in the Catholic church is changing now, for several very good reasons.

First of all, sitting as a bishop in the raised rows of seats down the centre of St. Peter's Basilica, I was struck by how many of the 2,400 bishops there were non-European and non-white. Moreover, these other faces predominated down where I was sitting, among the newer and younger bishops. The demographics of the Catholic church are changing. We are less and less northern and European, and more and more southern, from Latin America, Africa and Asia. There are now more Jesuits in India than in the United States.

Vernacular languages and evangelization

Partly in recognition of this, the council voted for vernacular languages in the liturgy. Non-European bishops won the argument that the use of only Latin was hindering their work of evangelization. It is important to add that the change was not restricted to language. Emphasizing the church's respect for the qualities and talents of various races and nations, the council opened the church to "anything in these people's way of life" that is true and authentic. This process, called inculturation, is far from ended, and moves in the direction of making our church evidently more universal, in the sense of Rahner's remark.

The images of sheepfold or vineyard are hardly adequate for our post-council self-understanding as church. Pilgrim people probably is the most adequate new term, for the moment. What other images would you add? One of the most beautiful images of the Trinity comes from the Eastern church. It shows God operating with two hands – Jesus and the Spirit. You can say of Jesus almost everything you say of the Spirit, and vice versa. Congar has noted a whole lot of parallel texts which show this.

+Remi

For Discussion

1. How do you understand the difference between updating and reform in the church?
2. In shifting from looking at the church as "a perfect society" untouched by history, to seeing ourselves as "a pilgrim people" moving through history with all of humanity, what changes are involved for individual church members? For the church as institution?
3. Discuss what it means for laity to be called to holiness as much as priests or religious are.
4. What signs do you see that laity are trying to direct temporal affairs according to God's will? Do you think you are hearing enough about Vatican II's teaching on the vocation of the laity? Who is chiefly responsible for increasing public awareness about the council?

5. This chapter lists Vatican II changes under 10 headings. Which of the 10 do you think is most apparent in your local church community?

6. Discuss what signs you see that people in your community are growing in their respect for Holy Scripture, the word of God.

For Action

1. Research what your diocese has done about renewing and enlivening the Sunday liturgy to encourage participation by young and old and those with differing cultural backgrounds.

2. Seek out some Eastern-rite Christians in your community and discuss how their understanding of the Holy Spirit differs from the general Western view.

3. Find out what goes on regularly in your diocese and in your parish about promoting Christian unity. Get involved in one initiative.

4. Read a book about one of the world's non-Christian religions.

5. Research what has been done in your diocese to implement the Vatican II teaching about the vocation of the laity.

Further Reading

Abbott, Walter M, ed. *Documents of Vatican II: With Notes and Commentaries by Catholic, Protestant and Orthodox Authorities.* New York: America Press, 1966.

Dulles, Avery. *The Reshaping of Catholicism: Current Challenges in the Theology of the Church.* San Francisco: Harper and Row, 1988.

Flannery,Austin,ed.*VaticanII:Constitutions,Decrees,Declarations.*Inclusive language edition, Northport, LI: Costello; Dublin: Dominican Publications, 1996.

John Paul II. *Christian Unity:* Encyclical Letter *Ut Unum Sint.* Sherbrooke, Que.: Mediaspaul, 1995.

McEnroy, Carmel Elizabeth. *Guests in Their Own House: The Women of Vatican II.* New York: Crossroad, 1996.

Tavard, George H. *The Church, Community of Salvation: An Ecumenical Ecclesiology.* Collegeville: Liturgical Press, 1992.

New Science, New Cosmology, New Theology: Serving a New World

One aim of Vatican II was to prepare Christians to be of greater service to the modern world. This chapter begins to explore some of the challenges facing members of the post-council church. (The following chapter continues this exploration.) The focus is on science and technology in this chapter. It looks at some of the things in the world that cause fear and hope. Will we humans destroy the world by weapons of mass destruction or by abuse of the environment? Are the developments of modern science and technology menaces or blessings? Who is shaping and directing change in the world? What new ideas about creation and the Creator are gaining attention? How is the relation between religion and science changing? What new moral questions are arising, and how are Christians preparing themselves to serve the world that is developing? The chapter concludes with a brief outline of one example of how modern science can be adapted and fitted into Christian faith life.

Dear Remi,

We're wondering what you think about some questions that seem to come up more frequently these days. Is the end of the world near at hand? Should any limit be set on science and technology and, if so, how and by whom? At first glance, these questions may seem unrelated, but they tie together at several levels.

Speculation about doomsday is fed in part by our profligate consumption of non-renewable resources. Many of our most wasteful habits involve use of the products of our most advanced science and technology, such as supersonic jets. The 1997 environmental conference in Kyoto, Japan, warned once more that we threaten essential natural systems and species by the way we consume resources and dispose of wastes. We have the awesome potential to make life on earth impossible for animals, plants and ourselves. Nuclear weapons alone could do that. At the same time, we are told that technological solutions, such as new genetically-altered foods, hold the key to human survival after conventional food supplies begin to fail because we have destroyed natural environments, caused global warming and so on. So, will the advances of science and technology bring us to destruction or save us?

Popular culture makes these questions both theological and scientific. For example, after early 1998 floods in California and ice storms in Ontario and Quebec, all blamed on the Pacific Ocean current El Niño, a tabloid newspaper sold at Canadian grocery store checkout counters had this headline: "Bizarre Weather Sign of Christ's Second Coming."

The questioning can't stop there. Recent scientific studies are changing the very way we look at the world. The universe is much older than had been thought. Its parts are more intimately connected than seen previously. We humans, as one species, cannot do things that threaten other species without endangering ourselves. Good scientific evidence requires us to take a new look at ourselves, how we behave, and what we believe. We must live within limits, we are told. At the same time, scientists also tell us that there are no limits to what we can do. They report that we are on the verge of being able to change ourselves at will by reaching into our own genetic makeup.

Conflicting messages, here. Some religious extremists say the end is near. Leading astronomers find no evidence that the expansion of the matter in the universe will ever end. High-tech growth is endangering life on earth, serious scientists say. Others, equally serious, look forward to achieving the technical ability to redesign ourselves and become the species that changes its own future.

Science and technology: part of being human

In the social teaching of the church – Vatican II, papal encyclicals, statements by the bishops of Canada and of other nations, etc. – science and technology are judged both positively and negatively. On the positive side, it is clear that the desire to know (science) and the determination to invent new ways to use new knowledge (technology) are part of what it is to be human. We cannot imagine what life would be like if the achievements of science and technology suddenly were wiped out. Moreover, we live in times when there seems to be no end to what might be discovered scientifically and developed technologically.

As one example of what leading scientists are thinking about, *The Guardian Weekly* has reported on the continuing high-level debate about the theories of Stephen Hawking, probably the world's best-known living scientist. Hawking proposed about a decade ago in his best-selling book *A Brief History of Time* that an initial explosion set the universe expanding with a force that is forever being slowed by the gravitational power of the matter in the universe. While Hawking and his Cambridge University colleague, Neil Turok, continue to wonder whether the universe's expansion will ever end, Russian physicist Andrei Linde is arguing that universes like ours are popping into existence all the time, so there is no point in trying to find a beginning or an end. The *Guardian* commented editorially: "The Hawking argument that time has a beginning but no end will make posterity sleep more soundly and ought in a small way to enhance the virtues of peacekeeping and environmental control since our stewardship of the Earth can no longer be seen as temporary. . . . Above all, it ought to give us all a sense of infinite humility at the awesomeness of all that has been happening." It also noted that the rival theories about how the universe began are broad enough to allow believers to hold that such a physical miracle as "the Big Bang" must have had an external cause, and to allow atheists to contend that we now have a complete explanation of existence and need look no further.

Meanwhile, astronomers have reported that various studies show that the universe is not dense enough to stop its own expansion. Three groups of scientists doing different tests reported to the American Astronomical Society late in 1997 that the universe has "only a fifth to a quarter of the matter that theory suggests would be necessary for it to stop the expansion of the Big Bang and fall back in on itself. . . . [W]e live in a universe that will expand forever . . . ," the report suggested. This agrees with theologian Diarmuid O'Murchu's general conclusion drawn from similar earlier scientific findings: "The cosmic evolutionary saga is far from finished. In fact, all indications are that this is a relatively young universe, which in evolutionary terms may still be growing through its adolescent phase."

Optimistic scientific speculation is not confined to the edges of space and the end of time. In March 1998, Hawking told U.S. President Bill Clinton in a millennium lecture at the White House that we humans likely will redesign ourselves completely over the next thousand years. At about the same time, New York physicist Michio Kaku was proposing in his new book, *Visions,* that we might get as far as genetically engineering wings for ourselves. In his new book, *Consilience,* Harvard evolutionary theorist Edward O. Wilson argues that we are about to decommission natural selection. From that point on, human evolution would be decided by our science and technology – except if tempered by ethics and political choice. Wilson at least suggests that perhaps we should set limits. Christopher Dewdney says we should not. In his new book, *Last Flesh,* he argues that the chess match in which the IBM supercomputer defeated Garry Kasparov was the dawn of the post-human era. At that moment, he says, we entered a transhuman era that will be shaped by genetic engineering and computer-based artificial intelligence. What should we do about all this? According to Dewdney, we should only prepare ourselves psychologically for our next, most momentous step, when human beings – "at least as we currently know them" – may well cease to exist, our DNA-based substrate left behind.

The role of religion

Obviously, this kind of speculation is optimistic that science and technology will continue to bring us new and marvellous discoveries and inventions. A key question is what part religion will play in this future. Some commentators are very pessimistic. For example, Prof. Michael Barber, head of a unit in England's department for education and employment, said that over the past

200 years "the belief systems which sustained Western societies have crumbled away" and that Christianity has become "a minority interest."

We can't just stand on the sidelines, mesmerized by the debate among high-powered scientists. As members of the people of God, we cannot settle for "a minority interest" in the future of the world. Questions about the future of science and technology raise faith questions which we cannot avoid. We have our own thoughts about that but are running out of time today. We look forward to your reactions.

Mae and Bernard

Dear Mae and Bernard,

As you know, besides reading about religion and science I have been involved as a founder of the Centre for Studies in Religion & Society, an interdisciplinary dialogue and research centre at the University of Victoria, BC. I want to stress two fascinating developments. One is the way science and religion have been coming closer together. The older attitudes that put science and religion into inevitable and perpetual opposition are fading. Equally important is the fact that science today is reshaping our view of the entire world. The physical sciences are probing ever deeper into the internal structure of matter, the shape of the cosmos and the history of time. You mentioned some of the developments planned or realized. My faltering steps into modern physics were made enjoyable by Robert Gilmore's delightful book, *Alice in Quantumland*. I still get confused, but am also somewhat consoled to learn that this is normal, given the complexity of these new endeavours.

The universe as a machine

For our Christian culture, for the way we think and act, our worldview is important. Science has been shifting how we look at the world, as you said. Our image of the universe until recently was that of a machine. Francis Bacon, considered the founder of modern science, urged future scientists to squeeze, mould and shape nature. Their aim, he said, should be to "enlarge the bounds of human empire to the effecting of all things possible." In other words, if it can be done, do it! This "technological imperative" still mesmerizes and almost controls us. That pretty well sums up the driving force behind modern science and technology. There is a moral question here: do we creatures face any limits to what we can do?

Isaac Newton and others in a long procession of scientists have tried to discover how the "machine" works. We figured that if we could discover the laws controlling nature we would have the world at our command. We wanted power and control over sickness, natural disasters, even the weather. God was the clock-maker, and our responsibility was to find out how the machine works, keep it running, and run it our way. If things broke down, our first reflex was to blame God: Why did God do this to me? For many, the aim was to get full control of the machine so that even the idea of God could be abandoned.

New discoveries in science

A shift in scientific thinking began with Einstein's theory of relativity and the realization that the universe is older than we thought and continues to expand. Scientists began to tell us that our old certitudes about time, space and matter had to be modified. The older concept, that the world is made up of solid objects governed by deterministic laws of nature, does not fit with new discoveries. A rock, for example, is not solid. It is a "sea-bed of minute, 'moving' particles . . . a pulsating conundrum of crystallized energy," as O'Murchu puts it. Matter is much older than we ever imagined. Outer space keeps expanding – expanding forever, some astronomers now say. And physicists looking into the atom for the ultimate particle of matter reach the point where they cannot say whether they are dealing with particles of matter or with waves of energy. They can observe one or the other but not both at once. One result is that the language of natural laws has given way to talk about sets of relationships.

So an entirely different conception of the world, of reality, is emerging. That in turn is leading to a fascinating new relationship between the most advanced science, on the one hand, and what can be called spirituality and the world of meaning, on the other. Everything is related to everything else. The universe will keep expanding whether we humans are there or not. Yet we have a very important relationship – that of being that element of the universe that has expanded to the level of consciousness. In a sense, we can help the universe be conscious of itself.

"Ultra-humanity": an evolutionary necessity

Teilhard de Chardin speculated that after slowly giving birth to life and then to humanity, the universe is itself being transformed by the evolution of humanity under the impact of Christ, leading to "ultra-humanity." The details of the Chardinian vision of the future are not important to us here. What we need to retain is that he foresaw humanity eventually reaching spiritual maturity through the influence of the Spirit of Christ. Scientists working since de Chardin's death have gone beyond his scientific knowledge, but they retain something of his hope for a better kind of humanity. The "ultra-humanity" that de Chardin projected only as an evolutionary possibility, today's scientists insist is an evolutionary necessity. Everyone sees that death, destruction and despair are widespread. If we continue our violent exploitation and desecration of the environment, we may be heading into chaos, destruction, and eventual annihilation. We have reached the point where we could destroy the whole enterprise.

Who can reverse the cumulative destruction that we humans are causing? At this point, environmentalists and Christian moralists converge in one reply. The onus is on us. The burden is ours to bear. We are the stewards of creation, but we must abandon any idea that we can render an account of our stewardship through the exercise of power and control. As British economist Barbara Ward used to say, either we learn to love – love the universe and love one another – or we will die. This ties in with Brian Swimme's view, that the touchstone of morality is the development of the universe according to its divine purpose. Everything we do as humans to help the universe achieve its divine purpose is good. Anything we do which destroys the environment and prevents it from developing to the glory of God is evil.

Vatican II made plain that our ideas about God are always culturally conditioned. When we had a machine view of the world, we talked about God from within that vision. Now, new views of the world open us up to new understandings of God. Now we see that God's plan for the universe is much more complex than we used to think. In 50 years, today's children will have an understanding of God and of the world that goes far beyond anything that we can talk about today. But even now we have to try to talk about that future view. I believe that the Holy Spirit continues to work to build up the church and promote the reign of God. The Holy Spirit is working through all people of good will in ways we don't recognize because we see things too much through the perspective of the institution, rather than from the charismatic side.

Modern Scripture scholars tell us that everything before the story of Sarah and Abraham is pre-history. The earlier stories in Genesis are about the meaning of how the world came into existence. These stories are about values such as truth, trust, constancy and fidelity, which now apply in our new cosmology, our new understanding of the cosmos. The Garden of Eden story is not about the difference between a primitive garden and a modern one. It is about fundamental values and relationships between God and humans, between creator and creation. It is about the expansive goodness of creation and the narrow selfishness of the sin into which human beings can fall. The story of Cain and Abel is about the sanctity of life and the concept of solidarity and responsibility for one another.

Our most crucial moral questions today are about how we build such values into the cosmos, even into cyberspace. We seem to grasp easily enough how freedom and power work in cyberspace. We know how to make this new technology fast, free and powerful. But how do we make it truthful, respectful, compassionate, tender? How do we use our new computer tools as instruments of solidarity and peace, knowing that almost all have been developed as instruments of war? Universal values have to be brought into play here: for example, truth in communications. The new media, which are controlled by a small number of corporations, can largely determine the nature of communications, our culture, how people think, how they react. Given the power of our new machines and systems, I would say that the need for truth, justice and compassion is stronger than ever.

The world as a garden

While some people continue to act as if the world is a machine that they can control and use as they wish, we have to start thinking of it as a garden. Force has no place when you are seeding a garden or teaching music to a child. You have to handle new growth and awakening interest and talent very delicately. Like a little flower. You don't go in with a bulldozer. All life has to be nurtured tenderly. That, too, is one of the stories in Genesis. We are given the world to cultivate and to tend. That means care and tenderness. Unfortunately, in the past many people distorted this Genesis story into a license to exploit, dominate, ravage and destroy. Environmentalists rightly condemn those who took this mistaken notion from the biblical story of creation. In a proper understanding of the Genesis story, nothing allows us humans to destroy other species, waste irreplaceable natural resources in the production of armaments, or build economic schemes that deprive millions of the possibility of having adequate food, housing, education, health care and other things needed for full human development.

You see, I am not negative about modernity, despite its obvious flaws. I remain hopeful, and my hope is constantly buoyed by learning from modern thinkers like Jennifer Cobb. In her book *Cybergrace,* she considers how divinity can inhabit the fruits of all human endeavours, including the machines we invent and the developing minds that emerge from modern science. She offers exciting new insights into the "cybergrace" that may be present in cyberspace, waiting for a new generation of reflective humans to probe its mysteries. I see emerging here a continued vindication of Teilhard de Chardin, so maligned by people who misrepresented what he sought to express, or rejected because they could not face the implications of what he thought is coming. How true it is that the "micro-phase" wisdom we have developed so far no longer suffices for the "macro-phase" awareness we need as our knowledge of the universe expands. Just imagine what kind of transformation will be required in our schools and universities, including Catholic ones, if we are to prepare new generations for the future we begin to perceive. That is one reason I am grateful that the University of Victoria accepted my proposal for a centre of dialogue between the sciences and modern world faiths. I believe it is unique in its field. It has already proven its worth and made a modest contribution to restoring dialogue between science and religion.

On this point, Ken Wilber, in his fascinating new book *The Marriage of Sense and Soul,* suggests that science and religion can be reconciled and integrated if art, morals, spirituality and science agree to respect the scientific discipline which lies at the heart of all human endeavours. Successful human undertakings in any discipline, he notes, require induction, experimentation and verification.

+*Remi*

Dear Remi,

We share your view that God put other creatures under our care. The key word is *care*. Death, destruction and despair dominate our world because we are not really *taking care* of the rest of creation. We are exploiting and desecrating, raping and violating, not "cultivating and tending." The problem is not that our Bible story set us on a path to destruction. The problem is that in our sinfulness we do not follow God's plan for creation.

We are addicted to false economic theories which lead us to chase after more and more material wealth through consuming still more of the world's natural resources. Look at how, in pursuit of economic growth, we kill off our cod and salmon, clear-cut our forests and put our best farm land under pavement. As Diarmuid O'Murchu warns, "we trip headlong into chaos, destruction, and eventual annihilation. It sounds too pessimistic to be taken seriously, so we resort to denial and rationalization. . . . We are immersed in a cultural death-wish of the gravest proportions, one from which we can only hope to escape from some divine miracle."

And, of course, we agree with O'Murchu that "the miracle has already happened! The Christ-event, with its climax of death and resurrection, with a special faith content for Christians, has a global symbolic significance of divine rescue." And now, "the onus is not on some divine, external agent who can reverse, with sleight of hand, the cumulative destruction we humans have caused. The burden is ours to own and to bear. We are the stewards of creation and the time is at hand to render an account of our stewardship." We join ourselves to this challenge but we do not share O'Murchu's pessimism. He says it is unlikely we humans will survive the impending global crisis. He suggests we may face virtual extinction "possibly within the next *fifty* to *one hundred* years." We believe, rather, that the Spirit will awaken and empower us to undergo the kind of conversion that will prolong human and other forms of life. Perhaps, as Cobb suggests, some kind of "cybergrace" is developing mysteriously; but what is certain is that we humans have to take better care of each other and of the universe. The urgency of doing this is evident, requiring no further evidence.

Indeed, our hope is in the Vatican II call for the laity to lead that kind of conversion and renewal, "by engaging in temporal affairs and ordering them according to God's plan" (LG, 31). We emphasize once again, that this key council teaching has scarcely been heard as yet.

Mae and Bernard

Dear Mae and Bernard,

I have no problem with your suggestion that the effective and practical church responses to questions of social justice and environmental protection will come mainly from the laity. That's where we pinned our hopes at Vatican II. We wrote: "It is to the laity, though not exclusively to them, that secular duties and activity properly belong.... Let them be aware of what their faith demands of them in these matters and derive strength from it; let them not hesitate to take the initiative at the opportune moment and put their findings into effect. It is *their task to cultivate a properly informed conscience and to impress the divine law on the affairs of the earthly city* (my emphasis). For guidance and spiritual strength let them turn to the clergy; but let them realize that their pastors will not always be so expert as to have a ready answer to every problem (even every grave problem) that arises; this is not the role of the clergy; it is rather up to the laity to shoulder their responsibilities under the guidance of Christian wisdom and with eager attention to the teaching authority of the Church" (GS, 43).

What teaching authority? Well, Holy Scripture, council teachings, papal encyclicals and episcopal conference documents which make up the literature that we call the social teachings of the church – "the church's best-kept secret," as some say. Moreover, if you laity think you are not hearing enough about these social teachings, you should demand more from your pastors – at every level in the church. The laity, we said clearly at Vatican II, "have the right to receive in abundance the help of the spiritual goods of the church" (LG, 37).

The end of the church?

I want to touch on what you said earlier about the religious visionaries who keep on predicting that the end of the world is just around the corner. Even more people are predicting that the church is coming to an end. At your suggestion, I have taken a look at George Tavard's book *The Church: Community of Salvation*. I want to pick up on what he says about whether the church is approaching an end or some kind of new start, a new Pentecost.

I agree with Tavard that there are both Protestants and Catholics who assume that the church is shrinking because the world is nearing its end. Some fundamentalist Protestants predict that the world will end in the near future. In Catholic circles, the concerns expressed take a different form – worry about declining vocations to the priesthood, nostalgia for past ages of faith, efforts to renew fervour by stressing that life on earth is not a supreme good and should be lived as a preparation for our resurrection and eternal life with God.

I also agree when Tavard indicates that he sees a great future for a renewed church. He projects two scenarios. We could destroy our habitat and that of all other species by poisoning the natural environment or destroying life altogether through nuclear war. In that case, the church ends if human life destroys itself. He inclines, however, towards the possibility of humanity converting from carelessness and violence and adopting an earth-saving lifestyle. In that case, "if the universe remains inhabitable for humankind, the church has an indefinite future ahead of itself, possibly for many millennia."

+Remi

Dear Remi,

We seem to be caught in a vicious circle about the future. Many of the advances in human science and technology are immensely beneficial. We want more of these new wonders, especially for the promise they hold out for assuring food supplies, controlling diseases, and much else. At the same

46

time, the threat to the natural world which sustains us and all other life also comes from the rapid advance of science and technology harnessed to industry. "An increasing number of scientists and engineers are speaking out but they cannot resolve the crisis," biologist Ghillean Prance, director of England's Royal Botanic Gardens at Kew, noted after the 1997 Kyoto meeting on climate change. This, he said, is because the threat to the planet involves moral issues of justice and stewardship that cannot be resolved by scientists, technicians and engineers. Modern science and technology raise two interlocked non-scientific questions: Should any limit be put on what we can do? If yes, by whom and just how will the line be drawn?

So, moral questions about whether we should limit human activity become political questions. Who sets the agenda for modern science? Who controls the budget? How do we post-council Christians read the "signs of the times" about new research and development? How do we engage in the temporal affairs of science and technology, and help order them according to God's will, as Vatican II directs us to do?

The role of democracy

To deal with such questions, democracy must be brought into decision-making about science and technology, according to Jeremy Rifkin, in his recent book *The Biotech Industry*. He argues that science and technology can and must be controlled and directed, by informed public opinion in democratic ways. "Until now," he says, "the debate over biotechnology has engaged a narrow group of molecular biologists, industry executives, government policy makers and critics. With the new technologies flooding into the marketplace and into our lives, the moment has arrived for a much broader debate over the benefits and risks of the new science." He calls for a debate as deep as it is broad, extending beyond professionals and "experts" and including the whole of society. It is a call which shows the shallowness of most political debate and most mainline information media. While legislators pander to vested economic interests with the power to influence elections, and newsrooms are overshadowed by related concerns about advertising revenues, who will raise the fundamental questions about our common future, such as those Rifkin discusses?

Bio-technology and ethics

An economist and social critic, Rifkin describes the new bio-industrial world that is growing out of a marriage of new life sciences and new global corporations. Computers are being used to organize vast new genetic information, which is being patented by global corporations. Their life-science complexes are poised to flood the world with new products of genetic engineering. The news media, themselves increasingly the products of a few transnational corporations, flaunt the wonders of a cornucopia of genetically engineered plants and animals to feed a hungry world, genetically derived sources of energy and fibre to expand trade and build a "renewable" society, wonder drugs and genetic therapies to produce healthier babies, eliminate painful diseases and lengthen human life. Mostly we hear about what are seen as the triumphs of this brave new world. We are told almost nothing about the issues of justice and good stewardship involved. We get almost no information, to take just one example, about continuous efforts by U.S. agribusiness to get laws passed in that country and throughout the world to control markets in favour of their own foods produced with growth hormones or by genetic engineering.

The trade in genetic products raises more troubling questions than any other economic revolution in history, Rifkin says. Will the artificial creation of cloned and transgenic animals mean the end of nature? Will the mass release of genetically engineered life forms cause catastrophic genetic pollution and irreversible damage to the biosphere? What are the consequences of laws that turn the world's gene pool into patented products controlled by a handful of giant corporations? What risks do we take in trying to design more "perfect" human beings?

Rifkin reminds us that the search for "better" genes resembles the eugenics movement that has been virtually edited out of American history books. It was U.S. President Theodore Roosevelt, not Hitler, who said "the great problem of civilization is to secure a relative increase of the valuable as compared with the less valuable or noxious elements of the population." It was a U.S. geneticist who wrote in the July 1934 *Journal of Heredity* that Germany was "proceeding toward a policy that will accord with the best thought of eugenicists in all civilized countries."

The issue, Rifkin says, is not to try to stop science and technology. The question is what kind of biotechnologies will we choose, and who will decide. It is a "limited" vision, he insists, to believe that the industrialized genetic engineering being planned today is the only way to apply new-found scientific knowledge. It "keeps us from entertaining other options which might prove even more effective in addressing the needs and fulfilling the dreams of current and future generations." Truly, as Rifkin concludes, "the moment has arrived for a much broader debate over the benefits and risks of the new science, one that extends beyond professional authorities and 'experts' on both sides of the issue and includes the whole of society."

This is a serious challenge for all Christians. The issue is to involve other people than those with a high-stake commercial interest in the new developments. This is also a central concern of Princeton molecular biologist Lee Silver in his book *Remaking Eden.* He has been attacked by other scientists for questioning how the knowledge of human genes may be used. His fear is not that genetic engineering is going to be used badly. "I think it is going to be used to prevent disease. The problem is – in the U.S. – that it is going to be controlled by the market place. And I am very cynical about the market place. . . . I think it's awful, this huge gap between the haves and the have nots, and genetic engineering just widens that gap." In this regard, Rifkin and Silver share similar concerns. They would agree with Dewdney that we are "approaching a terrifying, intoxicating and possibly dangerous threshold, a border of awareness of whose other side is a mystery as imponderable as anything we have yet wondered about." However, where Dewdney and others adopt an aggressively macho, let's-do-it optimism, Rifkin and others call for serious thought and broadly-informed choice.

Just getting the information we need for informed choice will be difficult. The news media are increasingly owned by just a few industrial complexes. Industries tend to hide bad news about their products. This was illustrated by a February 7, 1998, BBC television news feature about the effects of rising levels of the female hormone estrogen in lakes and rivers and even in treated public water supplies. Alarming results are being detected by concerned scientists. Among fish, turtles and alligators living in affected waters, increasing numbers of male animals have been found also to have female sexual organs.

These findings led scientists to wonder what else the stray estrogen might be affecting. After further research, some believe that estrogen in our water is also related to increasing incidences of breast cancer in women, and to three increasing male problems: testicle deformities in baby boys, testicular cancer at a later age, and, in men aged 20 to 45, sperm counts as low as a quarter of what used to be considered normal. In the BBC broadcast, the main sources of the excess estrogen were said to be industrial effluents, detergents and various plastics, including the linings of tin cans, all of which leach hormone-like substances into our water and food. There was no mention of research on any effects of increased use of estrogen in birth-control pills.

Industrial problems: who will speak out?

At the end of such an overview of world industrial trends and the problems they bring us, we tend to feel overwhelmed. It seems almost absurd to say that the church has an important role to play in the debate about the future of the world that science can shape. Where are the outstanding Christian centres where the future of science and technology is the major concern? Catholic schools and colleges may be forming a few critical and creative individuals, but no major church presence is notable in the debate that Rifkin says is crucial.

Christians are among the members of many small, scattered non-governmental groups that protest cases of injustice or pollution, but such groups are marginalized in most dioceses and parishes. From what activity we can see regarding justice and the environment, can we really say with Vatican II that "the joy and hope, the grief and anguish of people of our time, especially of those who are poor or afflicted in any way, are the joy and hope, the grief and anguish of the followers of Christ as well" (GS, 1)?

What we have in the Catholic church are many words but few well-informed and highly-trained Catholics who know what their duty is in this new age of high technology. We need to stir up the power of the Spirit dwelling in us. How might we bring this about, so that, in harmony with Matthew's vision of the last judgement, we will clearly see that what we neglect or refuse to do for neighbours in need, we fail or refuse to do for Christ?

The least we can say is that the new challenges from science and technology call for a new kind of response from the church. We need to educate ourselves in ways to promote awareness, concern, excellence and clear thinking. We have to purge ourselves of Western individualism, and replace it with compassion and solidarity. Obviously that ties in with what you were saying about the right of the laity to ask for the kind of pastoral services we need for our mission to shape science and technology and all other aspects of the temporal world "according to God's will," as Vatican II says.

Mae and Bernard

Dear Mae and Bernard,

You have reiterated several versions of a point with which I am in general agreement. Church teaching about the modern world is not well known, and most pastors are not busy promulgating it. However, that being said, I think it important to underline what the church *has* said, and to point out some positive new initiatives.

I think young people who are interested in science and technology will be open to what Vatican II said about religion and the modern world. The church has invited all people of good will to "engage with it in a conversation" about the future of humanity. Perhaps it won't be an easy conversation. For example, it was difficult at the 1996 Cairo world conference on population and development. Still, as church we are committed to continuing the conversation, one in which young people will be involved more and more. In doing so, we will be acting on what the council called our "responsibility of scrutinizing the signs of the times and of interpreting them in the light of the gospel" (GS, 4). We must not avoid the conversation just because we know that others will use different interpretive schemes.

One area where this appears to me to be particularly pertinent is the church's renewed dialogue with science. A profound misunderstanding took place during the seventeenth century. The "Galileo affair" is the best-known case. This really had more to do with faulty biblical scholarship than with a matter of faith. It also reflects the difficulties of the cultural environment of the time, when individual freedom was in short supply everywhere – not just in the church. In any event, great harm was done by what was seen as a clash between religion and science. The church, for its part, has now acknowledged its share of the blame.

Science and the church: a new dialogue

A new and promising dialogue has begun. Physics, cosmology, paleontology and psychology stand out among the sciences already involved. They have had a major impact on various domains of interest to the church. As you were pointing out earlier, some of the results and trends of modern science and technology are worrisome, and not just to us in the church. We must acknowledge, however, the positive results of science in general, and the work of particular individuals. Take, for instance, the influence of the Jesuit paleontologist, Teilhard de Chardin, on our Vatican II *Constitution on the Church in the Modern World.* More recently and closer to home, mention must be made of the work of Thomas Berry and Brian Swimme, summed up in their book, *The Universe Story.*

As you know, I have been pursuing a special interest in psychology. Self-understanding and self-development have become the goal of many people since the 1960s. A variety of disciplines have responded to this desire for more and better information about what makes us tick as human beings. Personality tests such as those developed by Myers-Briggs are one example. I have found these to be useful, but my preference is the Enneagram. It uses insights from Jungian psychology and links them with ancient Christian sources of spirituality dating back to the Desert Fathers in the fourth century. This combination has developed into an exciting new discipline which provides me with a powerful means of spiritual conversion and personal growth.

For authentic development as a human being, I need to know not only my strengths but also my weaknesses – my shadow side. What are the energies that drive me, consciously or unconsciously, and cause me to think, to feel and to act as I do? Why do I respond as I do to other people or to events that touch my life, and often to my own surprise? These questions, by the way, touch a key Vatican II teaching about human freedom. Human dignity, the council said, demands that we act "out of conscious and free choice, as moved and drawn in a personal way from within," and not from blind internal impulses or mere external constraint or pressure (GS, 17). Obviously, self-knowledge is central to conscious choice.

Head, heart and body: striving for balance

Psychology helps us to see that we have three primary sources of energy and inspiration – three "brains," if you will. This awareness leads us to a much more sophisticated understanding of human activity and interaction than we had before. Not only our head, but our heart and our body's vital forces govern how we feel and what we end up saying or doing. I have heard you, Mae, talk about this as the heart of the Kodaly method of music education which you have been promoting. Head, heart and body have indispensable roles to play. They need to be kept in balance and developed in their unique ways. Otherwise, one centre dominates and the others are misused or neglected or just follow along slavishly. How often have you heard someone say they let their heart run away with them, after they impulsively did something that they later regretted? Or, have you ever caught yourself saying something you would not have said if you had listened to your heart first? Or, indulged, as if compulsively, in feelings that you knew were wrong? These are examples of situations where a good grounding in the discipline of the Enneagram can make us better human beings, and bring peace and joy to our everyday endeavours and relationships.

My studies in the Enneagram began as a hobby but soon developed beyond that stage. To obtain certification in the discipline, I studied and worked with three pairs of experts in the field: Riso-Hudson, Hurley-Donson and Gotch-Walsh. Further inquiries and more experience led me into the fascinating experiment of using the Enneagram to open up the Sacred Scriptures. I worked with two friends in the Victoria diocese, Diane Tolomeo, a university professor, and Pearl Gervais, a consultant, to develop a novel program. Workshop participants are helped through self-analysis to locate themselves in one of the numbered "spaces" on the Enneagram chart. Then, by reading and discussing scriptural passages, the great persons we meet in the bible are similarly assigned "spaces," according to what they show of their personalities by things they said or did. Abraham and Sarah, Moses and Miriam, Job, Ruth, Peter, Paul, the Samaritan woman Jesus met at the well, the

Syro-Phoenician woman who pleaded for a cure for her daughter: these and many others can become our models or mentors.

Workshop participants gain self-knowledge from the exercise and also develop a more intimate relationship with some of our biblical fellow believers. I have learned a lot from putting myself in the place of any one of the biblical personalities. I reflect on how they relate to experiences and respond to God and to other people who influence them. For instance, I observe more deeply the exchange as Jesus warns Peter that he will betray his master. Peter is so impulsive and sure that he alone will never be a coward! Jesus tells Peter he has prayed for him so that his faith will not fail. Later, out of the experience of his own weakness, Peter learns to depend only on divine strength. Peter the betrayer is converted. I am awe-struck by the contrast with Judas! The faith of Peter, now tested and animated by the Spirit of the Risen Lord, makes him the "rock." He, with the entire college of bishops who will succeed the apostles, becomes an anchor for the faith of the body of believers down through the centuries. In this way, I try to deepen my own faith in Jesus Christ and to learn to count only on the Spirit of the Risen Lord to sustain me when things get tough. I hope to make good use of this approach to the Bible in future work as a counsellor and workshop director, after my mandate as bishop of Victoria has ended.

This is of more than just personal interest to me, of course. It is one example of how we believers can and should seek new ways to work with the findings of modern science. Indeed, I believe that in every field of science, believers can co-operate in creative ways, for the good of other people and of the entire universe. Perhaps one of the best ways to guard against the real threats involved in some new developments is for believers to plunge into science and technology in search of ways to serve "the least of these," our neighbours (Mt 25: 45). True followers of Christ have to become experts in their chosen field, where they can bring solid theological insights into rational scientific work. They must be expert in both fields. Hence the need for a new kind of Christian education, as you say.

We need balance and co-operation between science and religion for the reasons noted by John Paul II. "Science," he said, "can purify religion from error and superstition; religion can purify science from idolatry and false absolutes. Each can draw the other into a wider world, a world in which both can flourish." He adds other and deeper insights about this relationship in his 1998 encyclical, *Faith and Reason.*

+Remi

For Discussion

1. Discuss Francis Bacon's view that a scientist should aim at dominating nature.
2. How do you understand the idea that there are both threats and promises in the advances of science and technology? Should there be any limits on science and technology? If so, who should decide those limits, and how should they be decided?
3. Discuss the concepts of progress and growth. Can a distinction be made between scientific advance and economic development?
4. Discuss what aspects of Christian teaching are most helpful for deciding the future directions of science and technology.
5. What do you think is the appropriate modern view of the relation between God, as Creator, and humankind, as collaborator in creation?
6. In what ways do we have common links with all of nature? In what ways might we feel set apart from other creatures?

For Action

1. Explore the causes of some local environmental problem – soil, water, air, noise. Try to determine and weigh natural and human factors.
2. Research the concept of "the common good," and how it relates to private enterprise.
3. Meet with members of some local group who are concerned about environmental issues to discuss what motivates them and what opposition they meet.

4. Seek out a scientist or an engineer to discuss if they put any limits on their work, and how they set limits. Do they feel free to do everything they can do?

5. What are the main issues being debated in your community about medical research and practices? Explore the views of both the practitioners involved and those who question them.

Further Reading

Hawking, Stephen. *A Brief History of Time: From the Big Bang to Black Holes.* New York: Bantam Books, 1988.

Hurley, Kathleen, and Theodorre Donson. *My Best Self: Using the Enneagram To Free the Soul.* San Francisco: Harper San Francisco, 1993.

John Paul II. *Faith and Reason,* encyclical letter. Ottawa: CCCB Publication Service, 1998.

Kaku, Michio. *Visions: How Science will Revolutionize the 21st Century.* New York: Doubleday, 1997.

O'Murchu, Diarmuid. *Quantum Theology: Spiritual Implications of the New Physics.* New York: Crossroad, 1997.

Rifkin, Jeremy. *The Biotech Century: Harnessing the Gene and Remaking the World.* New York: Tarcher/Putnam, 1998.

Riso, Don Richard and Russ Hobson. *Personality Types: Using the Enneagram for Self-Discovery.* Rev. ed., New York: Houghton Mifflin, 1996.

Silver, Lee. *Remaking Eden.* Toronto: Hearst Book Group of Canada, 1998.

Swimme, Brian, and Thomas Berry. *The Universe Story.* San Francisco: Harper and Row, 1992.

Wilber, Ken. *The Marriage of Sense and Soul: Integrating Science and Religion.* New York: Random House, 1998.

"All My Relations":
How We Treat Other People

This chapter continues an exploration of the modern world which, according to Vatican II, Christians are supposed to serve by bringing gospel values to life. Whereas Chapter 3 looked at how people are treating nature, this chapter looks especially at how we are treating other people. The focus here is the growing gap between the excessively rich and the desperately poor. The concept of right relations as a moral principle is discussed. The sexual revolution and the rise of consumerism are sketched as examples of how identifiable people have changed the modern world. This raises questions about who is causing poverty. The role of representatives of the rich, developed countries in shaping international agreements to the advantage of people who are already wealthy is sketched. More details about Catholic social teaching are introduced, particularly what Vatican II and the post-council popes have taught about the laity's particular vocation to shape temporal affairs according to God's will. A Canadian study about how religious and cultural values can be integrated in plans for economic development is introduced. The chapter concludes with a reflection on teachings of the Canadian Catholic bishops about how Christians might better serve the poor.

Dear Mae and Bernard,

Canadian Natives will often end a public statement with the words "All my relations." They say it the way we might say "Amen" at the end of a prayer. I've heard that a number of times. They say it out of respect for all the other creatures of which they are a part. They recognize that we are creatures among creatures and we are all in relation with one another.

Apart from all else it signifies, their expression is for me an embarrassing mirror reflecting my own innate prejudices towards my Native sisters and brothers. I know I have often commented on Third World issues far from home while not paying enough attention to the racism underlying our relations with Canadian Natives.

Although I remember my parents as being kind towards people who were then disparagingly called "the Indians," I can see now that the Manitoba culture of my childhood gave me negative feelings about these marginalized people. Around the village of Swan Lake, as I grew up, non-Natives rarely spoke to them. We children kept our distance. Later, when I came to Vancouver Island as bishop, I found that a large segment of the Catholic population was Native. They greeted me warmly and honoured me with adoption into their race, with the name "Great Priest White Swan," which I treasure. I regularly visited Native communities and made many dear friends.

I also visited the two residential schools the church administered at that time. I did not hear of any cases of abuse, but now I see more clearly the unconscious cultural abuse that was taken for granted as part of the educational pattern. I learned more of these realities as chair of the British Colombia Human Rights Commission from 1974 to 1977. I had many occasions to see first hand what damage discrimination against Native people can cause. And now we know much more about the extent of that abuse, after the allegations and criminal convictions that have clouded our recent relations with Native sisters and brothers.

We need to face these abuses, our innate racist attitudes and our cultural blindness. We need to make appropriate amends to Native people. We need to do this as part of a "dialogue of conversion" with Natives, through which both we and they can be liberated from attitudes and prejudices that keep us from mutual respect, friendship and solidarity.

A civilization of love

What values should Christians try to bring into our future relations with Natives, with other peoples and with all of the universe? One answer is given in the liturgy for our Feast of Christ the King. The preface speaks of building a kingdom of God on earth that is marked by truth and life, holiness and grace, justice, love and peace. We must pray that all the baptized will strive to bring these values into all their relationships. This is what the civilization of love, often mentioned by John Paul II, would look like.

I wish that, as we go into our secular vocation in an expanding cyber-space world, all the baptized would try to think of ways that people can be less individualistic, less atomized, especially in the industrialized countries. It is deeply contradictory that just when scientists are showing that the whole universe is a network of relationships, human beings feel they are more and more separated and isolated from one another. This is seen in increasing loneliness and even homelessness, with more people just living on the street. The high rate of suicides also shows this. Worse, modern business depends on us seeking our self-interest as consumers. Competition is the norm, not co-operation and solidarity. Everything about our industrialized culture inclines us to neglect the needs of others, the common good. For example, as we build our cities our first concern is how to move goods and services at minimal costs for maximum profits. The results for human relationships are secondary. People may have to travel many lonely, boring hours to get to work. That does not matter so long as a new widget or a gallon of oil can be sent as quickly as possible to where it is needed in order to make a dollar.

The values currently dominating the marketplace seem to me very destructive, retarding the growth and development of human beings. I distinguish between the values at play in the market and those on which most of us base our behaviour. I believe that by nature, human beings are good. Furthermore, through our baptism we are gifted by the Spirit to share and to build a civilization which truly reflects the goodness and beauty of God. This brings us back to what we were discussing earlier about the call for the laity to live out gospel values within our society. This is the counter-cultural challenge we face.

God is love. God's love is a creating love. Creation comes out of God's love. Made in the image of God, we too are creators, as parents, artists, architects and engineers and in all the other ways that we live and work. If we are to approach the divine, our creating work has to have something of the quality of God's. How much of what we create comes out of love? Love for other human beings? Love for all other creatures? Love for the whole of the universe? Is it not true that most human creativity is directed toward self-gain, self-love?

This is part of the crisis we face. We are not sufficiently concerned about how rapidly the natural environment is being destroyed. But worse, we seem even less disturbed by how much people are hurt by widespread unemployment, massive poverty and other forms of human degradation. Certainly, in business, money comes before people. If there is a choice between making a certain level of profit or giving a person a job, priority is given to profit. In trade missions around the world, the Canadian Prime Minister and U.S. President have steadfastly refused even to talk about human rights' violations in countries where they hoped to do more business. There can be no clearer examples of the priority of pragmatism over moral principles. As St. Paul says, the love of money is the root of all kinds of evil (1 Timothy 6:10).

Right relations: the key issue

To me, the fundamental issue is right relations. We start from the idea that God created heaven and earth. We are creatures ourselves. Right relations mean that we put ourselves in that position of creatures, of receiving life and all else from the creator. As Christians we also remember that no matter how much we love God's good world, our first commandment is to love God and to love our neighbours as ourselves. Much as we care about the environment, we must care more for fellow human beings in need. Do we, like Adam, refuse to trust God and try to have it our way, to set the norms for ourselves? And thereby alienate ourselves from the source of our being? Do we, Cain-like, take the law into our own hands? Or do we, like Christ, the second Adam, place total trust in God's plan even if we can't understand it? That's the ultimate question. Jesus on the cross didn't fully understand, and yet he trusted.

Jesus received the fullness of the power of the Spirit in the resurrection because he trusted.

Now, right relationships require that, as we see the universe expanding, we collaborate with the universe to work towards restoring or maintaining right relationships, starting with caring for neighbours in need, to build up a civilization of love. That's another version of Brian Swimme's insight that whatever contributes to the proper unfolding of the universe according to God's will is good. Anything against it is evil. That's the fundamental basis of morality.

+ *Remi*

Dear Remi,

We especially liked what you said about Canadian Natives stressing "all my relations." Our Christian tradition calls us to the same sense of respect and solidarity, if we respect and live by that tradition. From the opening lines of the Bible we learn that God created the world, and judged it to be good. God put the world into our hands, for us "to cultivate and to tend" it. The things we see around us, both the marvels and the miseries, are mostly man-made. This is our culture. Is this what God intended? We can say yes, when we look at the natural beauty around us, and at the technology that eases human suffering, speeds communication and reduces drudgery. But we must add that God does not want us to reduce millions of neighbours to grinding poverty, waste resources on tools of war, and despoil water, air and soil.

Too many people, we find, steer away from naming those who cause social or environmental change. They tend to speak instead of anonymous social trends, market pressures, and the like. We heard recently of a retreat director who led participants into a reflection about "polar shifts" as an explanation of social changes. Others talk about "paradigm shifts." Any such analysis makes social change seem impersonal, evolutionary and inevitable. If, instead, the leaders of social change are named and stripped of anonymity and mystery, we are empowered. If we don't like the values they espouse and the direction in which they are leading us, we can react. We know whom to work against to change direction. Often it is only in the longer view of history that we see clearly who has been shaping our world, and in what direction. We will expand on just three examples out of many that could be chosen: the sexual revolution, the rise of consumerism, and the creation of poverty. People who can be named were the leaders in all these developments.

The sexual revolution

What we call the sexual revolution was launched in the 1950s and 1960s. Because of their personal efforts to change public attitudes, Alfred Kinsey and Hugh Hefner are rightly regarded as symbols of the attitude that we can see and think and do whatever we want. This is a change from what our grandparents valued, and it is labelled sexual enlightenment. We know how this change was brought about. Kinsey's 1948 report on American sexual behaviour inspired sex-education programs in schools, encouraged therapists to tell patients that "if it feels good, do it," helped launch new sex industries including the Playboy clubs that made Hefner fabulously wealthy, and led to the repeal of laws against such actions as sodomy.

Kinsey's influence grew in part because he was able to maintain a myth until his death. More truthful recent biographies show that "Kinsey was not quite . . . the simple empiricist disinterestedly reporting his data." In a recent *New Yorker* magazine article, James H. Jones draws attention to a harsher side of Kinsey. He was "a covert crusader . . . who created around himself a kind of utopian community in which sexual experimentation was encouraged," Jones writes. What really inspired Kinsey's crusade "was his own secret life. . . . From the very beginnings of his research into sexual behaviour, the Americans who most persistently engaged Kinsey's attention were people who were either on the margins or beyond the pale: homosexuals, sadomasochists, voyeurs, exhibitionists, pedophiles, transsexuals, transvestites, fetishists. . . . [His] methodology and his sampling techniques virtually guaranteed that he would find what he was looking for," Jones recalls. Of course, latter-day exposure of bias in Kinsey's research will not of itself undo the results of his crusade – especially after Hefner, in turn, helped to build voyeurism and pornography into a transnational industry. Also, we know from ancient art and literature that Kinsey and Hefner did not invent interest in eroticism, but they led the social change that makes it a dominant part of popular culture today.

Consumerism and the great American dream

Similarly, consumerism as we know it is an invention of the leaders of big science and big industry. Until the 1920s, consumption was just another name for tuberculosis. Since then consumption has been changed from medical spectre to commercial necessity. Part of the great American dream has been shaped by utopian visions of men and women early in the twentieth century who looked to a future world where machines would replace human labour, creating a near-workerless society of abundance and leisure. Science fiction writers made a huge contribution to this dream. So did the organizers of world fairs with their dazzling displays of technical wonders. Oh, how our grandparents marvelled at the new technology of their day! Some of our parents and we ourselves dreamed that one day science and technology would free us from a life of hardship and toil and usher in an earthly kingdom of leisure and abundance. And now our grandchildren dream of travelling at nanosecond speeds along information superhighways, entering worlds of virtual reality and cyberspace.

As this world of technical wonders developed, the capacity to produce goods soared. Early twentieth century industrialists worried especially about how to increase consumption. Our ancestors were too thrifty. Careful use of money, self-sacrifice and saving were hallmarks of both the American Protestant tradition and of the new immigrants coming to Canada and the U.S. American business leaders therefore set out to change people from investors in the future to spenders in the present. It was in their interest to convert North Americans from thrift to spend-thrift. This became the industrial goal. For this as for everything else, they turned to engineering techniques which were applied in two new industries, advertising and marketing. Common people were enticed to emulate the rich, to take on the trappings of wealth and prosperity previously reserved for the business aristocracy and social elite. For example, consumption economist Hazel Kyrk argued in 1923 that overproduction and technological unemployment could be mitigated, even eliminated, if only the working class could be re-educated toward what she called "the dynamic consumption of luxuries." "Luxuries for the well-off," she said, had to be "turned into necessities for the poorer classes."

As a result of the success of this effort, the average North American today consumes twice as much as at the end of World War II. We use about 30 times as much of the world's resources as people in a favella in Peru or Brazil or a mountain village in El Salvador. We take conspicuous consumption for granted, both as a personal right and as a necessity for a healthy economy. When we start to spend less on ourselves, economists who work for the banks and other large corporations complain that there is a failure of what they call consumer confidence. It is no mystery, then, why we spend and consume at such a rate. We are simply responding to the intentions of those who manipulate us through advertising and marketing techniques. We consume resources at a rate the world cannot sustain. And, as we use up resources so greedily, we create poverty for others. However, our consumerism, and the advertising and marketing that stimulate it, can be countered, and changed!

A similar analysis can be made of who causes poverty. World-wide, unemployment is now at the highest level since the Great Depression of the 1930s. Yet, some of our brightest minds are at work at this moment planning how production costs might be cut still more by using ever-more sophisticated computers, robots and other cutting-edge technologies to replace human workers in virtually every sector and industry. The new information technology – the Internet – could raise educational levels everywhere, but we are not using it primarily for this purpose. Instead, the info-revolution "is producing a new breed of billionaires who are worsening inequalities both in terms of financial rewards and in dividing the world into info-rich and info-poor. It's a new form of highway robbery," the *Guardian Weekly* has commented.

Causes of poverty: overpopulation or economic policies?

We saw first-hand how public opinion in the industrialized countries is manipulated when Bernard was a non-governmental participant at the 1974 United Nations (UN) population conference in Bucharest and the 1976 UN human habitation conference in Vancouver. The "plan of action" that was to be approved in Bucharest was drafted mainly by U.S. officials, with the support of representatives of the governments of the major industrialized countries, including Canada. It stressed the need for population controls, especially in poor countries. At Bucharest, once the debate began, representatives of poor countries moved and passed more than 160 amendments. The final text at Bucharest therefore said, in general, that the roots of Third World poverty are to be found not in Third World over-population but in the after-effects of colonialism and the impact of trade and fiscal arrangements under the Bretton Woods agreements which set up the World Bank, the International Monetary Fund (IMF) and the General Agreement on Tariffs and Trade (GATT). The Third World countries said at Bucharest that they wanted a New International Economic Order (NIEO), not population controls. The representatives of the rich countries therefore left Bucharest defeated, with a final "plan of action" vastly different from the one they wanted. The Western press soothed them with reports that the Third World had "ignored reality" at Bucharest. Efforts began immediately to discredit the Third World campaign in favour of a NIEO. By the 1976 UN conference in Vancouver, on human habitations, a defence against the Third World agenda had been prepared. In every committee and at plenary sessions, we watched Canadians vote with representatives of other rich countries to delete from the final statement all references to the need for a new and more just international economic order. The rich allowed no talk of change in the system that makes them rich. If the poor were ever to have better housing, clean water and safe sanitation, they'd have to find other means. By the time of the 1994 UN population and development conference in Cairo, the Holy See's delegation was ridiculed for even trying to get a serious discussion of Third World development needs. Any changes in world systems, such as new free trade agreements, have been in favour of those who are already rich.

The world is increasingly being polarized into two classes. One is an elite, skilled in the new information technologies, who control and manage the high-tech global economy. The other class is made up of the growing numbers of permanently displaced workers around the world. These women and men have few prospects and little hope of meaningful employment in an increasingly automated world. And, within our cities, which already divide and isolate people too much, the number of people living on the streets grows, while the wealthy move even farther from the poor by withdrawing into guarded or gated communities.

In fact, we humans are causing social and environmental disintegration in nearly every country, as David C. Korten notes in his book *When Corporations Rule the World*. We are breaking down both the social fabric that sustains human community and the regenerative capacities of the ecosystem. This destruction is accelerated by our continued quest for economic growth as the organizing principle of public policy. Yet, despite the signs of breakdown, "an active propaganda machine controlled by the world's largest corporations constantly reassures us that consumerism is the path to happiness." We are told that we will be better off if there is even less government control of market excesses. Economic globalization is promoted as both inevitable and a boon to the human species. We are, in fact, being fed a steady diet of myths that are propagated "to justify profligate greed and mask the extent to which the global transformation of human institutions is a consequence of the sophisticated, well-funded, and intentional interventions of a small elite whose money enables them to live in a world of illusion apart from the rest of humanity," as Korten puts it.

How, then, are we to judge this world, as members of the post-Vatican II Catholic church? What resources from our faith could help us to join in building instead a civilization of love? We cannot look to the Scriptures or other faith sources for exact plans for government or industry, but the principles to guide action are clear. How do we as Christians draw on our tradition and inner strength to face up to this situation? How do we encourage one another to live more simply?

Mae and Bernard

Dear Mae and Bernard,

Your latest letter outlines a rather full agenda for Spirit-inspired, post-council laity. As John Paul II noted in *Christifideles Laici*, Vatican II was the first church council ever to deal with the "nature, dignity, spirituality, mission and responsibility" of the laity (CL, 2). The council "went beyond other interpretations [of the lay role] which were predominantly negative. Instead, it opened itself to a decidedly positive vision [of the laity] and displayed a basic intention of asserting the full belonging of the lay faithful to the church and to its mystery" (CL, 9).

The council stressed that the church in its deepest nature is a participation, a sharing, in the life of the trinity of persons in one God. It presented the church as a God-given, Christ-centred, Spirit-empowered community of salvation. Some may still favour a pyramidal view of the church as a clergy-led structure, but this is not the main Vatican II vision. Nor is the emphasis on salvation of isolated individuals. Christ "willed to make men holy and save them, not as individuals without any bond or link between them, but rather to make them into a people who might acknowledge him and serve him in holiness," Vatican II teaches (LG, 9).

Lay participation in the mission of the church

Mention of the participation of the laity in the mission of the church probably starts most Catholics thinking about parish activities, such as pastoral council member, eucharistic minister or reader. But, the primary mission of lay people is outside church walls. There is more to the lay vocation than co-operating with priests and bishops in parish and diocesan affairs. When the council called lay people to full participation in the church, it also insisted on the unique character of their vocation, which is in a special way to seek the kingdom of God by engaging in temporal affairs and ordering them according to the will of God (LG, 31). Vatican II noted that everything said of the people of God "is addressed equally to laity, religious and clergy. Because of their situation and mission, however, certain things pertain particularly to the laity, both men and women, the foundations of which must be more fully examined owing to the special circumstances of our time" (LG, 30). What pertains particularly to the laity is their secular character, their vocation in temporal affairs. The question, then, is not whether the laity have a mission in the world and in the church; it is whether they are taking their mission seriously.

In the autumn of 1987, the Synod of Bishops studied the role and mission of the laity in the Church and in the world. As usual, John Paul II later published a major document, *Christifideles Laici*, summing up the Synod's conclusions. What he said is dramatic, but is virtually ignored today. The pope said the Synod showed that since Vatican II, the laity have been plagued by two main temptations. One is the temptation to separate faith from action – to profess belief in Jesus and then act like non-believers. The second is the temptation of getting so involved in church affairs that the laity's primary role in secular society is forgotten (CL, 2). Temptation is a strong word in Christian circles. We pray constantly that we may not be led into temptation. Yet here is the pope himself warning that involvement in church affairs can be a temptation – "the temptation of being so strongly interested in Church services and tasks that some fail to become actively engaged in their responsibilities in the professional, social, cultural and political world" (CL, 2).

The vocation of the laity

In saying this, the pope was simply building on Vatican II teaching that certain things pertain especially to the laity. Everyone in the Church is called to holiness. The laity's first and special vocation is to seek the kingdom by engaging in temporal affairs. The council stressed that the laity have a "secular character" that is proper and peculiar to them. "They live in the world.... There they are called by God that, being led by the spirit of the Gospel, they may contribute to the sanctification of the world, as from within like leaven, by fulfilling their own particular duties" (LG, 31).

The council went on to give even more specific direction to the laity: "It is their task to cultivate a properly informed conscience and to impress the divine law on the earthly city. For guidance and spiritual strength let them turn to the clergy; but let them realize that their pastors will not always be so expert as to have a ready answer for every problem (even every grave problem) that arises; that is not the role of the clergy; it is rather up to the layman [and woman] to shoulder their own responsibilities under the guidance of Christian wisdom and with eager attention to the teaching authority of the Church" (GS, 43).

Just in that sentence there is a whole agenda for laity: to cultivate an informed conscience; to act on one's own initiative; to bring God's law to life in the earthly city where the Spirit may be working in hidden ways. This notion, that the Church through its lay members has a secular dimension, has been little discussed and even less taught in the years since Vatican II. We should hear it more often from pastors and faith educators. Emphasis on the laity's secular vocation is also neglected in other aspects of our faith education. How prominent is this teaching in high school religion classes, or in the materials for adult faith education? The working paper for the special synod for America late in 1997 discussed the laity's involvement in local church affairs but is silent about their secular vocation. Worse still, no bishop at the synod made a major issue of the omission, although the Canadian delegation was alerted to the oversight. The laity's secular vocation is played down even in the new *Catechism of the Catholic Church*. It is as if what John Paul II said about the laity's vocation in the world was censored by the authors of the catechism, which has only three minor footnote references to *Christifideles Laici*.

The church's secular character

We say frequently that the church has a spiritual aspect but rarely that it also has a secular character or dimension through its lay members. Building on Vatican II teaching, Paul VI referred to this mission in a 1972 talk to members of secular institutes. The church, he said, "has an authentic secular dimension, inherent in her inner nature and mission, which is deeply rooted in the mystery of the Word Incarnate, and which is realized in different forms through her members" (CL, 15).

Four years later, in his apostolic exhortation *Evangelii Nuntiandi*, summing up the 1974 Synod on evangelization, Paul VI returned to this topic. He specified that the laity, "whose vocation commits them to the world and to various temporal enterprises, should exercise a special form of evangelization. Their principal and primary function is not to establish or promote ecclesial (that is, church) communities, which is the special function of pastors, but to develop and make effective all those latent Christian and evangelical possibilities which already exist and operate in the world. . . . It follows that the active presence of the laity in temporal affairs is of the greatest importance" (EN, 70).

In the same document, Paul VI did note that the laity are "to co-operate with their pastors in the service of the ecclesial community." However, Paul

VI stressed, co-operation with their pastors in the service of the church community is not, for the laity, "their principal and primary function."

John Paul II dramatically reiterated this teaching when he reported on the 1987 Synod on the lay mission. As I noted earlier, he began by talking about the laity's temptation to be so interested in Church work that some fail to become actively engaged in their secular responsibilities. He went on in the same document to a deeper discussion of the laity's secular role. He wrote: "To understand properly the lay faithful's position in the church in a complete, adequate and specific manner, it is necessary to come to a deeper theological understanding of their secular character in the light of God's plan of salvation and in the context of the mystery of the Church" (CL 15).

The Church, in fact, lives in the world, he continued, "even if she is not of the world. She is sent to continue the redemptive work of Jesus Christ which (as Vatican II said) 'by its very nature concerns the salvation of humanity, and also involves the renewal of the whole temporal order.' Certainly *all the members* of the Church are sharers in this secular dimension but *in different ways*. In particular, the sharing of the *lay faithful* has its own manner of realization and function, which, according to the Council, is 'properly and particularly' theirs. Such a manner is designated with the expression 'secular character.'" (CL 15, emphasis in original)

The pope continued with further emphasis: "*The world thus becomes the place and the means for the lay faithful to fulfill their Christian vocation*, because the world itself is destined to glorify God the Father in Christ . . . ." (CL, 15) To clarify still more the term "secular," he took the unusual step of quoting in full one of the propositions recommended to him by the bishops at the 1987 Synod on the Laity. It said: " . . . The term *secular* must be understood in the light of the act of God the creator and redeemer, who has handed over the world to women and men, so that they may participate in the work of creation, free creation from the influence of sin and sanctify themselves in marriage or the celibate life, in a family, in a profession and in the various activities of society. The lay faithful's *position in the church*, then, comes to be fundamentally defined by their *newness in Christian life* and distinguished by their *secular character*," the pope stressed (CL, 15).

This is the task, then. As Paul said in his letter to the Romans: "The whole created world eagerly awaits the revelation of the children of God. . . ." And, as Clare Short, British secretary of state for international development, wrote recently: "In every generation people who believe in social justice and compassion must struggle to try to build a fairer world. . . . It is not good enough for any of us just to say that we believe in morality and compassion. We have to work to create the conditions where goodness, morality and compassion are triumphant." As your letter showed, given the world's social problems, lay Christians do not lack opportunities to work at building a civilization of love.

+*Remi*

Dear Remi,

Jesus once said: "The wind blows where it chooses, and you hear the sound of it, but you do not know where it comes from or where it goes. So it is with everyone who is born of the Spirit" (John 3:8). This account of how the Spirit moves about bringing hope came to mind while we were rereading our recent exchange of letters. So much about today's world seems beyond the power of ordinary folk. So much just lands in our lives, coming from big business and big science and big government. But just as pessimism begins to rise, the Spirit seems to send a spark of hope. We got that feeling from news of how local groups around the world are trying to take back control over their lives.

Development projects: looking for an alternative vision

A bit of background about a research project of Canada's International Development Research Centre (IDRC) in Ottawa, to set the scene. Early in 1994, the IDRC sponsored Canadian Jesuit William Ryan to do a 28-country study, interviewing nearly 200 persons in East and Southeast Asia, Africa and Latin America about development projects and processes in their countries. He explored what relationship they see between scientific and cultural development, on the one hand, and religious values and systems, on the other. His findings have been published. The IDRC has launched a continuing in-depth study to find a framework and language to relate or integrate faith, scientific knowledge and experience in the area of human development.

In general, he asked people what outside values they saw being foisted on their countries through development projects such as those of the World Bank and International Development Fund. What local values did they see being neglected or suppressed? Ryan reported he found general agreement, among people with many different religious backgrounds, that the global free-market approach is not viable ecologically in the long term, and is not adequate in the short term to meet the basic needs of all peoples for human development. He found no ready-made alternatives, but Third World people are searching for alternative approaches to development, ones that include a positive handling of cultural and spiritual values.

Why do these people seek an alternative vision? It is because they see that the global free-market model – through such agents as structural adjustment programs and uncontrolled transnational corporations (TNCs) – "is destroying local values and identities by slowly homogenizing them into narrow Western market values, and thus into a nonviable global future."

Ryan found that "what people seem to be rejecting today – consciously or not – is exaggerated secularism that begins by setting up a dualism of convenience between matter and spirit, body and soul. This dualism separates religious faith and knowledge from 'science,' and ends up, in practice, by denying the reality of all that is not measurable or marketable." Most of those he interviewed believe that a viable global future cannot be shaped by today's dominant western development model. It narrowly defines market "rationality" as the individual maximization of "want satisfaction." They see the immense and growing influence of this model spreading world-wide, as the general form of all human organization. This socially impoverished conception of the individual is being promoted as the "universal" model for all people. "The international economy is out of control, at least beyond the control of individual governments, if not of the larger TNCs!" Ryan concluded. "But instead of hastening to build up new global regulatory institutions, rich countries blindly urge one another to compete economically even as they play at the game of international co-operation. This is a nonsense situation in which only the TNCs win. . . ."

The quest of all religions, but especially Asian religions, for harmonious and consensus approaches to social change is seen as sharply at odds with the present conflict model so prominent in the West. Generally speaking, in the Asian perspective, "social responsibility" takes priority over "individual rights."

Religion and development

He found that in Asia, as in Latin America and Africa, most non-government organizations (NGOs) had their inspiration, roots and initial funding in religion. In Asia, within Buddhism, Islam, Hinduism and the minority Christianity, there are many enthusiastic groups championing the cause of compassion, solidarity, social justice, and ecological concerns. Third-World people see that religion can have negative effects, for example, when it causes sectarian divisions that become violent. However, they don't want to have religion completely left out of plans for development. Most of those Ryan interviewed attribute to religious roots the very strong bonds of extended family, which still characterize societies in Asia and Africa and, to a lesser extent, Latin America.

The values that Ryan found in Asia were confirmed by what the bishops from that vast area told the 1998 Asian Synod in Rome. There is hope for a better world, for a civilization of love, among the world's poorest people. If only we who are rich can be open to what they have to teach us!

Mae and Bernard

Dear Mae and Bernard,

Yes, we do find the world full of wonders, despite the terrible poverty and suffering that is the lot of most people on earth. I agree that to keep us from utter despair the Spirit, going we know not where, does stir up projects such as those reported in Bill Ryan's study. Throughout the Third World, local groups are organized and busy, providing for poor people what their governments and corporations, mostly transnationals, fail to provide.

These groups involve peoples of all faiths, depending on their country. Many of them are the basic Christian communities found throughout Latin America and elsewhere. In the Philippines there are nearly 50,000 of them. During the 1998 Asian Synod in Rome, several Filipino bishops described these groups. They meet, usually under lay leadership, to worship together, to discern the challenges and opportunities which life offers them, and to act in response. As Archbishop Orlando Quevedo of Nueva Segovia explained: "They progress from the ritual celebration of the sacraments to deep awareness of the social and political implications of their faith. They remain very aware of the importance of traditional works of charity, but their faith impels them to do more and, therefore, to act for justice and social transformation." Where Christians live among people of other religions, they try to build what they call "basic human communities."

Perhaps our high standard of living and our assimilation into the alien culture of individualism are limiting the formation on a large scale of similar basic ecclesial communities in Canada, the U.S. and other industrialized countries. We must pray constantly that the Spirit will convert us, too, and stir us to action in solidarity with the poor – who are poor because of the economic systems which produce our wealth.

Acting in solidarity with the poor: a few suggestions

And, of course, we can do more. I will not try to outline a complete program of action, but I have some suggestions. On a personal level, a first step is to steep oneself in scriptural and council teachings about how Christ works in the world and about the specific lay role in temporal affairs. If you are a lay person, strive to understand that your primary and particular vocation is to "impress the divine law on the temporal city." If you are a priest or faith educator, prepare yourself to help lay sisters and brothers to develop the spirituality they need to follow their own way to holiness in the world. As part of this, laity must begin demanding that pastors and religious educators not keep hidden what Vatican II and the post-council popes have to say about the primacy of the laity's secular vocation.

We have neglected in recent years one of the best church programs for preparing laity for action in secular fields. Catholic Action, widespread before Vatican II, featured the see-judge-act approach. In English Canada it was best known through the Christian Family Movement, Young Christian Students and Young Christian Workers. These movements cannot simply be relaunched, but the basic Christian communities in Third World countries

74

prove the continuing relevance and importance of small groups meeting regularly to pray, reflect on the Scriptures, discern and act for justice and social transformation.

The same see-judge-act approach is basic to the work for justice that we Canadian bishops outlined in many post-council teachings, including our 1996 social statement. We proposed six steps which are to be reviewed regularly, as in a cyclical process:

1 - We listen to the stories of the poor and marginalized, and identify with them as fellow human beings and pilgrims before the Lord.

2 - With them we read the Scriptures and learn how God is revealed as liberator on the side of the poor, who accompanies us always, as *Emmanuel,* God *with, for* and *among* us.

3 - In the light of Revelation we compare the divine plan of salvation with the experience of the poor and downtrodden today.

4 - Together we explore and formulate alternatives to the systems, structures, policies or plans which cause poverty, mindful that those who suffer the consequences are in some ways the true experts.

5 - We work in solidarity with the poor, bringing our gifts to add to theirs as the poor liberate themselves, becoming gradually agents of their own destiny. This is where political activity, which has been called "love in action," comes in.

6 - We help to establish the groups, networks and coalitions, with local and international connections, which can actually make things happen to overcome wrongdoing and achieve justice.

In keeping with our social nature, we need to form or join groups to work with others in seeking to direct temporal affairs according to God's plan. What you may already be doing in this way about building a civilization of love with the poor around you likely is what you should be doing. And you can take heart from the good news that, around the world, poor people are joining together to help themselves. And religion is at the centre of this new work everywhere. Catholic laity should not feel alone, as in a ghetto. Increasingly they can find themselves in solidarity with other believers of all religions who are beginning to realize that the spirit of God is at work in us and in the world, giving us new but genuine possibilities of building a civilization of love together.

Poverty and injustice: beyond our control?

Related to this is a point made by Anne Alexander, an adult educator in Thunder Bay, Ontario. In her book about the late Monsignor Moses Coady of Antigonish, Nova Scotia, Alexander shows that in the late 1930s, as now, many people believed that the poverty and injustice around them resulted from forces beyond their control. With other pioneers of the Antigonish Movement, Coady had a different vision. He urged people to change themselves and their society through adult education. Alexander's book recalls the values and methods that distinguished Coady's efforts for social change. She also launches a serious critique of today's adult educators, who no longer form a social reform movement. Her critique is particularly timely now, when the free market system and big governments still fail to meet what was Coady's main concern: the growing gap between rich and poor.

Finally, while champions of the free market continue to bash our governments, we must as citizens and voters support those poverty-ending steps that can be done only by states, or between states, such as at the United Nations level. A Nobel peace prize went to those seeking a world ban on land mines. Other proposals are being made to lighten the multi-billion dollar debt burden of developing countries and to stop trading in armaments. These things *can* be done. The 1997 report on poverty by the United Nations Development Programme concluded that the world can afford and achieve the elimination of poverty. All that is lacking, it said, is the political will.

It is our Christian duty to help generate and sustain the political will needed to educate all children in the world, end illiteracy, bring everyone clean water, adequate food, sanitation and basic health care, and create economies which offer everyone the opportunity to work. We must build up the ideas and movements that make it possible for individuals to help to create a more moral and sustainable future. It can be done.

+Remi

Dear Remi,

This is just a footnote about a concern we have from our experience with trying to stir up interest in local or parish social justice groups. We could take Development & Peace (D&P) as an example, or one of the inter-church coalitions which the Canadian Conference of Catholic Bishops (CCCB) supported. Such projects never seem to get enough support in a diocese, or parish, or local community. The response to D&P's national education and social animation programs is spotty, at best. You recalled the six-step anti-poverty program of the Canadian bishops. Our impression is that only a few bishops went home from the CCCB meeting that approved that plan and started to promote it throughout their dioceses. Of course, it shouldn't just be up to the local bishop to launch and promote social justice work. Most parish priests and leaders of pastoral councils know about Development & Peace or an inter-church coalition to aid refugees, for example. Why are there so few self-starting parish groups? Why isn't material on social justice, such as the six-step program you mentioned, much more prominent in the adult education material from the CCCB's National Office of Religious Education? If Third World people who have so little can get themselves organized, perhaps it is our comfort and even luxury that impede us.

Mae and Bernard

For Discussion

1. What are the causes of poverty in your community? Would you distinguish natural from human causes? Assess who is responsible for the human causes – the poor themselves, or someone else.

2. Discuss how the Internet and other new communications media may be causing a new and deeper gap between rich and poor.

3. Discuss how advertising feeds consumerism by turning luxuries into necessities. What things have you and your friends bought recently which you don't really need? Analyze why you bought them.

4. Do you agree that Christians should be leaders in trying for a more equitable distribution of wealth between rich and poor? How do you assess what your parish is doing in this regard?

5. What do you think of the trend to reduce public services provided by governments and to increase pay-for-service private businesses?

6. What do you think inhibits people from acting on the Canadian bishops' six-step plan for solidarity with the poor?

For Action

1. Read John Paul II's *Christifideles Laici,* on the vocation and mission of the laity, with particular attention to what he says about building up the world as "a civilization of love."

2. Meet with local church groups working for refugees or other poor people to discuss what they are doing and what difficulties they meet.

3. Invite your federal or provincial representative to meet a group of you to discuss the government's role in dealing with poverty.

4. Keep track of how often you hear something in church about solidarity with the poor in your community, and discuss your findings with your pastor and other members of your parish pastoral council.

Further Reading

Cobb, John. *Sustaining the Common Good: A Christian Perspective on the Global Economy.* Cleveland: Pilgrim Press, 1994.

Dorr, Donal. *The Social Justice Agenda: Justice, Ecology, Power and Church.* Maryknoll, NY: Orbis Books, 1991.

————. *Option for the Poor: Catholic Social Teaching.* Revised edition, Dublin: Gill and Macmillan, 1992.

Durning, Alan. *How Much Is Enough? The Consumer Society and the Future of the Earth.* New York: Norton, 1992.

Goudzwaard, Bob, and Harry de Lange. *Beyond Poverty and Affluence: Towards a Canadian Economy of Care.* Toronto: University of Toronto Press, 1995.

Hill, James H. "Dr. Yes." *The New Yorker,* August 25 & September 1, 1997.

John Paul II. *Centesimus Annus: The Social Teaching of the Church.* Sherbrooke, Que.: Editions Paulines, 1991.

Korten, David C. *When Corporations Rule the World.* West Hartford: Kumarian, 1995.

Rifkin, Jeremy. *The End of Work.* New York: Tarcher/Putnam, 1995.

Ryan, William F. *Culture, Spirituality and Economic Development.* Ottawa: International Development Research Centre, 1995.

Sheridan, Edward F., ed. *Do Justice: The Social Teachings of the Canadian Catholic Bishops, 1945-1986.* Sherbrooke, Que.: Editions Pauline; Toronto: Jesuit Centre for Social Faith and Justice, 1987.

5

Created Man and Woman:
Equal Sharers in the Divine Image

This chapter continues the exploration of how human relations correspond to Gospel values. The focus here is on relations between men and women. The Bible shows that God created man and woman as equal sharers in the divine image. Throughout human culture, however, women are treated as inferior. This is true also inside the Christian church. The suggestion is made that male-female relations are perhaps the aspect of human life still least influenced by the commandment to love others as we love ourselves. Some present-day examples of abuse of women by men are explored. The role of the feminist movement in raising public awareness is noted. The question is raised whether male aggressiveness results from nature or from nurture. The emphasis here is on nurture, and on the question of how little boys are taught to respect others and to control their own behaviour. The chapter ends with a return to the discussion of right relations as a key moral principle.

Dear Remi,

You said on the phone the other day that we should write something about what the Gospel says about relations between men and women. We think this area, especially how men treat women, is perhaps the aspect of human life least touched by the Gospel so far. If there is any part of life that cries out for a new evangelization, as church leaders say today, it is this.

We have pop names for how men typically act – macho, Rambo, biker. How many men in any culture have nothing in them of this aggressive attitude toward women? You find the resulting problems not just in bedrooms or harems, but perhaps even more in corporate offices and the rooms where wars are planned. Not just women, but the world's natural resources and entire nations of poor people are, all of them, exploited in the sense of being raped. Abused women, endangered species, threatened ozone! Macho behaviour is widely destructive.

Of course, we also have some positive things to say about sexual intimacy, and we'll come back to that, and to more about the Gospel message. But first, let's look at some harsh realities. Nowhere in the world do men really treat women as their equals. Not in the church, not in the professions, not in politics, not in business. And not in the home! Organized feminism has resulted in more talk about this, and some corrective action, but we are still far from true social equality of the sexes.

Violence against women: abuse of male power

Rent a copy of the movie, *Zorba the Greek*. When you come to the scene where the young widow is stoned and stabbed to death, rewind and watch it a couple of times. Are you struck by the hypocrisy of that event? Only the woman pays, and pays the capital price. How different the Gospel story, where Jesus says the first stone can be thrown by a sinless man, and none is to be found! So, no stone is thrown and Jesus sends the woman away, after telling her to sin no more. The ancient custom of blaming the woman also shows up in the way most police forces treat prostitution. The women are hassled and arrested. Male customers and pimps get off with a rap on the knuckles, or sometimes only a wink!

Even if women are no longer routinely stoned to death, some of today's violence against women is almost as shocking. We saw an example of this in a CBC television documentary in March 1998. It showed the horrors that result from men in Bangladesh throwing acid in the faces of young women who resist their advances. There also has been a lot of media coverage of that other horror, female circumcision. We can't go into all the cultural complexities of this practice, which is part of a social system in which men try to control and dominate women, even though, ironically, where female circumcision is performed it is usually older women who do the mutilating.

In Canada, men have their own ways of dominating women. Look at our figures for wife beating! And most of what is going on in this country is not documented. Who knows how many girls are the victims of teenage date rape? Rape in general is underreported. So are other kinds of sexual assault, especially incest in families, which ruins the lives of daughters, sisters, nieces, cousins. For all the increased awareness of child sexual abuse in Canada, there is still almost no discussion of incest as part of the general problem of male-female inequality. What is called sex education in the schools doesn't even scratch the surface of the real problem of the domination of women by men.

Acid throwing, female circumcision, rape and incest are the extreme examples of abuses of male power over women. There are more subtle examples that are perhaps more common, but no less demeaning for women. One time, friends of ours went to a neighbour's house; they were going out together. The husband answered the door and let them in, but the wife upstairs did not know the other couple had arrived. They heard her call out: "Can I get dressed now, or do you still want to use me?" That story really brought out the big picture for us. Wow! This was the way some marriages worked? The wife was there to be used and that was it?

Do you remember the sort of guffaw that rippled through the world media in the fall of 1980, when the pope said a man could commit adultery with his wife? This was in one of a series of great talks John Paul II gave on the teaching about marriage in Matthew's Gospel. He was speaking of Christ's teaching, that a married man who looks lustfully at another woman may commit adultery with her "in his heart," even if he does not touch her. The pope said no man should look on any woman in this way, as a mere sex object. And, he added, a husband can treat his wife as a mere sex object. He can, in this sense, commit adultery with his own wife. Abused wives everywhere knew exactly what the pope meant, but the male-dominated media could only laugh at the idea!

Contraception: the cost for women

One general effect of all contraceptive technology is that it renders the woman's body "safe" against a man's sperm at all times. Her body thus

82

becomes available for sexual intercourse at any time without any worry about possible pregnancy. That idea is part of our culture now. Most people seem to look on this as a positive development, enabling women, like men, to enjoy casual sex without personal consequences. Women can let themselves be used without risk, and some women find enjoyment in that. But there are costs for women who are used in this way by men. This harsh reality gets blurred these days, when fear of AIDS has put the focus on avoiding HIV infection as the main concern. Women can avoid infection or pregnancy and still be hurt, demeaned, abused, while being used "safely."

An episode in Brian Moore's novel *The Luck of Ginger Coffey* illustrates something about contraceptives. He pictures a married couple who get caught up in the urge for intercourse while dressing in the morning. The husband, however, does not respect and accept her as she is. She must go to the bathroom to make herself "safe." Then, he uses her. Here is how Moore describes the scene:

> Obediently she leaned into the closet to get the suit and at that moment the sight of a fold of her slip caught between the cleft of her buttocks aroused him to a sluggish, familiar desire. Married as long as they were, desire was not something a man could waste. He dropped his own dressing gown and pulled her down on the bed. He kissed her, fumbled her slip off her, then remembered. He looked at her, and, obedient, she went to the bathroom. He shut his eyes, carefully nursing his desire until she came back. Then, forgetting her years of complaints about his roughness, his selfishness, he took her, tumbling her naked beneath him. Animal, his breathing harsh in the morning silence, he labored towards that moment of release and fulfillment. And afterwards, fell down beside her, pulling her on top of him, crushing her face against the reddish, graying hair on his chest. He exhaled in contentment; dozed off to sleep.

Before we go on with some of the more positive things we want to say, or touch more on Gospel insights, we'd like some feedback. Are we being too negative, too out of touch with modern young people? Are we missing important things?

Mae and Bernard

P.S. I want to add a couple of related points. The high school girls in the family life class I taught in Grenada were aware of being used as sex objects, but they thought they couldn't do anything about it. In that culture, virginity is regarded by men as a sort of weakness, immaturity, and lack of fulfillment. "Correcting" this situation is a source of male pride. Most Grenadian girls grow up unable even to imagine that they might have reasons or ways to resist what boys and men want to do to them. And the girls pay most of the costs, and not just in the extremely high rate of young unmarried mothers. For many who escape pregnancy, the sense of growing up as used, sullied, second-hand goods is the highest cost. This lack of self-esteem spills over into all aspects of their lives later on.

Another point. Men have to learn that just because they get married they don't have the privilege of "using their wives." It's a two-way bargain. Unfortunately, so many "good" Catholics never learn that. I think they still don't mention these things in pre-marriage courses. I really think that marriage gives some men the idea that they can do whatever they want, and pay no attention to what their wives want. I've heard people say: "that's the way men are made." It's not so; and even if it's "natural" it's not acceptable! Men need to learn to control themselves in that area as much as in any other.

One of the priests we know used to say to Bernie: "Don't try to tell me that you go off to Rome for all that time and don't have a little bit on the side." It was a big insult to Bernie and a bigger one to me.

It is not so that men have a kind of compulsion to need to rape their wives. I know this idea is around. Ask any woman with six, eight, ten kids and you'll get the same reply. It doesn't matter how holy the husbands were. That is, for sure, being taught somehow: that boys just can't help themselves. That's wrong. And some women really believe that. So in the most intimate area of life, the whole thing is being skewed. So how can you talk about how holy and all the rest marriage can be, when that's the whole picture you're into? It's just not right.

Then contraceptives are said to make all this "safe" for the woman! They say, oh, good, we won't get pregnant, so they go ahead and fall into that trap, too. How do you deal with all that? It's hard.

I wanted to stress these points myself.

Mae

Dear Mae and Bernard,

No, I don't think you are being too negative. I don't know how younger people will react, but these are your experiences so they have their own validity.

You made me aware that some of these things are part of my experience, too. I remember overhearing a woman cousin bitterly resenting the fact that she had become pregnant at a time when she didn't want to, and saying that she felt her husband had raped her. I'll never forget that. Even in the confessional some women who were effectively being raped by their husbands were told, "That's your marital duty. That's how you're going to get to heaven!"

But even when we denounce these things we must be compassionate. We have to accept that wounded people perceive reality in wounded ways. You're talking about wounded men – and women. So there will never be a perfect presentation. The only answer is for us to speak out of our experience. We're not preaching at anyone. We can't find the perfect language whereby everyone will be taught and will accept it. Wounded people will hear as wounded. That all colours what they hear and see through their own perceptions. This is generally recognized in psychology. So we need to speak from a position of compassion, not condescending, but suffering with them. We can speak of our pain as couple/pastor that these difficulties touch others. Instead of affirming things, we can raise a lot of questions.

Difficult choices and the need for compassion

Over the years, a number of spouses or couples have told me of relying on some form of birth control to feel personally fulfilled without getting discouraged as family burdens and responsibilities increased. Women especially have spoken of wanting, even during child-bearing years, to continue developing their natural gifts beyond only physical motherhood, to continue maximizing their personal contribution to society in a career from which they could not just walk away. I frequently experienced the deep pain of faith-filled couples faced with difficult choices and not able to find the spiritual counselling they hoped for from their clergy. Simply telling couples what moralists say is not always helpful. Failing to assist them in forming their conscience can leave them with intolerable burdens, compounding their feelings of inadequacy. I believe compassion applies in a particular way to people who are faced with difficult choices, or who have committed themselves to painful situations, where confusion and discouragement are the daily routine.

I look forward to hearing more from you.

+Remi

Dear Remi,

What you wrote about being compassionate and not preaching at people made us think of the see-judge-act method we followed in the Christian Family Movement (CFM). We could write a lot more about negative things we see, but maybe we should say a bit here about why we think male power trips are wrong and what we think might be done about all this.

In our view, what men do to women is probably the area of human life that is still least touched by the message of the Gospel. The message seems clear, but even many Christians don't live by it. Take, for example, the most general commandment: Love your neighbour as yourself. Do to others only what you would want done to you. Leaving aside masochists who are very sick people who enjoy pain, men do not like to be put down, or used, or abused. They are no different from women in this regard. Why, then, don't they respect and treat women as equals, the way they themselves want to be treated? But this is not what men talk about in locker rooms and bars.

Don't bring up that business about men having more muscle power. Of course, most men are physically stronger, and there is a place for their strength. But do we therefore concede that power should be the dominant value in male-female relationships? Gender equality is the message we should take from the Bible story that when God created humankind, "man and woman he created them" – as equal in dignity and worth. Mutual respect and solidarity between the genders is what it means to love your neighbour as yourself. By the way, we know that the present scientific fad is to try to find a gene for everything, even male aggression, and to put more stress on nature than on nurture as an explanation for human behaviour. Clearly, we emphasize nurture. In fact, behind the drive to master even our genes, don't we see that same old ambition to manipulate and control everything and everyone?

In our last letter we mentioned John Paul II's talks about what Jesus taught about marriage, as recorded in Matthew's Gospel. The pope also gave an earlier series of talks about the vision of man-woman relations that can be drawn from Genesis, the first book of the Bible. We hope that some day the key ideas in these talks will be presented in more popular language. A married couple would be best suited for this task.

The original biblical vision as presented in Genesis shows man and woman as equals. In many other passages, the Bible condemns abuse of women by men. It speaks frequently against licentiousness, adultery, fornication, harlotry. We know that a woman can be active and even aggressive in all these matters. However, every type of such behaviour is also characterized by some element of male abuse of women. To the ancient biblical list we can add such present-day evils as pornography, the exploitation of the female body in advertising, "topless" clubs and sex tourism. We believe our Christian faith says this kind of male behaviour is wrong. Even those who will argue that it is natural should be able to see that it is hurtful and unacceptable.

The masculine viewpoint: shaping the culture

Feminist literature has been helpful in showing how much our understanding of our culture is shaped by masculine points of view. Even in the Bible a male perspective dominates the stories about where we come from and who we are. Human culture, including male behaviour, is largely passed from generation to generation by telling stories. And, in all of recorded literature, the works of men, and therefore their opinions, clearly outnumber those of women. But we can't forget all the unwritten stories that are passed on orally, and how important they are in shaping attitudes and behaviour. In this area, the stories mothers tell their children have a privileged place. Babies, including baby boys, hear their mother's voice first and most often. Mothers almost always spend more time than fathers do with small children, including the little boys who become dominating men. In no culture are men the primary child-rearers, or the first and most important shapers of a child's imagination. What are we to say, then, about the role of women in the development of aggressive male behaviour? Gender stereotypes that favour male power and domination begin with "big boy" crib talk by proud mothers who, perhaps unconsciously, contribute in this way to the macho male stereotype. Fathers are involved, too, of course. Where do boys get the idea that once they have the potential they have to go out and "sow their wild oats?" These notions come from fathers and other older men. Back in the locker rooms and bars!

This is an area in which the Catholic church needs reform as much as "the world" does. Many – perhaps most – Catholic men are assimilated into the woman-dominating male culture. When you hear a Catholic man seriously argue that a woman's place is in the home, it's because that's the way he was brought up. Why does he have that idea? Because someone in the church said men were supposed to be the breadwinners and work outside the home, and women weren't. And, look anywhere, if you want to see men in charge of everything, it's in the church! And what are we doing about correcting this? Not much, it seems. Some even continue to believe there are theological reasons to support the exclusion and subjugation of women!

We can't look to current church practice for the ideal of male-female relations, but we believe it is to be found in the good news that Christ brought us. Moreover, we believe that working to bring this good news to reality is a primary task for lay Christians. It is perhaps the first effort to be made in fulfilling the Vatican II teaching that we laity are called by our baptism to engage in temporal affairs and order them according to God's plan. Striving to put male-female equality high on the world's moral agenda is a foremost Christian duty.

We realize that this idea will be dismissed by many as being impossibly idealistic and impractical. Persuade men to control their hormones? You've got to be kidding! Yet control of male sexual domination is directly linked to control of hedonistic consumerism and pollution and global warming and weapons of mass destruction. There can be no peace and right order anywhere without self-control. In every case, it's a question of right relationships. The will to dominate, to use power to indulge self and gratify desires and achieve goals, is all of a piece. The main difference between a battered and raped woman, a polluted ecosystem, a devastated rain forest, a hole in the ozone layer, and a burned-out war zone is the victim involved. The aim and lifestyle of the aggressor are similar in every case.

Are we preaching an outmoded sexual asceticism based on fear or hatred of bodily pleasures? Not at all. Later we may have something to say about intimacy as a source of joy and gratitude in marriage. For the moment, we are stressing the evils that arise when men ruthlessly pursue pleasure and power as ends in themselves. For example, people express shock at how women and children are abused in the sex tourist trade. Harsher laws are being enacted in a number of countries as a result. However, this kind of evil cannot be eradicated or even controlled by criminal laws alone. The widespread culture of wilful male dominance has to be faced on all fronts, starting with recognition that it is a basic social problem that begins with baby boys.

The shaping of gender behaviour: nature or nurture?

In human sexuality, some things are genetically given, but most of what we think and do is learned. How to copulate is not instinctive knowledge with us, as with all animals. At some point in childhood, each of us has been told where babies come from, and most people can remember who told them. Bernard remembers hearing a girl in Grade 1 with him at Wanganui School tell a little group sitting by the swings at recess. He discovered later that she didn't have every fact straight, but she enlightened him about the fascinating essentials. Parents typically are slow to tell their children, and popular literature makes fun of parental talks about "the birds and the bees." Eventually, everyone learns from someone, and there are even how-to-do-it books and films, something your cat or dog would laugh at, if they could think about it, or could laugh! Sexual behaviour in animals follows constant, instinctive patterns. In contrast, the study of different races shows that, as sociologist Peter Berger put it, "in sexual matters, man is capable of almost anything." Learning, nurture, and cultural conditioning are by far the main shapers of gender behaviour, including every form of male abuse of girls and women. The time and place to start changing how men abuse women is as each baby boy comes out of the birth canal. Why isn't there talk of this in prenatal classes? In marriage preparation classes?

We come back to our opening question. Is there any aspect of life on earth in which the gentle good news that Jesus brought is more needed than in man-woman relationships? Our faith alone should show us this and urge us to action. Instead, like Thomas the Apostle, we wait obstinately for still more evidence. Meanwhile, women suffer.

Mae and Bernard

Dear Mae and Bernard,

I especially agree with where you ended up in your last letter. Morality is a question of right relationships. I made that point earlier about how we humans look on the rest of the universe. As creatures we must love and respect all the rest of creation. It is no different in man-woman relationships.

Back to Genesis. "Male and female he created them." It is of the very essence of the human being to be female and male. Why? Because the human being is made "in the image of God." God is love, John tells us. God by definition is relationship. God created humans female and male so that they would reflect the divine image by being in relationship. Falling in love, loving even an enemy, we become more like God. Creativity also comes from relationship. We need to point that out as basic. From that starting point you can distinguish male and female sexuality. People are sexual because they are in relationship. Relationship requires the presence of other. Woman and man have to be there for each other or they cannot have a relationship. I cannot relate to myself. In terms of relationship, I am incomplete without the other. This is like the mystery of the Trinity. The divine is relationship – three persons in one God. God is love. I don't relate to women as to a wife, but even as a bishop I must relate to women in loving ways. I can't go around scared to death they'll lead me into temptation.

As you pointed out, a lot of things in the church have to change before women are respected and treated as they should be. There has been far too much emphasis on what Paul said about women obeying their husbands, but almost complete neglect of the fact that he first said husbands have to love their wives. And, you're absolutely right; when Paul said husbands should love their wives, he didn't mean the kind of behaviour that some people today call lovemaking but is more like sexual assault! Love the way Christ loves the church, Paul said. Totally, constantly, faithfully, mutually, forgivingly, gently. I suppose most wives would settle for that kind of love.

And, yes, our new evangelization to bring about the civilization of love desired by God must emphasize serious efforts to evangelize male-female relationships. Difficult as that may seem, we can go forward in faith. What you are talking about is the will of the Spirit for human relations. And in this struggle the Spirit will be with us (and with our successors, for we will not see the final victory in our lives, I suppose); and the Spirit will prevail!

+Remi

For Discussion

1. After reading the first two chapters of Genesis, discuss whether men today are treating women as God wants them to do.
2. Discuss whether men in your community treat women as their equals more than men in other cultures do. How do you account for differences and similarities?
3. Discuss the influence of popular media – films, television, music – in advancing or retarding equality for women. How does the influence of the media compare with the influence of the Gospel message?
4. What signs do you see at schools, recreation centres, shopping malls, etc., that boys and young men are being helped to respect and treat girls and women as their equals?
5. What do you think of the sources from which modern young people get their ideas about what is right and wrong in relationships between men and women?

For Action

1. Research, through social workers and your local police, the kinds and amount of violence by men against women in your community.

2. Make a study of local schools to find out how much violence at schools is by boys against girls. How do the schools handle this issue?
3. Check religious education programs used by elementary and secondary schools in your area to see how much attention they pay to equality for women.
4. Interview the owners of a local newspaper, radio and television station about their concerns on man-woman equality, and what they are doing about it.

Further Reading

Chittister, Joan D. *Heart of Flesh: A Feminist Spirituality for Women and Men.* Grand Rapids, Mich.: Eerdmans; Ottawa: Novalis, 1998.

John Paul II. *Theology of the Body: Human Love in the Divine Plan.* Boston: St. Paul Editions, 1997.

McKeen, Jock, and Bennet Wong. *The Relationship Garden.* Gabriola Island, BC: PD Publishing, 1996.

Intimacy and Family:
Exploring and Managing Fertility

Birth control has been the Catholic church's most difficult question since Vatican II. John XXIII set up a secret commission to study this issue. Paul VI kept the question out of the council and expanded John XXIII's commission study. This chapter notes what Vatican II did say about marriage, conjugal intimacy and responsible parenthood, and notes the contributions of Canadian bishops to the council's discussion. It goes on to present a detailed account and critical analysis of what is known about the work of the papal birth-control commission. It compares what the commission proposed with the 1968 encyclical, Humanae Vitae, *in which Paul VI repeated previous papal teaching that Catholics should not use artificial birth-control methods. It outlines the case for a new church study of human love and fertility, with more emphasis on the experience of married couples and on health and environmental concerns.*

Dear Remi,

Everyone agrees that birth control has been the Catholic church's most difficult issue in recent years. There is no other question on which the church's teaching authority stands as isolated in public opinion. No other papal teaching has been as openly rejected, by both church members and outsiders, as Paul VI's 1968 encyclical, *Humanae Vitae.*

As a couple, we have always opposed birth-control drugs and devices. We do so mainly for reasons not even mentioned in the encyclical. We agree with its broad vision of marriage. We know, however, that its arguments and language about birth control are not persuasive for many couples. It was developed by a closed process which drew criticism, especially from bishops and theologians, quite apart from what it taught. Paul VI acted alone, not collegially with other bishops. We hope the church will revisit the birth-control question soon. We are convinced that another process, and another way of reasoning, some day will win much wider support for the church's basic teaching on contraceptives.

The long-term goal should be to give couples the will and the capacity to manage their fertility in a way that conforms to God's original vision for human intimacy. If they are to manage their fertility in this way, couples have to grow in freedom in several different aspects of their lives. We mention them as three steps, but in real life they don't necessarily come about separately or in the order listed here. First, couples have to overcome today's almost universal lack of understanding about their fertility. Despite all the explicit talk about sex, real knowledge – especially knowledge about female sexual functions – is not a common commodity. Second, what couples understand about their conjugal sexuality has to be freed from the negativity of a certain kind of church moral teaching. Third, they have to be freed from the manipulations of mercenary transnational corporations who market contraceptives aggressively with an eye on only one consequence – the billions of dollars to be made from the millions of couples who use contraceptives more than they need to do, often at grave risk to the woman's health and the couple's real conjugal happiness.

The church's teaching on sexuality

Where to begin, since you have never heard us argue our point of view? We will start with a critique of the church's teaching on sexuality during its first 2000 years. Later, we will analyze what was lacking in the process leading to Paul VI's encyclical, and present another way to sustain similar conclusions. In this letter we probably won't have time to get past the first historical point.

The church has yet to speak in a complete, positive and informed way about the meaning of sexual intimacy in marriage. As a result, Catholics are crippled if we try to speak out against today's sexual hedonism. Two things stand out about church teaching in this area during its first 2000 years. One is that the experience of couples living chaste and permanent marriages has been given no place in the formulation of the church's message to the world about human sexuality. Overwhelmingly, official teaching has come from men who, by their vocation, have vowed not to be sexually active. St. Augustine, for example, spoke from experience but not experience from within a sacramental marriage. In addition, during its 2000 years, the church has not developed a comprehensive and positive moral teaching about intimacy. A review of the history of its teaching shows that its disciplinary and doctrinal statements have always been in response to this or that heresy or some moral crisis. The tradition developed in argument and conflict with heretics such as the Gnostics, Manichaeans, Cathari and Jansenists. Each time some group taught that matter was evil and marriage therefore base as compared with vocations less involved with things of the flesh, the church did stress that marital intimacy is God-given and procreation is good. On each such occasion, however, the point of the teaching was mainly to reject the heresy rather than to present a full, open and positive Christian teaching about marital intimacy. The most basic point, that God created conjugal sexuality and said it is good, is lost. Vatican II began to change that, but there is still a way to go.

Did you read an excellent review of this matter in *The Tablet* of March 1, 1997, presented as a letter from Harman Grisewood to a friend? He stresses the discrepancy between the positive Catholic philosophical position on sexuality, and the contrasting negative cast of what he calls "the character and trend of Catholic exhortation and the officially promulgated moral code."

He proposes a reading of the *Life of Tiberius Caesar* by Suetonius for a description of sexual behaviour of the pagans among whom the first Christians lived. For those who seldom read histories, the video of *I, Claudius* will give the same picture. Such depravity was also the moral climate of Ephesus and Corinth at the time Paul was writing his epistles, and was still the situation three centuries later in the Carthage and Rome that Augustine knew. "Even the most depraved of brothel keepers would today I believe be horrified by those practices," Grisewood writes.

The prevailing philosophy of those early centuries was Platonism. It implied a sharp distinction between spirit and matter. Spirit was seen as elevated and matter as degraded. This Platonic dualism, Grisewood argues, "did something to encourage the brothelized sexuality" in the great Roman and Greek cities. "In the prevailing climate of those days," he says, "it was easy for the Christian to identify 'matter' with the body; and 'spirit' with the soul. It was easy to see matter and body as abhorrent, while soul and spirit constituted the true dignity of man. And so it was – crudely put – that the church became launched upon its course of presenting to the faithful a picture of the good Christian fighting the good fight against the flesh and all that pertains thereto." Early church teaching about sexuality thus contained an "antagonism to enjoyment of the physical world and the greatest enemy was sexual pleasure."

It wasn't until the thirteenth century that St. Thomas Aquinas discovered Aristotle and began to pull the medieval church out of the rut of Platonic dualism. Aquinas christianized Aristotle and proclaimed that the whole of the created universe is good. This included matter and the human body. God created all, including human sexuality, and all is good. The teaching of Aquinas did not enjoy a steady rise to ascendancy, however. Aquinas himself went through condemnation and later rehabilitation. Eventually he was given primacy among the doctors of the church. However, St. Bonaventure, his contemporary and a philosophical opponent, was also held out as a model to be revered.

"With the simultaneous exaltation of these two," Grisewood notes, "it is not fanciful to see two somewhat divergent streams of tradition: the one philosophical, flowing in one direction, and the other a stream of pastoral theology and spiritual exhortation flowing in a different course." And, over the centuries up to Vatican II, the Thomist view of matter – the "approval" of matter – grew dim and was replaced by the old pietistic dualism in which the spirit was exalted and the body degraded. This was clearly the prevailing view when we married. Had we become nun and priest instead of marrying, we would have been seen as choosing "higher" vocations. A nun made that remark to Mae even after our first son was born in the fall of 1949.

Sex in marriage: a new teaching from Vatican II

One of the most important aspects of Vatican II for married Catholics is that it turned a corner and began to give us positive teaching about the goodness of sex acts in marriage. However, we still do not have a complete, positive theology of conjugal intimacy. We still do not have a catechism setting out the basic Catholic belief that the joys and pleasures of sex in marriage are God-given, to help the couple build up, and show forth, each partner's spiritual capacity for total giving of self and unreserved accepting of the other, learning to love another as one loves oneself. Meanwhile, because of the sexual sins of some clergy (and many other men), the public image of church teaching is further tarnished by yet another round of focusing on the negative. Most theologians, for their part, seem more interested in issues such as homosexuality and the AIDS epidemic than in the goodness of marriage. We have some ideas about ways to overcome this neglect, but more about that will have to wait for another letter.

Mae and Bernard

Dear Mae and Bernard,

There is no doubt that the dichotomy between spirit and matter, between the spiritual and the secular, is one of the church's oldest and most difficult problems. The historical overview by Grisewood in *The Tablet* is helpful; thank you for pointing it out to me. But there is more to be said. That is why I made this problem central to my own interventions at Vatican II.

You will recall that Bishops Charbonneau, Power and I spoke about the lay apostolate early in Vatican II's third session in 1964. (Paul-Emile Charbonneau of Hull, Quebec, William Power of Antigonish, Nova Scotia, and I lived in the same house in Rome during the council.) In my talk, I stressed that God's creative plan was not set aside by God's plan for the redemption of the world. That's how insidious Platonic dualism is for our faith. It even leads some to think that creation is somehow incomplete or secondary or faulty. Rather, as I said in the council, creation and redemption "are united as one in Christ inasmuch as Christ himself is both the source and author of salvation and the crowning glory of the whole created universe." I went on to argue that every Christian therefore has a two-fold vocation: "to work for the completion of creation and the perfection of the universe" and also "to co-operate with Christ in the restoration of all things according to the divine plan of redemption." These two aspects, the natural and the supernatural, are inseparable in the vocation of the lay apostolate. We must not oppose first and second when talking about the tasks of transforming the universe and proclaiming God's kingdom.

At the council, we also were trying to end another dimension of this dichotomy when we stressed that baptism makes all Christians sharers in the three-fold priesthood of Christ. Ordination after baptism is a call to special service, not to higher rank. That principle underpins the council's teaching about the church as people of God.

We had to attack Platonic dualism at still another level when we wrote the *Constitution on the Church in the Modern World,* and in particular the chapter on marriage and family life. Cardinal Léger, then archbishop of Montreal, and I were the two Canadians who spoke about this during the third session. I made the more general point: That Christ's spirit requires a positive attitude towards the world, not one of condemnation. Therefore, "Christians should be instructed to avoid any dichotomy or split between the natural and supernatural missions which are part of their vocation." No one can effectively collaborate in building Christian community unless they participate actively in building the human community. The final council text said this beautifully: Nothing that is human fails to find an echo in the hearts of the followers of Christ (GS, 1).

Léger applied this principle more specifically to marriage in his October 29, 1964 intervention. It was one of an historic series of talks about marriage. Spread over two days, this debate marked the beginning of important new teaching about the goodness and holiness of human love in marriage. The discussion continued into the fourth session the next year, when I was able to report what couples in Victoria diocese had told me about what love meant in their marriages. All this is reflected in the final council text. It says that "the acts in marriage by which the intimate and chaste union of the spouses takes place are noble and honourable; the truly human performance of these tasks fosters the self-giving they signify and enriches the spouses in joy and gratitude." The council even warned that "where the intimacy of married life is broken, it often happens that faithfulness is imperilled and the good of children suffers" (GS, 51). Church teaching therefore cannot be called anti-sex, or anti-pleasure. That still leaves room for talking, as I know you do, about abstinence as a way of expressing love at times.

A remark that Léger made during that debate touches directly on what you were saying about a harmful dichotomy stemming from Platonism. Referring to pre-council teaching, Léger said that "a certain pessimistic and negative attitude regarding human love, attributable neither to Scripture nor to Tradition, but to philosophies of past centuries, has prevailed and this has veiled the importance and legitimacy of conjugal love in marriage." Now, he voiced that criticism in 1964. The final council text published a year later goes a long way to overcome such pessimism and negativity. Still, what we were doing at Vatican II was more about opening up new visions than giving a full, positive theology of conjugal love. You're right. We still do not have that kind of teaching about human sexuality and marriage.

This is as important for us dedicated to celibacy as for you who are married. I recall how we were cautioned in seminary against "particular friendships," without any clear explanation or teaching. It left me with a negative attitude towards relationships, especially with women. We joked that the day we were ordained subdeacons and committed ourselves to celibacy we "put on tin shorts." It is obvious now that my professors and directors did not teach us to distinguish between intimacy and sexual excitement. Other rules of the day didn't help. A cleric was never to be seen "alone with a woman alone." Once, when I was a deacon, when I borrowed the family car to drive my own sister, an Ursuline nun, from her convent to a neighbouring village, she was expected to sit alone in the back seat. I now see that all this left me emotionally impoverished for many years. For some priests, as recent criminal cases show, this confusion is disastrous.

Intimacy and sexual contact: making a distinction

I still remember how painful it was to learn, as a bishop, that some women religious with whom I worked thought me cold and distant. Thanks to some dear friends, who had the courage to confront me about this, I set out on a path of discovery which has proven very rewarding. In this process I was helped by many friends, among them Jock McKeen and Bennet Wong and their book, *The Relationship Garden*. It has taught me how important it is to distinguish between intimacy and sexual contact. They describe intimacy as "a deep knowing and understanding of one another's interior lives that is achieved through vulnerable revelations and a shared sense of closeness and caring." They warn not to equate intimacy with "sexual charge." We are misled and impoverished by popular use of the expression "having intimate relations" to describe sexual contact.

That's why I'm interested in hearing your further thoughts, as a couple speaking from experience and conscience.

+Remi

Dear Remi,

Probably the next step is to set out our own birth-control experience. We have never used contraceptive drugs or devices. When we got married, there was some information available about so-called calendar rhythm. It was some time before we learned just why it is so unreliable. We learned that after discovering the SERENA method of natural family planning, which is both fully reliable and easy to follow.

SERENA: A natural family planning method that worked!

We learned around 1959 that, four years earlier, Rita and Gilles Breault of Lachine, Quebec, had developed a method for helping couples to know and follow their own fertility cycle on a day-to-day basis. (She was a social worker and he an aircraft technician.) By the time we heard of it, a number of couples around Montreal were using the Breaults' method to space births or to achieve pregnancy. Besides, they were organizing groups of couples trained to teach the method to other couples. They called their project "Service de regulations des naissances" (in English, a service for the regulation of natality) – SERENA, for short. We began using the method as soon as we heard of it, and by 1963 had qualified as an official teaching couple in the first English-speaking SERENA group. More than 40 years later we still recommend it, and SERENA continues to spread slowly, especially among environmentally-concerned couples.

Let us stress that SERENA (like other scientific ovulation methods of natural family planning, including the Billings and Creighton methods) must not be confused with "calendar" rhythm. That rhythm method was based on the inaccurate theory that a woman ovulates every 28 days. In fact, shorter and longer cycles are regular and normal. Calendar rhythm therefore is a blind guessing game, for good reason called "Vatican roulette" by some. The SERENA method has nothing to do with guessing when ovulation might occur. It involves precise observation of the changes that occur in a woman's body day by day during her menstrual cycle. Her cycles can and do vary in length a great deal, from cycle to cycle, but the physical signs of each stage of the ovulation cycle can always be read and charted accurately. By reading her chart, the couple can follow precisely where they are in her menstrual cycle. If we go into some detail, it is because we believe factual information is central in moral decision-making. Grace builds on nature!

It is important to note that we discovered SERENA before the birth-control debate hit the Second Vatican Council in 1964. Of course, the debate had begun to heat up as soon as the birth-control pill was invented in the 1950s, but inside the church it remained somewhat tentative or speculative until the council began to discuss marriage and the intimate lives of couples. That discussion started the widespread expectation that the Catholic ban on contraceptives as voiced by Pius XI and Pius XII might be reversed.

Vatican II gave us important new teaching about marriage, as we noted earlier, but Paul VI removed the birth-control question from council debate and gave it to a special commission, which John XXIII had set up secretly early in 1963. We felt we had a ringside seat as Bernard was covering the council and brought home the latest news after each session. As we discussed it, we did so as a newly trained SERENA couple. We had more knowledge than young doctors typically receive about the working of a woman's fertility cycle.

The fertility cycle: the key to the SERENA method

We learned through SERENA that the woman's pituitary gland in her brain controls how the ovarian hormones estrogen and progesterone alternate in her bloodstream. At the beginning of each cycle, estrogen is dominant. During this phase, the ovary is preparing for release of an ovum. Also, the lining of the womb begins to thicken in anticipation of a possible pregnancy. After the ovum is released, progesterone becomes the dominant hormone. Among other effects, it blocks further ovulations (that it why it is a key ingredient in the pill).

If sperm and ovum meet and unite successfully to begin a conception, that new group of living cells soon nests in the womb. In that case, progesterone continues as the dominant hormone, maintaining the blood as a rich carrier of nutrients for a baby. However, if fertilization does not occur for any number of reasons, the ovum quickly dies and the womb receives that message. It then sheds the blood-filled lining it had been preparing, and this becomes the menstrual flow. Then, estrogen again takes over and begins once more to prepare for another ovulation.

The SERENA method is helping thousands of couples to follow the workings of this exquisite system in the woman's body by reading and charting simple, normal signs. There are daily vaginal mucous changes, easily observed by the woman in the course of her personal hygiene. Also, it is easy to note a distinct shift in the body's basal temperature, when estrogen gives way to progesterone after ovulation. Keeping a daily chart of this information is no more time-consuming than cleaning one's teeth properly, and no harder to learn.

Obviously, one main reason for learning and charting this information about the woman's inner ecosystem is to fix the time of ovulation. The lifespan of male sperm in a woman's body is about three days. The woman's ovum lives less than one-third this time, or about 24 hours. Therefore, avoiding intercourse for about three or four days before ovulation and one day after it, is a sure way to avoid pregnancy. Or, if they want a child, a couple can use the same information to have intercourse just before and during the time of ovulation, to increase the chances of sperm meeting ovum. We know couples who talk of the ecstasy of "conscious creation." Knowing their cycle, they tried to conceive on a chosen occasion, and succeeded!

The woman's system: complex and balanced

But the couple gains much more than control over spacing births. Both partners, and especially the man, learn to marvel at how complex and balanced the female system is. The man's sexual organs and functions are simple in comparison. They are always the same, time after time. Not so the woman's. In fact, if they had intercourse every day of a cycle, the environment the man entered each time would be different from the time before. Her hormones, alternating once during each cycle, are constantly changing her ovaries, womb, cervix and vaginal canal in subtle but real and consistent ways. Her basal body temperature shifts levels, the consistency of her vaginal mucous changes from day to day (part of a mechanism for either aiding the sperm or resisting it), an ovary discharges an ovum, her womb prepares and (if there is no fertilization) then sheds a blood-filled lining, and she experiences accompanying mood changes. Most couples never develop a sense of wonder about all this. Ignorance inhibits their appreciation for its complexities and marvels. Sadly, the woman's exquisite interior ecosystem usually is dismissed as "inside plumbing" or ridiculed as a nuisance.

One time, as we discussed the pressure being put on the church to accept contraceptives, Mae burst out: "I don't care what they decide. You're not going to get me to put any of that stuff in me!" As part of our SERENA training, we had examined and discussed the "birth-control kit" that a drug company was promoting. It contained every device: condoms, applicators for spermicidal foams, cervical shields (diaphragms) of various sizes and shapes, an assortment of intrauterine devices (IUDs) meant to disrupt the process of nidation, and empty pill dispensers, to introduce the drugs in a general way. All were great money-makers in the eyes of the drug company. In Mae's eyes, all were invaders of her inner space and violators of its marvellous processes.

Colette and Laurent Potvin of Ottawa were one of three couples eventually named to the papal birth-control commission. Two other couples, the Crowleys of the U.S. and the Rendus of France were also named. The Potvins had some SERENA background, and he was a doctor. Before going to commission meetings, they met in Ottawa with some of us SERENA couples. In general, we urged that the Potvins should tell the commission that the greatest need was not a doctrinal statement on the morality of contraceptives. Rather, the church should launch a world-wide teaching effort to help couples everywhere learn about the marvels of the female body and how to manage their fertility without invasive drugs or devices. Obviously, our wish was not heeded by the commission, if the Potvins pressed our point.

Other reasons for using the SERENA method

It was no surprise to us that at that time, in the mid-1960s, growing numbers of couples were being attracted to SERENA for ecological reasons. The method did give Catholic couples a way to follow church teaching by spacing births without contraceptives, but every couple who used it also saw that it did much more besides. It fully engaged the man as partner in using the method and so overcame the notion that fertility control was a woman's problem and pregnancy a female pathology. It led the couple and especially the man to see positive aspects of abstaining from intercourse for a time during each cycle. They learned to value other ways of "making love" – doing other things together tenderly and with more attention to each other. It awakened both of them, and especially the man, to the wonder of the miniature ecosystem of the woman's fertility cycle.

This was a time of awakening awareness to the widespread damage being caused in many natural environments by careless industrial activities. We were learning that air, water, soil, food chains, and entire species were being polluted, endangered, even destroyed. All over the world, people demonstrated against projects that harmed the natural environment, whether in the Amazon rainforests or in British Columbia's stands of Douglas fir. Everywhere, alarms were going up against indiscriminate use in the wilderness of such machines as chainsaws and bulldozers. In the woman's womb, however, drugs and devices as powerful as bulldozers and as violent as chainsaws are still used without regard for what they really do in and to her inner ecosystem.

The fertility cycle: still a mystery to many

Most people are uninformed about the workings of the woman's fertility cycle. Even if environmentalists have aroused growing concern and respect for intricate natural systems, that awareness and concern does not extend to what goes on in the woman's body. It is only in the 1920s that the Ogino-Knaus medical team documented the process of human ovulation. For generations, people did not talk about these "intimate" facts. Teaching girls in a junior high school in Grenada, Mae found that they knew about the external signs of menstruation but nothing about the entire natural process of which it is a part. Their mothers and other teachers either did not know or did not tell them. When Mae taught them the basic facts that we have sketched here, they developed a sense of wonder about their own bodies, followed by new self-respect and a determination to insist that boys and men should respect them more. They began to see in a new light that male ignorance and aggressive pleasure-seeking are major problems for women.

We had a similar experience as SERENA teachers with the couples who came to us to learn the method. The facts of the woman's cycle are generally unknown. Men in particular are uninformed, especially about how a woman's biological cycle, with its regular pattern of hormonal changes, is related to her psychological moods and, indeed, her personality. Every woman's cycle is unique to her in some details, even if every woman also has generally shared experiences. And because the cycle's workings mostly are interior and hidden, few women or men have any idea of what really happens to the ecosystem in her own body when she takes a pill that inhibits ovulation by changing the natural pattern of the hormones in her blood, or inserts into her womb a device as radical as an IUD. Spermicides, vaginal shields and condoms are only somewhat less invasive for the woman. Most violent of all is the new RU-486, the so-called morning-after pill, which causes an abortion by blocking the cells in her womb from receiving progesterone, the natural function of which is to prepare the lining of the womb to receive and sustain a fertilized ovum.

Gospel values and human sexuality

We are convinced by our experience about conjugal intimacy and birth control that Gospel values concerning human sexuality have not yet taken root as they are meant to do. In general, the double commandment to love God and love our neighbour as ourselves is ignored at least as much as it is lived. And, as we said earlier, man-woman sexual relations are the area of human life perhaps least influenced by the Gospel vision. Vatican II says (GS, 17) that human dignity demands that a person act according to a knowing and free choice – a choice motivated from within, and not as the result of blind instinct or mere external pressure. A knowing choice – one that is made by a person who is fully informed about what they are doing and fully aware of the consequences of the choice made. A free choice, one in which there is no coercion or manipulation. Women will quickly tell you how often intercourse for them is only a matter of giving in to "mere external pressure." That is what date rape and spousal abuse are all about. Intercourse can be pleasurable for women too. However, the violence of battered women and abortion shows to what extent the burden of careless intercourse and unwanted pregnancy rests on the woman alone. Those who do important social work campaigning against abortion seldom have anything to say about compulsive, instinctual male sexual behaviour as a cause of abortion. Even the most ardent anti-abortion campaigners are, in our experience, inclined to go along with the common expression that "boys will be boys," which shows how widely we accept the idea that a man's sexual behaviour is little different from a rooster's or any other barnyard animal's. Just listen to men's locker-room talk sometime.

More later on the way that the papal birth control commission worked, and on what we wish it had done. And we think there is more to be said about your council intervention on conjugal love.

Mae and Bernard

Dear Mae and Bernard,

Yes, we tend to forget – and younger people have no easy way of knowing – the excitement that we felt by the end of the third session of Vatican II. We were studying the text that is now called the *Constitution on the Church in the Modern World*. I had spoken during the third session in 1964 about the apostolate of the laity and about the church in today's world. For the latter text, I urged that Christians should be instructed to avoid any dichotomy or split between the natural and the supernatural missions which are part of their

106

vocation. I am satisfied that the final text caught some key points I was stressing.

The drafting of that text continued into the fourth and final session in the fall of 1965. Between the third and fourth sessions, I invited about 30 Victoria-area couples to meet to tell me what conjugal love meant to them. I knew that the section of the council text dealing with this topic would come up for further discussion during the fourth session. When it did, I was able to feed in what the couples on Vancouver Island had shared with me.

Looking now at my September 30, 1965, intervention, I think three points stand out. The first is one on which the church still has not made much progress. "The whole Christian people," I said, " must contribute to the solution of the grave problems that affect conjugal love. Married life is the vocation of the vast majority of Christians; and the mind of the faithful (*sensus fidelium*) has a special function not only in matters of doctrine or belief but in matters of Christian morals or practice as well." Well, the laity, including married couples, still are rarely found around the tables at which our church discusses faith and morals. The Spirit does not come to dwell only in bishops and priests. My recent experience of our diocesan synod (I'll get back to details about it later) convinces me that we have to make greater use of mechanisms such as synods to give you laity the means to help us shape what we say to the modern world. Including what we say about human sexuality, but not just that.

Another concern I had when I stood up in the council was to emphasize the positive. We should insist "on the positive vision of the riches of human love and the heights it can reach through grace," I stressed. We should set aside too great a preoccupation with the pitfalls of married love and its ever possible abuses. This ties in with a point you made in an earlier letter – that, historically, church teaching about marriage has developed more from dealing with problems than from exploring the fullness of the Gospel's positive teaching about human love. I know we have to point out the evils of such things as abortion and marriage breakdown. But we shouldn't follow secular culture into the trap of concentrating more on pathology than on good health. The best way to attack things like divorce and abortion is to help people grasp the full goodness and beauty of faithful and fruitful human love.

That was my third main point, and it was mostly a presentation of what the couples had told me. They said that marital intimacy gives rise to a unique communion by the couple of their complete lives and persons. Unless this "central truth of prime importance is clearly recognized," I said, "Christian spouses know that their conjugal union cannot be really understood." Here I was speaking against "a certain dualism" that treated procreation and loving union as separate purposes or ends in marriage. Procreation, I noted, "requires that the parents be the authors of more than physical life. . . . They must also be a source of love for the entire family."

Loving sexual intercourse: "like a sacrament of the married vocation"

That brought me to what I considered one of the most important things I had heard from the couples. In various ways the couples had told me that, for them, loving sexual intercourse is "like a sacrament of the married vocation because it both signifies and nourishes this vocation." Therefore, I told the council,

> we ignore or distort reality if we consider merely one or the other gesture of conjugal love apart from the whole of daily family life. For the expressions of love proper to conjugal life fit into a total complex outside of which they lose their full and true meaning. Physical attraction alone fails to define married love; pleasure alone cannot describe its bounds. . . . Married couples tell us that conjugal love is a spiritual experience of the most profound kind. It gives them their deepest insight into their own being, into what they mean to each other, into their mutual communion in unbreakable union. Through this love they grasp as in a synthesis the mysterious purpose of their life as one, as well as the bonds that link them to God the Creator. In an almost tangible way they commune in God's love and through their activity as spouses they see intuitively that God is the source of life and happiness.

The creative function of marital intimacy involves not just the couple and their children, I had been told, but "spreads its influence beyond the home as well." Besides, we should recognize also "the healing values of marital intimacy. Husband and wife find it is often indispensable when spirits are dejected, when a partner labours under some extreme difficulty, when home life has lost the serenity so necessary for the children's welfare." Church laws on marriage, I concluded, "must not inhibit the full development of Christian married love in all its dimensions. And we must promote and emphasize positively the unique redemptive values of Christian conjugal love." I stressed how much all humanity needs the positive values of conjugal love.

Looking back on that talk, two things strike me now. First, I was overly optimistic. We achieved a certain breakthrough in church teaching about marriage at the council, but since then we have also seen thousands of couples turn towards the hedonistic culture around them, with no sense that the church can teach or help them. Second, I very much share your conviction that couples must be helped to come forward to be the first evangelizers of the good news concerning marriage. What those Victoria couples did to help me in 1965 was a foreshadowing of the great work couples can do to promote the Christian understanding of marriage and family life, if only they are helped to speak in and for the church, and with real knowledge about their own marvellous complexity, as persons and as a couple.

+Remi

Dear Remi,

Back to the matter of the papal birth-control commission. We think it very important as background to remember that public pressure for change in the church's ban on contraceptives did not start with Catholic couples. We even tend to forget that the Criminal Code of Canada outlawed the promotion and sale of contraceptives until it was amended in 1968. Other jurisdictions had similar laws, which had been enacted for other reasons than to support Catholic teaching.

Birth control: public pressure versus Catholic teaching

The pressures to change civil laws came from various sources. Margaret Sanger, heralded now as the pioneer of the planned parenthood movement, launched her campaign for public support of birth control as an American eugenicist. Her target was not church teachings but U.S. civil laws against birth control. Her aim was to reduce the ranks of the poor and other lower classes in U.S. cities. Her main complaint was that "the very types which in all kindness should be obliterated from the human stock, have been allowed to reproduce themselves and to perpetuate their group." Criminal sanctions against birth control gradually lost public support, especially after the Anglican decision at the 1930 Lambeth Conference to remove its moral sanctions against contraceptives.

In his 1931 encyclical, *Casti Connubii,* Pius XI set out Catholic teaching. The pope stressed that artificial or "unnatural" means of birth control are immoral. Seen as a reply to Lambeth, and later reiterated by Pius XII, this teaching was what came under fire just before Vatican II. Who fired the first serious public shot against this teaching? Many people point to the 1961 article in *Good Housekeeping* magazine by John Rock, a Boston doctor who had helped develop the progesterone pill. Actually, in the article and in a 1963 book, *The Time Has Come,* Rock was not so much attacking the church's position as promoting his pill. He argued that it operated in a way that the church should find acceptable. He knew how much money would be made if he could convince Catholics that his pill was not immoral.

Whatever Rock intended, his pill was quickly seen as a scientific development for which the church's traditional position was not an obvious or even adequate reply. It was in this context that John XXIII secretly accepted Cardinal Suenens' suggestion to set up a Pontifical Commission for the Study of Population, Family and Births. It had met three times in secret when Paul VI announced its existence on June 23, 1964. When the council's third session opened later that year, the topic of birth control was reserved for Paul VI and his commission. When Léger and you and others talked about marriage, as you recalled in your last letter, it was about other aspects of the question. The matter of birth control, as such, was not on the council agenda.

Married couples as interpreters of God's love

Still, you touched on it in a general way; and the *Constitution on the Church in the Modern World* says some things that should be recalled here. The language is very general but sets out important criteria for deciding about family size. It tells couples that they are "in a certain sense" the interpreters of love of God the Creator. "This involves," the council says, "the fulfillment of their role with a sense of human and Christian responsibility, and the formation of correct judgments through docile respect for God and common reflection and effort; it also involves a consideration of their own good and the good of their children already born or yet to come, and ability to read the signs of the times and of their own situation on the material and spiritual level, and, finally, an estimation of the good of the family, of society, and of the church. It is the married couples themselves who must in the last analysis arrive at these judgments before God," the council said (GS, 50).

What we are talking about here is not just hopping from bed to bed for "safe" recreational sex, as they do in soap operas – what Grisewood calls "brothelized sexuality." Vatican II invites married couples to see that "the exercise of the acts proper to marriage" makes us in a sense "co-creators" with God and interpreters of God's love. Birth control thus involves saying yes or no to God's creative love. And, to repeat, the council says "it is the married couples themselves who must in the last analysis arrive at these judgments before God." That is why they can't "simply follow their own fancy."

The papal commission on birth control: a summary

Official records of the papal commission are not available yet. However, several books have been recognized as accurate accounts of its discussions. The commission's composition, agenda and results are worth a closer look.

Composition: For its first meeting, October 12-13, 1963, three priest specialists (sociologist, demographer and diplomat) and three lay men (neurologist, internist, economist) were convened. Six months later, April 3-5, 1964, these six reconvened, along with seven others – two lay men (sociologist, demographer) and five priest theologians. Two months later, two more priests – a parish pastor and a theologian – were added. They met June 13-14, 1964. Two weeks later, on June 23, 1964, Paul VI revealed for the first time that the commission existed. About four months later, during the council's fourth session, as you recalled, the bishops began discussing marriage, with the understanding that the birth-control question was reserved to the commission. For the commission's fourth meeting, March 25-28, 1965, the total number invited rose to 58. Among the 43 newcomers were 23 lay men, 13 priests, five women and two bishops. Three of the lay men and three of the women were married couples. The commission's work ended with a fifth meeting – actually a series of sessions – from April to June 1966. Fourteen bishops, seven of them cardinals, were added; they were designated as members, with all the others called advisers. Thus, over the course of the five meetings, those invited were 42 ordained men (16 of them bishops, of whom one did not attend), 28 lay men and five women – three married to three of the men invited.

Agenda: At the first meeting, their main topic was demography – the relation of church birth-control teaching to population growth. One lay doctor also stressed his view (agreeing with Dr. Rock) that the pill should be accepted since it did not put a physical barrier between ovum and sperm and its effect was not permanent. They concluded, however, that previous papal teaching stood firm, calendar rhythm was the Catholic way, and the pill needed more study. At the second meeting in April 1964, the discussion was mainly theological and philosophical: the "ends" of marriage, the scope of natural law and, especially, whether contraceptives are "intrinsically" evil. They concluded that natural law by itself was not adequate to answer their questions; that rhythm was the most desirable method; and that love in marriage could not be considered secondary to procreation.

For the June 1964 third meeting – nine priests and five lay men attending – three questions were put on the agenda at the outset: What is the relationship of the primary and secondary ends of marriage? What are the major responsibilities of married couples? How do rhythm and the pill relate to responsible parenthood? Discussions concluded with two votes: Is the pill morally acceptable? Nine no, five unsure. Should the pope approve the pill? Fourteen no.

For the 1965 much enlarged fourth meeting, some "immediate action" questions were introduced. Among them: Has sufficient progress been made on doctrine for a pronouncement to be made? If there are changes, how should they be announced? Is the teaching of Pius XI and Pius XII reformable? Are some forms of birth control intrinsically evil? Should the magisterium speak about rhythm and legitimate uses of the pill? Even if no pronouncement is made, can pastors and confessors be given some advice? Also setting the tone at the opening was a two-hour summary by John Noonan, a U.S. lawyer, of the history of contraception and of how church teachings had changed at times regarding love and marriage. The participants were divided into three main groups: theologians, medical professionals, and social scientists. New members included three married couples, and two other women professionals. Pat and Patty Crowley of Chicago, world leaders of the Christian Family Movement, tabled 100 letters from CFM couples in the U.S. about their hopes for an expanded, positive theology of human love and marriage, and their difficulties with calendar rhythm.

For much of the four days, the theologians debated whether church teaching could be reformed. They ended up voting 12-7 that earlier papal pronouncements could indeed be changed. Their other main topic was the morality of the pill, on which no vote was taken. The medical professionals produced 17 reports on the benefits, liabilities and probable moral implications of every form of contraception. The social scientists again discussed world population issues, but had no answers about how to promote responsible parenthood across diverse cultures.

The meeting concluded with informal votes. The pope should not just repeat past condemnations of birth control. He should issue a "basic" document on marriage. It should stress that parenthood should be responsible, conjugal love is central to marriage and not secondary, sex is a value apart from procreation, and young people should have better education about marriage.

The two-month final session in the spring of 1966 developed by stages. First, the 19 theologians again discussed natural law, the limits of church authority, and intrinsic evil. They voted on two questions: Is past papal teaching irreformable? Is artificial contraception an intrinsically evil violation of the natural law? By 15-4 counts, they voted no to each question. Some participating doctors criticized how past church teachings had been decided, and stressed problems that they saw with the calendar rhythm method. The Crowleys tabled a larger survey of CFM couples about their negative experiences with calendar rhythm. The five women were asked to speak about their personal views on love in marriage and birth control.

Influences on the commission

By all accounts, the presentations by Patty Crowley of Chicago and Colette Potvin of Ottawa were major influences in the commission's final work. Patty Crowley presented a summary of their CFM survey. Respondents generally reported dissatisfaction with calendar rhythm. "Marital union does lead to fruitfulness, psychologically as well as physically," she said.

> Couples want children and will have them generously and love them and cherish them. We do not need the impetus of legislation to procreate. It is the very instinct of life, love and sexuality. It is in fact largely our very love for children as persons and our desire for their full development as committed Christians that leads us to realize that numbers alone and the large size of a family is by no means a Christian ideal unless parents can truly be concerned about and capable of nurturing a high quality of Christian life. We sincerely hope and do respectfully recommend that the Commission redefine the moral imperatives of fertility regulation with a view toward bringing them into conformity with our new and improved understanding of men and women in today's world. We realize that some may be scandalized: those who have no awareness of the meaning of renewal; those who disagree with the conciliar emphasis on personhood and those who do not understand that the Church is the living people of God guided by the Holy Spirit.

Colette Potvin said it was time "to change directions, to find the true meaning of sexuality in the Christian life; to see how sex is embodied in the great commandment – love your neighbour as yourself. To understand woman, one must stop looking at her as a defective male, an occasion of sin for man or an incarnation of the demon of depravity; but rather, as Genesis presents her, a companion for man. . . ." Periodic continence, she added, "can have a positive value if it is agreed on by both husband and wife for the good of one or the other and if it doesn't upset the tranquillity of the family. But if it impedes the couple from living a serene, intimate conjugal life, one has to question its value. . . ." She asked whether it was human or Christian to "sacrifice the psychological benefits of marital relations in order to preserve the biological integrity of an act." She concluded that "a morality that emphasizes the biology of an act in all circumstances is unfair, especially to the woman. It should be adjusted to take into account the good of the marriage, the good of the couple, the good of the children and of the whole family community."

A text is drafted

At the end of May, the bishop members asked some of the theologians to draft a text outlining the commission's majority view favouring some change. A dissenting group undertook to write a minority report opposing any change. Some of the first group also were asked to comment on the minority report, and their third text came to be known as the majority rebuttal. All three texts eventually went to the June 20-26 meeting of 15 cardinals and bishops (one invited bishop, the future John Paul II, did not attend, because of the political situation in Poland). After two days of study and debate, the bishops authorized the editing of the majority report, to include some elements of the minority report. It was again debated and three votes were taken June 24 on the following questions: Is contraception intrinsically evil? (Nine bishops said no, three said yes and three abstained.) Is contraception, as defined in the majority report, in basic continuity with tradition and the declarations of the magisterium? (Nine yes, five no, one abstention.) Should the magisterium speak on this as soon as possible? (Fourteen yes, one no.) Then Bishop Dupuy from France was asked to write a brief pastoral introduction. His text and the majority report were presented to Paul VI. The commission disbanded on June 28, 1966.

Those who supported the texts sent to Paul VI saw them as the basis for an encyclical that would bring some change to the Catholic position on birth control. When *Humanae Vitae* was finally published 25 months later, on July 29, 1968, it was clear that the pope had decided instead to base it on material prepared by supporters of the commission's minority view, led by Cardinal Ottaviani.

We want to say something about the majority report that was discarded and the encyclical that was issued, after taking a moment to analyze what the commission did and failed to do. The commission did not discuss a complete and positive theology of Christian marriage and marital intimacy. This crucial matter was raised only at the last session when the five women were asked to speak, and came out especially in what Patty Crowley and Colette Potvin said. Their moving, emotional comments were not a full and positive study, however, and are not presented in any official texts. Throughout its work, the commission's main concern was whether official church teaching was reformable. This was seen as the real issue, even when days were spent on other topics, such as intrinsic evil or the natural law on the ends of marriage. It is clear, too, that the commission got hooked into John Rock's argument in favour of his pill – that it was as moral as rhythm. The rhythm method discussed by the commission was "calendar rhythm" which, as we noted earlier, we and hundreds of other Canadian couples knew by then to be scientifically flawed and unreliable. The Crowleys brought to the commission only the negative views of users of calendar rhythm who seemed to ignore the breakthroughs by SERENA in Canada and by the Billings in Australia. In its final report, the commission accepted the view of dissatisfied users of unscientific calendar rhythm: that they had been condemned "to a long and often heroic abstinence," as the Crowleys put it.

What was missing

If the Rendus from France, the third invited couple, gave the commission some information about the highly reliable ovulation methods of natural family planning, there is no evidence that it was discussed seriously. Moreover, we know that the Crowleys went to the commission with closed minds about what we were learning through SERENA. As the Canadian couple on the CFM program committee, we persuaded the committee that the program book we were writing at that time should include material to start husbands and wives learning about their own fertility and discussing how to manage it. The other program committee couples accepted our material for three CFM meetings. However, when the draft book went as required to the Crowleys and Monsignor Reynold Hillenbrand, the lead CFM chaplain, for final approval, our three meetings were rejected. Substitute material had to be written at the last minute. Hillenbrand and Pat Crowley in particular found our suggestions for discussions about sexual intimacy unacceptable, and even distasteful.

Moved by what CFM couples told them about their difficulties with calendar rhythm, Patty Crowley later talked frankly to the commission about the positive values of sexual intercourse in marriage. But none of the women who spoke said anything about her wonderful interior ecosystem and how contraceptive drugs and devices invade or disturb that system. None of them spoke about helping a husband to understand and respect the delicate and constantly changing female environment which he enters, sometimes in unwelcome and even violent ways.

All accounts of Patty Crowley's presentation highlight her statement that "we think it is time that this commission recommend that the sacredness of conjugal love not be violated by thermometers and calendars." Clearly, that remark summed up the Crowleys' negative report about the rhythm method. No mention is made of similar critical comments about the effects of artificial contraceptives. We are left to wonder, therefore, if anyone asked how human love can be enhanced by blood-altering pills, devices and drugs that render the womb uninhabitable for babies, and procedures that put one's spouse into a class with neutered pets.

Whatever else it did, the commission did not discuss a pedagogy for human love and control, including the positive values of abstinence. Their main focus was on past church teaching and whether to change or retain it.

The commission's majority report versus the later encyclical

Many Catholics who have not read the full texts of the commission's majority report or of the later encyclical nevertheless have strong views about Paul VI's decision not to agree with the commission's majority. In fact, each text draws from the same Vatican II teachings about marriage, conjugal love and the values to be considered when making decisions regarding size of family. Each text puts the same "gravely sinful" label on abortion, sterilization and what the commission called a "truly contraceptive mentality," which is opposed to having any children at all.

On two basic points, the two texts disagree. The encyclical stresses that "just as man does not have unlimited dominion over his body in general, so also, and with more particular reason, he has no such dominion over his specifically sexual faculties, for these are concerned by their very nature with generation of life, of which God is the source" (HV, 13). The commission adopted a different view of technology. It said it is natural for humans to use their skill "in order to put under human control what is given by nature." This would have opened the way to some use of artificial contraceptives. On a second point, Paul VI rejected the "principle of totality" accepted by the commission's majority. This is the idea "that procreative finality applies to the totality of married life rather than to each single act" (HV, 3). According to the commission, a couple could block conception at some times so long as they did not refuse ever to have children. They would be procreative as a "totality" but not necessarily every time they had intercourse. Not so, said the pope. Conception, or at least its possibility, can never be blocked. Intercourse must always be open to new life.

While stressing this point, the encyclical does not deal with an important aspect of what we learned through SERENA, and what couples using other ovulation methods also learn. Any couple using these "natural" methods will know for sure that at certain times intercourse is not "open" to conception simply because there is no live ovum to be fertilized. Intercourse at those times may serve other ends, but it makes no sense to suggest that it is "open" at those times to procreation, strictly speaking.

When Paul VI issued his encyclical, we SERENA couples were not disappointed. We knew that life without contraceptives was not only possible but could be rich and rewarding. We even thought that the Pope's reinforcement of a continuing official ban on contraceptives for Catholics might increase support in the church for our method. That did not happen. Some in the church criticize SERENA couples for not being more ardent promoters of papal teaching about birth control. They forget that SERENA began as a Canadian lay initiative 13 years before Paul VI's encyclical was published in 1968. Indeed, instead of being upset by his teaching we felt that up to a point he was confirming our approach. We know, from the experience of teaching other couples, that what *Humanae Vitae* says does not help couples to discover the wonders of their bodies the way our teaching methods do. The encyclical proposes an ideal of conjugal love and calls on people to live up to it. We welcome and subscribe to that, of course. But it does not show them in practical terms how to make knowing and free choices regarding their fertility. It calls for obedience that is virtually blind for lack of know-how.

Wanted: church support for fertility management

For some in the church, avoidance of contraceptives is used as a test of loyalty to the church's official teaching authority. We think this is not a fair test. Most Catholics receive no help from the official church regarding how to manage fertility without contraceptives. In general, the papal ban is perceived as "mere external pressure." Vatican II makes clear (GS, 17), as we noted before, that "mere external pressure" cannot be the basis for a truly human informed free choice. Dioceses and parishes spend little or no money for programs to inform people about how contraceptives really work in the internal female ecosystem. How many priests or others giving marriage preparation courses, or counselling couples, can speak in informed and intelligent ways about how contraceptives really work and about modern scientific natural methods? SERENA couples continue with their own limited personal means to spread their couple-to-couple method, and other individuals promote other natural family planning methods (Billings, Creighton, etc.) with equally slim resources. Meanwhile, the information flooding the media and shaping public opinion and behaviour comes almost entirely from the manufacturers of contraceptives. We are not surprised when surveys show that Catholic couples respond to that advertising in much the same way as anyone else. Their knowledge of the church's official teaching is too skimpy and general to help them make informed and free choices in the face of the barrage from the drug companies. No wonder Catholic couples get assimilated into the alien culture that the drug companies spend millions to promote for their own billion-dollar profits!

Couples as official teachers of intimacy

Church teaching about marital intimacy will not be renewed, will not be put into language that will convince and move millions, until couples are given first place as official teachers of intimacy. The main evangelizers of sexual intimacy must be those who by their vocation live that intimacy. Christian couples still have no real status in the Vatican circles where official teaching about intimacy is written. But there is one place where couples are the official teachers of what their faith tells them about sex. That place is their own home. The women and men who make up each generation are given their first understanding of their sexuality while babes in arms. Gender stereotypes begin in the crib with the way parents and other relatives talk to and play with girls and boys. Obviously, certain male and female characteristics, both physical and psychological, are shaped by nature – by genes, hormones, body types and other such factors. But it is nurture, not nature, that shapes understanding, gives meaning, assigns roles. Rape, wife-beating and incest are cultural realities not because "boys are like that" but because men are brought up to believe that kind of behaviour is acceptable and that they can get away with it. Male stud-like behaviour starts with child-rearing and continues through later stages of development. It is not "just natural," and it is not acceptable. All this has to do with the morality of birth control, too.

The feminist movement has made some progress in raising awareness of women's rights to counter rape and wife beating. It has remained mostly silent, however, about how many women suffer side effects from birth-control technology. The popular news media also say little about this. Occasionally, however, the truth will come out. For example, the January 28, 1998 Toronto *Globe & Mail* had an article which acknowledged that hormone levels in contraceptive pills worry a lot of women. The newspaper was reporting the release of "a new birth-control pill that has fewer side effects than the dozens of other brands on the market." As many as 50 percent of women who try birth-control pills stop using them within a year because of side effects, the article said. The new pill, it added, combines chemical forms of the female hormones estrogen and progesterone found in many other oral contraceptives "but at greatly reduced dosages." The general silence about the ill effects of birth-control technology is another example of the problem of truth-telling in contemporary society.

Human sexuality: different from animals?

A central issue in all discussions about human sexuality is whether we see any difference between people and animals. Are women and men just other animals? What do we make of the few words in Genesis which tell us that

120

Adam looked over all the animals and did not find his mate among them? (Genesis 2:20) The story continues that when God created woman, Adam recognized her at once as "flesh of my flesh" (2:23) – and the two became one. Catholics often recall this story in our teaching about divorce. Rarely do we try to tease out what these words might mean about our sexuality in a more general sense, or relate them to the morality of the new reproductive technologies.

We humans resemble animals biologically in our sex organs and in the way we mate and give birth. Perhaps it is no surprise, then, that what farmers and veterinarians have learned to do to animals is now being done to human beings. So we won't be overrun with pups and kittens, female dogs and cats are routinely neutered, and now women have their fallopian tubes tied. Especially for selective breeding, male animals of all species are systematically castrated and, snip, snip, men now are vasectomized. Even more, all the old techniques of artificial breeding perfected by veterinarians for animals – gathering eggs and sperm, fertilizing eggs outside the body, freezing sperm and embryos, using surrogate mothers and artificial wombs – are now the "new technologies" of human reproduction. Is it really all the same? Is the only difference the fact that animals have no choice and we do? After perfecting techniques for subjecting farm animals to genetic manipulation and even cloning, do we simply proceed to selecting human genes for preferred characteristics in our babies or to the cloning of superior humans? Were we mistaken in the past to react negatively when the Nazis, for example, used animal husbandry techniques to implement a national eugenics policy? Were the Nazis wrong only in their choice of the particular human features they tried to obliterate?

When we try to draw a line in these matters between human beings and animals, several things become evident. For one, we find support in the Judeo-Christian tradition. The psalms and other Old Testament writings, starting with Genesis, set humans apart from animals. Christian literature continues the same line. Our personal experience as wife and husband confirms us in the conviction that we are not just animals in our intimacy. We resist the very idea of using farm-based fertilizing or sterilizing techniques on ourselves; indeed, we find it abhorrent. This reaction, in turn, is our starting point for rejecting the mass-produced stuff of the contraceptive industry. Unlike those social scientists who theorize that we are naked apes at best, driven by the same instincts and appetites as all animals, we believe we can bring gospel values into human sexual relations as into any other aspect of life. How far we are from having achieved this ideal is a sign of how much work we still have to do before the reign of God is a reality.

Mae and Bernard

Dear Mae and Bernard,

All I want to add at this point is a comment about something one of your earlier letters noted. We cannot say now what difference it might have made if Paul VI had asked all the bishops, or a representative group of them, to join him in finalizing his encyclical on birth control. As you said, he acted alone, setting aside the principle of collegiality. In that sense, he reverted to the view of the Roman minority at Vatican II, who opposed the idea of collegiality. As we noted in earlier letters, the council deliberately included in the end the two views of authority in the church – pope with all the bishops, and pope alone. Strictly speaking, therefore, no one can question Paul VI's authority to act alone on the birth-control question. However, we can see now that by acting alone on so crucial a question less than three years after the close of the council, he may have lent support to those who now seem bent on undermining Vatican II's teaching about collegiality. Thus, quite apart from moral questions related to birth control, his encyclical raised questions of ecclesiology, questions about the theology of the church and how it is governed.

I can't go into all the details here, but the main issue for us bishops in Canada after *Humanae Vitae* was published was what pastoral guidance to give couples and others who dissented from the papal teaching. We tried to teach people the importance of openness to God and respect for church teaching as they tried in conscience to balance what seemed to them conflicting values in their family life, making the decisions that only they could make. Each couple must decide for themselves. However, contrary to some of our constant critics, we did not say that following one's conscience is just doing whatever one likes.

+Remi

For Discussion

1. Why do you think there is so little in the popular news media about the negative effects of birth-control drugs and devices?

2. How much should the church be concerned about sexual morality? More than it is, or less?

3. Discuss how wider use of birth control by women might leave them open to more sexual violence from men.

4. Are you satisfied with how the church has studied human love and sexuality? What do you think should be stressed?

5. Discuss what links you see between natural family planning and the environmental movement.

For Action

1. Read the majority report of Paul VI's birth-control commission and his 1968 encyclical, *Humanae Vitae,* and note the points on which they agree and disagree.

2. Read the Canadian bishops' 1968 Winnipeg statement about *Humanae Vitae,* and their April 1969 follow-up statement.

3. Research medical literature about health risks and side effects associated with birth-control drugs and devices.

4. Discuss with local promoters of natural family planning what support they get and what difficulties they face. Also discuss similar issues with those who promote artificial contraceptives.

Further Reading

Kaiser, Robert B. *The Politics of Sex and Religion*. Kansas City: Leaven Press, 1985.

_____. *The Encyclical that Never Was*. London: Sheed and Ward, 1987.

McClory, Robert. *The Turning Point*. New York: Crossroad, 1995.

Parenteau-Carreau, Suzanne. *Planning Your Family the S-T Way*. Ottawa: SERENA-Canada, 1987.

_____. *Love and Life: Fertility and Conception Prevention*. Ottawa: SERENA-Canada, 1989.

Paul VI. *On Human Life: Encyclical Letter* Humanae Vitae. In *Vatican Council II*, Austin Flannery, ed. Northport, NY: Costello, 1988. Volume 2, 397-416.

Plenary Assembly of Canadian Catholic Bishops. "Statement on the Encyclical *Humanae Vitae*, 27 September 1968." *Love Kindness*, Edward F. Sheridan, ed. Ottawa: CCCB, 1991, 142-146. See also "Statement on Family Life and Related Matters," *Love Kindness*, 154-155.

The Holy Spirit:
Presence and Power

The Catholic church teaches that the Holy Spirit comes to dwell in a person through baptism and confirmation. This chapter takes up in more detail what Vatican II taught about the Spirit. It looks at the contribution of the Eastern church to this teaching. It discusses the difficulties Christians have in appreciating the presence and power of the Spirit in their daily lives. It looks in particular at the way baptism is celebrated in the typical parish. New opportunities for teaching about the Spirit at the time a baby is born and brought to baptism are explored. A number of lay-initiated parish activities are suggested which might make the entire Christian community more aware of the role of the Spirit in their lives. Awareness of Christian oneness in the Spirit is discussed as an antidote to the excessive isolation and individualism of today's dominant culture.

Dear Mae and Bernard,

One of my favourite descriptions of Vatican II is that it started us breathing with our other lung – the Eastern side of the Church. Vatican II heard the voice of the Eastern church from a number of outstanding pastors, including Archeparch Maxim Hermaniuk, the Ukrainian Metropolitan of Winnipeg, who died a few years ago after making a huge but unheralded contribution to the church in Canada and throughout the world. The Council recognized that we so-called Latin rite Catholics need to put more stress on the work of the Holy Spirit in the church. Someday we may look back and see that one of the council's greatest contributions was to deepen our appreciation of the Spirit. And there's no better place to start than by trying to get a broader and deeper understanding of our own baptism.

What do we understand when we say baptism "makes us members of the body of Christ"? It means a great deal more than just a sort of social membership in the local church. Vatican II emphasized that baptism gives each person a full share in Christ's prophetic, priestly and sovereign mission. It's hard for anyone to grasp fully what that really means. Even after 36 years as a bishop I keep learning new things. As members of the body of Christ, we are all equal in dignity and equally called to serve the Gospel. "For in one Spirit we were all baptized into one body" (1 Corinthians 12:13), and we are "members of one another" (Ephesians 4:25). The words seem simple. The mystery they try to convey is awesome.

Baptism: a community celebration

Today's typical baptism ceremony tries to help us see into the depths of what's involved. Baptism used to be an almost private ceremony, involving just the immediate family. Part of the social pressure for that came from an inordinate fear that a child might die without baptism. Thanks to Vatican II, we are losing that fear. Now, if a child does die before baptism – which should be very rare, because any believer can baptize – we know that child is not condemned to limbo. Therefore, now, much more often than before the council, baptism takes place in front of the whole worshipping community. That crowd of other Christians is as important a baptismal symbol as are the water, oils, lighted candle and white garment. The newly-baptized becomes a member of the entire believing community throughout the world, represented by the local congregation. The new Christian will live and grow in this body of Christ, this community of believers. Most of us need to be much more alive to the fact that our Christian friends and neighbours are members of Christ's body in this way.

But there is much more than that to it. The body of Christ, the church, continues in history to do great things through us – or, more precisely, through the Spirit of the Risen Lord, imparted to us through baptism and confirmation. We Western Christians have had the impression that somehow there is a kind of continuous incarnation, a continuous presence of Jesus with us. It was almost as if we ignored Christ's death, resurrection and ascension and kept thinking about Jesus still walking with us. Jesus is not walking with us. Jesus in his glorified flesh has returned to the Father. He even stressed that he had to do that or the Spirit, the other Paraclete, wouldn't come to us. Now it's the Spirit of Jesus dwelling in us that makes us, in that sense, "other Christs," members of Christ. That's why we have to try harder to understand and appreciate the work of the Spirit.

The baptism of Jesus

We're talking here about receiving in baptism the same Spirit that Jesus first received from the Father. This is where the baptism of Jesus comes in. We have placed a lot of emphasis on the incarnation, birth, passion and death of Jesus. We tend almost to forget that in the flesh Jesus was baptized by John in the Jordan. The Christmas story tells of the incarnation, the once-for-all inbreaking of the divine into our human flesh. Then, moving along past some well-known incidents in the early life of Jesus, there comes that critical moment when the full-grown human Jesus begins his public ministry. He is recognized by John the Baptist. Despite John's protests, Jesus insists that John baptize him, in solidarity with the people called to repentance.

Jesus is conscious at this point of accepting publicly the mission of his Father, to establish the reign of God. Then comes the theophany, that manifestation of the Trinity, when the voice of the Father says "This is my beloved Son," and the Spirit, in the form of a dove, descends on Jesus. From that moment he is a marked man. He receives the divine commissioning in his flesh. He begins his ministry under the guidance of the Holy Spirit, being led into the desert to be tempted.

The Spirit of the Risen Christ, living in us

At the end of his life, as he is completing his mission, he says to his astonished disciples, It is good for you that I leave, because if I don't leave – if I don't take my human flesh back into the divine embrace; if I don't complete the cycle of coming from the Godhead and returning to the Father – then the

Spirit will not come to you. But I will send you another Paraclete, and he will help you to understand everything that I have told you.

In this sense, it has to be clear to us that the Catholic church is not a continuing incarnation of Jesus. The incarnation is complete. We are no longer talking about Jesus somehow mysteriously walking beside us. But the Spirit sent by the Risen Christ is with us. Jesus first receives the Spirit, and is led by the Spirit in his mission, leading to the crucifixion. After the resurrection, Jesus as Lord sends his Spirit; and it is the Spirit of Christ who now develops and leads us, the church.

You and I through our baptism receive from Christ the same Spirit Jesus received at his baptism. Through faith and baptism, we're now the extended body of Christ. About this, Jesus says: "The one who believes in me will also do the works that I do and, in fact, will do greater works" (John 14:12). We are to carry on Christ's work with the help of the Holy Spirit. But that's the same Spirit that Jesus first received from the Father.

All Christians need to come alive to this fact. We have received the Spirit, and we can and must carry on Christ's work here on earth. But we don't do that automatically, as it were, or in spite of ourselves. We're not spiritual robots. We have a part to play in consciously welcoming the Spirit into our lives. Paul in his letter to the Corinthians talks about that – the release of the Spirit. That awakening of the Spirit in each of us is critically important. It is that Spirit, then, that enables us to become eucharist for others, to go out into the world, as the apostles and disciples did after Pentecost.

Christ is head of the church. All its members must be in communion with its head. To be in communion means to live through and experience all that Christ did. Can we see ourselves in that great circular movement – coming from the Father, witnessing to the world, sharing in the passion, and returning to the Father? The circle moves through the incarnation when Jesus took on our flesh; through the coming of the Spirit on Jesus at his baptism; through his transfiguration on the mountain; through his passion and death on the cross, his resurrection and ascension, and his bestowal of the Spirit at Pentecost. It is through being part of all this that we are empowered to transform the whole world and bring about the reign of God, through Christ. That is what being baptized means. Awesome, as I said.

One result of the current fascination with apparitions in various parts of the world is that it distracts us and impedes our realization that through baptism, confirmation and the eucharist the Spirit of Christ comes to live in us and we are supposed to be busy bringing God's reign to reality. Mary, woman of faith, Mother of God, exemplar of discipleship, is *not* a substitute for our own responsibility. We down-play or, worse, ignore the Spirit who is alive within us when we ask the Blessed Mother herself to do the work we are supposed to be doing, to build a civilization of love.

A footnote before I close: Vatican II, as I said earlier, began reawakening our awareness of the Spirit, something we have to relearn from Eastern Christians. The council also turned us back to Holy Scripture, the word of God, as the source of our faith. By reading God's word prayerfully each day, and by reflecting on it, we will meet the Spirit at work in our lives. This is how we do our part to awaken the Spirit that is within us from baptism. Let us be totally open to this intimate divine personal presence.

+*Remi*

Dear Remi,

Several times we have participated at baptisms during the Sunday mass. It seems to have happened more often while we were visiting in Grenada than living in Canada, but that may be just an accident of timing. Each time in either country, however, we've had something of the same experience.

For one thing, you sense a certain tension or restlessness in the regular congregation. It's as if the regular churchgoers are uncomfortable. The added baptism ritual keeps them in church longer than usual. Some people seem to look on it as an interruption of the standard liturgy. We are more used to other sacraments performed within the mass, such as weddings or funerals or ordinations. We even have names for wedding, ordination or funeral masses. But all these were taking place before Vatican II. Baptism during mass has become common only since the council. Another important difference is that for a wedding, ordination or funeral, the congregation comes for that occasion out of personal interest; they know the party involved in the special ritual. It is different when young parents bring their child for baptism during a regular Sunday mass. Except in very small parishes, usually they are strangers to most present.

This is why we think the birth and baptism of a child is a special challenge and opportunity for each local Christian community. A few years ago some research was done on this around Quebec City. It pointed to promising new pastoral initiatives that still await full development. The challenge lies in overcoming individualism and isolation in our modern industrial society in general, and in the so-called nuclear family in particular. The opportunity arises when a young couple brings their child from their nuclear home into the large parish community for baptism.

Many young couples live in a very private and isolated way. Their life can be limited to work, contact with family and a few friends, and a narrow round of favourite social activities. Even if they go to church regularly, they can opt for minimal involvement. Radical change begins when their first child is on the way. They may face the prospect of living on a reduced income with added expenses. Probably they'll need to begin thinking of moving to a larger home. New parental preoccupations and tasks change their relations with friends and family. New social patterns emerge. If they go to prenatal classes, and later to baptism-preparation courses in their parish, they are put in touch in new ways with familiar institutions such as hospitals and churches. New needs arise, such as for baby-sitters. New parents are quite different from newlyweds. And the poorer they are, the more difficulty they'll have dealing with their new needs.

The birth-baptism event: a key moment for the community

Pastors and catechists sometimes discuss what they call key moments when people are open to new faith experiences. We have given the name "birth-baptism event" to what we see as one of those special times for young couples and for the entire Christian community in which they live. By deciding to give life to a child and to bring him or her to be baptized, the couple are signalling a new and special kind of openness on their part. Their need for new relationships and services gives all their neighbours new opportunities to reach out to them and to serve them. Befriending and helping couples around the birth-baptism event could become an important way to serve new life. That could include helping new parents with very concrete, material needs, such as housing, a better job, transport, or childcare.

We have never come across a parish where people seemed fully aware of all this and were doing something about it. A parish program of the kind we are imagining would start with an invitation to mothers-to-be to make themselves known to the local Christian community. They would be announced, welcomed and offered any assistance needed. There would be special prayers with and for them and for their babies. Later, the birth would be announced and celebrated appropriately, as support of the new parents and as a pro-life witness. A Christian community open to the Spirit alive in their midst would want to do such things even for new parents who may be somewhat distant from the church. Such gestures are the least that can be done to "love one's neighbour as oneself" and to "share each other's burden."

Such solidarity on the part of the larger community should take on special qualities of warmth and generosity when young parents decide to bring their child for baptism. During a baptism at mass, the ritual usually calls for everyone present to renew their baptismal promises and to affirm that they will try to help the new parents raise their child in the Christian faith. Too often this promise is forgotten before we leave our pews at the end of the liturgy. Or, we make the promise as if we don't intend it to lead to real involvement and help. But it should extend even beyond supportive friendship to real help, if necessary. And, of course, the needs of new parents may be greatest after the birth of their second or third child.

We Catholics talk about how other faith groups "look after their own" more than we do. We know that the most general criticism of our churches is that people do not feel truly welcomed when they walk in. Usually we don't get to know one another well enough. New parishioners talk about going to a church for months and never being approached and greeted. When we were living in Toronto for a couple of years, we preferred assisting at mass in the Caribbean parish because people there were more friendly to us as newcomers and strangers.

Who can be a more welcome newcomer than a new baby? Around each child's birth and baptism we see many opportunities for members of the

Christian community to stir up the Spirit within them, and to "love their neighbours as themselves."

Mae and Bernard

Dear Mae and Bernard,

Two things strike me right off about your birth-baptism vision. It is truly counter-cultural, for it involves a sense of solidarity that is not typical of Catholics who have been assimilated into Western individualism. Latin Americans have a much deeper and richer sense of community, solidarity and participation than we have. And you found Caribbean people to be like that, too. Second, it is the kind of activity that lay Catholics can and should initiate. For it to succeed, a pastor must see the point and get involved, but such a project can be organized and launched mainly by the laity – *by* the laity (all the parishioners), *for* the laity (the new parents and babies).

Obviously it could seem to be just a social project to organize temporal support and assistance for new parents in their new family responsibilities. I would hope that it would be started and continued in a way that would bring out very clearly that the presence and work of the Spirit is central. The activities that would develop would be truly the work of evangelization, in the sense of bringing the Gospel to life in our midst. I assume, too, that if people really started in this way to love their neighbours as themselves, they would come to see other opportunities in other situations – such as poverty, sickness, old age and loneliness.

Vatican II stresses the right of laity to ask for the kinds of pastoral services that they think are needed for the good of the Church. It said the laity should disclose their needs and desires to their pastors "with that liberty and confidence which befits children of God," who are sisters and brothers of Christ (LG, 37).

Baptism and confirmation

If we are to become fully alive to the Spirit we received in baptism, many and varied educational and inspirational efforts will be needed. You spoke one time, Mae, about the usefulness of the Rite of Christian Initiation of Adults

(RCIA) program. I agree it would be good if every Catholic could "graduate" from such a course at about high school age. But I would not call that graduation "confirmation." We need another follow-up ceremony, more like a "solemn communion," as we used to call it. Confirmation and the gifts of the Spirit are linked to baptism. Only through the Spirit do we fully understand the eucharist.

A Ukrainian Catholic nun told me once: "We baptize and then bestow the gifts of the Spirit (in confirmation) so that people can be properly eucharisted." Unhappily, all too often in the Western church, we baptize, give first communion, and then wait a number of years for confirmation, to receive the gifts of the Spirit which help people to understand the eucharist. It is not that we haven't received the gift of the Spirit at baptism; but in a sense it is just there, taken for granted, and not fully appreciated. So in a sense we need to awaken that gift of the Spirit, and bring it to the level of awareness and action.

Charismatics used to talk about what they called baptism of the Spirit. The impression was given that this is a second baptism. It is not! If they mean there can be two baptisms, they're wrong. But it's fine if they mean that at a given moment, through deeper prayer and contemplation, the release of the gift of the Spirit is facilitated, and the baptized person is inflamed with the fire of the Spirit. Today the more mature charismatic movement talks of a "releasing" of the gift of the Spirit. This is still a somewhat ambiguous word. However, it can happen that a person, after prayer and perhaps a retreat or some special ritual such as laying on hands, is suddenly raised to a new level of consciousness and exclaims: "Yes, I am baptized. I am converted. I have the gift and the power of the Spirit. I now commit myself to active discipleship!"

Falling in love with the Spirit

Sometimes that is accompanied by extraordinary experiences. These phenomena are really secondary. Such a person may do wonderful things for a time, such as speaking in tongues, a gift of which Paul speaks (1 Corinthians 14) – although some who claim to speak in tongues may simply be psychotic, babbling away. That's why there must also be discernment and order. My recent experience is that the charismatics in Canada have matured and settled down. I recently met with a group of Western Canadian charismatic leaders. It was delightful. They recognize earlier weaknesses and have grown beyond their excesses of zeal. To me, the charismatic movement is now a positive, maturing movement in the church. Still, the power of the Spirit is very great, and when people are awakened to it, it's like a revelation. It's marvellous; you want to tell everyone! Would that every Christian would fall in love that way and shout from on high the gifts of the Spirit. The hierarchy would have no problems with that, or very few. At the moment, we're trying to awaken and empower the laity – "the sleeping giant."

The main point here is that everyone has to be converted in some such sense. As Mark says (1:14-15): "Jesus, after John was arrested, came to Galilee proclaiming the good news of God and saying, 'The time is fulfilled. The reign of God has come near. Repent and believe the good news.'" That's at the beginning of Mark's Gospel, the first, primitive gospel. And that's the fundamental movement for every Christian. Everyone has to turn around, saying in effect: "Hey, we've been going the wrong way, but we're turning around. We were lost and now we rejoice in being found."

If you are stone-hearted and stiff-necked, you can refuse the gift of the Spirit. One sin against the Spirit is to refuse to accept what God did in Jesus. God is love, and love is freedom. God is a courteous visitor, who knocks but does not enter until I say, "Come in." If I say "No" (and nobody can force me to say yes), God does not enter my life. God is respectful of our freedom. This is because it is the nature of love to be reciprocal. You can't walk up to someone and say, "I command you to love me." To say that prevents it happening, as many frustrated lovers have discovered in cases of unrequited love.

Prayer to the Holy Spirit

In the breviary, in the Ordinary of each day, there is a beautiful prayer to the Holy Spirit.

> "Holy Spirit, come, confirm us
> In the truth that Christ makes known;
> We have faith and understanding
> Through your helping gifts alone.

Holy Spirit, come, console us,
Come as Advocate to plead,
Loving Spirit from the Father,
Grant in Christ the help we need.

Holy Spirit, come, renew us,
Come yourself to make us live:
Holy through your loving presence,
Holy through the gifts you give.

Holy Spirit, come, possess us.
You the Love of Three in one,
Holy Spirit of the Father,
Holy Spirit of the Son."

(Text composed by Brian Foley)

The Spirit given to the church is the Spirit of Christ. It is given to us by Christ through his glorified humanity, his glorified flesh, after his return to the Father. That is why he told his disciples that it was important that he return to the Father. The Spirit given to us by Jesus in our baptism was first received by Jesus. The rediscovery and development of the theology of the Spirit, as I said, is one of the highlights of Vatican II. That theology is implicit in council teachings but is not fully developed there because we were especially concerned about an ecclesiology, with the focus very much on Christ. It is clear, however, that in a certain sense what you can say about Christ you can say about the Holy Spirit – as of two sides of a coin, so to speak. Jesus received the Spirit from his Father at his baptism. Having received the Spirit, Jesus can transmit the Spirit to us. We receive the Spirit in faith and baptism and we, in turn, can transmit the Spirit to others.

The gift of the Spirit

The Poor Clares recently told me a story about a girl in Korea who was baptized by a friend of her aunt. The girl grew up without knowing she had been baptized. She was living in a Buddhist community when the time came for her to get married. They were about to find her a Buddhist husband when the aunt's friend said, "You can't marry her to a Buddhist. She was baptized a Christian. You have to find her a Christian husband." And the Buddhist community respected that, and she married a Christian. The Poor Clares also knew of laity who baptized people they thought were going to die. They did not die, and years later discovered in themselves the power of the Spirit which they did not know they had.

This is not some kind of magic. The girl in the first story did not know, but the gift of the Spirit was there. It lived on in the community, so to speak, in this case in the aunt's friend; and it was up to the community to help transmit it. The intervention by the aunt's friend awakened it. Similarly, the parents and godparents awaken an infant to the presence of the Spirit with which it was gifted at baptism. All other baptized members of their community can and should be more involved in this same mission, and also in supporting and sustaining one another in their material, social and cultural needs.

These stories involve lay initiatives. We know of many other examples of the church surviving without the hierarchy. The church is wounded and incomplete in such cases. But faith is a gift, given to the people. A major responsibility of the hierarchy, in its broadest sense, is to discern the gifts of the Spirit. That's a special gift in itself, and also a necessary one. As Paul wrote (1 Corinthians 14:40), " . . . all things should be done decently and in order." Seeing to that good order is a charism primarily imparted to the bishop. But that discernment follows after, and does not come before, the gifts bestowed upon the people.

Service to the Gospel does not originate with the hierarchy, contrary to the popular belief of so many people. Service, or ministry, begins with the gift of the Spirit and the call that each Christian receives at baptism. And one of the gifts of Vatican II is to have clarified and emphasized that once again.

+*Remi*

Dear Remi,

We have a sort of hodgepodge of thoughts after your latest letter. Not long ago, Fr. Ron Rolheiser published an interesting newspaper column about how the term "mystical body of Christ" gives rise to a problem of perception among Catholics. We use the word "real" to talk about our Lord's presence on the altar and in the tabernacle. But we use the word "mystical" to speak about the indwelling of the same Spirit in each of us through baptism. As a result, we do not perceive the Spirit in us to be as *real* as in the eucharist. As a further result, we do not appreciate or revere our baptism the way we do the eucharist. St. Paul doesn't seem to make that sort of distinction when he says, "Because the bread is one, we, though many, are one body, all of us who partake of the one bread" (1 Corinthians 10:17).

After the Vatican document on the Jewish holocaust was published, Radio Canada televised an interesting discussion of the text by Cardinal Turcotte and Victor Goldbloom, Catholic and Jewish, both Montrealers. The question of the relationship between an individual and the community came up. For example, to what extent should an individual Catholic in Canada today feel responsible for what the Catholic community in Germany did or did not do during the Nazi regime? Cardinal Turcotte noted how our sense of individual and community can change over time. There are many examples in church history of a whole tribe or nation accepting baptism after their chief or ruler was converted. Today people would not follow in a similar way if a prime minister or president changed religion. Personal responsibility and individual freedom are stressed more these days. However, we cannot lose sight of the importance of community solidarity. Individual and group values have to be held in tension, and both kept alive.

Building communities of faith

This touches on what we were saying earlier about trying to involve the whole community when a baby is born and baptized. Vatican II begins its discussion of the people of God by stressing that God has willed to make us holy and save us, "not as individuals without any bond or link" between us, but rather to make us "into a people who might acknowledge him and serve him in holiness" (LG, 9). In other words, we can't settle for individual salvation, important as individual conversion is. We have to work at building communities of faith and love. Training in community development is essential for all pastoral workers.

At the same time, the value of each person has to be respected and built up. The uniqueness and infinite value of each single person risks being lost sight of in our global conformity and mass consumerism. Ironically, group conformity and crass individualism go together in modern industrial society. I can care only about myself, even as I try to dress like everyone else, go to the same rock concerts, and eat the same junk food.

The meaning of baptism brings a healthy tension into today's cultural mix. In the eyes of faith, the Spirit dwells both in each person and in the entire community. We are talking here in terms of mystery, yet also reality, though not just sociological categories. The Spirit transforms us into members of Christ. We thus enter the community, but not as individuals added only as separate entities. Pentecost reverses the Babel of independent, selfish individualism. Both person and community have to be respected and built up. Every family knows how hard this can be – to build unity as a family with common values and rules, and at the same time to create space for unique and free individual persons. Only in the Spirit can it work.

Mae and Bernard

For Discussion

1. Discuss with some friends who comes to mind first at the mention of God. Is it God the Father, or the Son, or the Holy Spirit? Why do you think as you do?
2. Why is it difficult, even after baptism and confirmation, to have a lively awareness that the Spirit dwells in each of us?
3. Discuss how concern for individual rights can work against a sense of solidarity among Christians.
4. Vatican II opened Christians to an awareness that other religions also have signs of the Spirit in them. Discuss what implications this awareness should have for local relations among peoples of different faiths.
5. At a baptism ceremony, why is it easier to think of a lighted candle as a symbol of the Spirit than to see the gathered congregation as a similar symbol?

For Action

1. Attend a parish pastoral council meeting and suggest that more be done to celebrate births and baptisms, and to give greater community support to new parents.
2. Study how the theology and pastoral practices for baptism differ in Eastern Christian churches from those in the Western church.
3. Meet with leaders of local charismatic groups to explore their concerns and experiences.
4. Read a book by a contemporary theologian about the work of the Spirit.
5. Draw a picture, or represent in some other medium, what you think would be an appropriate new symbol for the Holy Spirit.

Further Reading

Kavanagh, Aiden. *The Shape of Baptism: The Rite of Christian Initiation.* New York: Pueblo Publishing, 1978.

Osborne, Kenan. *The Christian Sacraments of Initiation: Baptism, Confirmation, Eucharist.* New York/Mahwah: Paulist Press, 1987.

Searle, Mark. *Christening, the Making of Christians.* Essex, Great Britain: Devin Mayhew Ltd., 1977.

Sacred Congregation for Divine Worship. *General Introduction to Christian Initiation.* In *Vatican Council II.* Austin Flannery, ed. Northport, NY: Costello, 1988. Volume 2, 22-28.

_____. *Introduction to the Rite of Infant Baptism.* Op. cit., 29-34.

World Council of Churches. *Baptism, Eucharist and Ministry.* Geneva: WCC, 1982.

8

All Are Called to Holiness

This chapter returns to a key Vatican II teaching: that all the baptized are called to holiness. It looks in particular at the importance of this teaching for lay members of the church. Holiness for those who spend their days in secular settings and temporal occupations is explored. Emphasis is placed on scriptural insights into the meaning of holiness. The difficulties raised by modern culture are noted. The heroes for most modern young people are those who excel in amassing fame and fortunes, starting with the stars of sports and popular culture. Holy people are not similarly honoured. Different views of saints in the Eastern and Western branches of the church are explored. The chapter concludes with a discussion of holiness and prayer.

Dear Remi,

The council has a whole chapter on holiness in the *Constitution on the Church*. It stresses that all the baptized are called to holiness. Most Catholics still don't take this as serious teaching that applies to them personally. Most of us laity still think of holiness somewhat along monastic lines – that holiness involves withdrawing from the world, being quiet, taking time off, dropping our worldly tools.

We were looking the other day at the article Bernard wrote from Rome in November 1963, about the Vatican II discussion that had just ended on the draft text about holiness. "The 47 speakers who commented on the text," he wrote, "left no doubt that they wanted to get rid of any notions that sanctity is just for a special few." One of the speakers was Cardinal Léger of Montreal. He noted that for a long time in the church, the ideal of holiness for monks had been held up as the model for all Christian life. While this had some happy results, the life of lay people today is so different from that of monks and religious that sanctity has seemed to many people to be unattainable. The monastic formula has also served diocesan priests badly, the Cardinal added, and a great loss of spiritual force in the Church has resulted. The same point was made one way or another 20 times during the four-day discussion.

As we know, these wishes of bishops at the council are reflected in what Vatican II taught about holiness and its impact on the world. "All Christians in any state or walk of life are called to the fullness of Christian life and to the perfection of love, and by this holiness a more human manner of life is fostered also in earthly society," the council said (LG, 40).

Holiness: part of our ordinary lives

Even if we have heard retreat talks about how you can pray and be holy while doing the dishes or changing diapers or working in a factory or office, we still usually think of holiness as something special added on. We don't see that just doing our job is part of holiness. We think of holiness as an extraordinary gift or quality that is not usually part of ordinary lives. The council seems to have something else in mind when it stresses that the call to holiness is universal, for everyone. This surely is another part of Vatican II teaching that we still have to catch up with.

However, it is easier to say, as Cardinal Léger did, that monastic spirituality does not suit today's lay people than it is to spell out just what a modern lay spirituality should be. Any thoughts?

Mae and Bernard

P.S. When I was teaching religion in a secondary school for boys in Grenada, the young men all insisted that they were not as holy as their parish priest. Just the fact that he was a priest made him holier, in their eyes. Perhaps they were right in saying their pastor was holier than they, but if so it was through his way of life and not just because of ordination. And they were mistaken if they meant they were not called to holiness as much as he.

I have always resisted the idea that I should do something "spiritual" or join some group in order to be a good Christian. I'm not sure who gave me the idea, but I always believed I could be holy doing a good job of the things I had to do without "spiritual" extras – as a mother, or a teacher in the classroom, or when I sang or taught music. I resented being pressured to join the Catholic Women's League or the Charismatics or make a Cursillo. You don't have to do more than trying to do your best at whatever you already have to do!

I think the other idea comes from the fact that a lot of people don't think they are good, let alone holy. They think they don't have anything, that they're nobodies, somehow worthless. So they think they have to do something extra. Or, they just turn away, from the church or whatever, because they think they just don't fit into that model of being spirit-filled. Both younger and older people have this sense of unworthiness, of lack of fulfillment, that their life is not worth much. I think this is especially true of people who have been through something like a failed marriage. There's a terrible feeling of nothingness, of worthlessness. How do you get that feeling turned around into something positive? You have all those suicides because people give up. Nobody says to them, hey, you're not perfect but you're not worthless, either. That's why it is important to give everyone a sense that they are of value, and that God wants them to be fully who they are – and who they can become, because we can all do a better job of what we have to do.

Mae

Dear Mae and Bernard,

The world would be a very different place if all baptized Catholics really understood and accepted their personal call to holiness. The problem you raised in your last letter is very real. The council says we are all called to holiness, according to St. Paul's saying, "For this is the will of God, your sanctification" (1 Thessalonians 4:3; cf. Ephesians 1:4). So we are called to holiness; but, as you say, what is holiness?

What is spirituality? Maybe I can illustrate with the story about a friend of Ken Dryden, the famous goalie for the Montreal Canadiens. Dryden's friend, so the story goes, took his son to see a hockey game. After the game, Dryden invited his friend and the boy to have breakfast with him the next morning. The boy, of course, was speechless with delight. During breakfast, his dad asked him what he thought of it all. It was a great spiritual experience, the lad replied. Surprised, his father asked what he meant. "Well," the boy said, "here we are, all together: Father, son and goalie host."

So, in a sense, that's what spirituality means: Being alive to the whole dimension of other-worldly; being aware at all times that we are in the presence of Father, Son and Holy Spirit. It means acknowledging that we are more than just earthbound creatures. It has to do with the sense that everything is ultimately gift from God; and that everything coming from God is meant to return to God. And it means, as you said, Mae, being sure that we are of infinite worth, just as we are!

What is spirituality?

To me, spirituality is being in tune with that complete dance of the whole of existence. It means entering into the divine, trinitarian mystery – the choreography of divine love – that goes out from and returns to the Father. Spirituality deals with the recapitulation of all that in Christ, which is so magnificently presented in Ephesians and Colossians. It has to do with us being part of all that movement, that dance of divine love.

Contemplation is entering into that dance, in terms of being open to the gift, present to the gift, not obsessed with our own human achievements or failures, but rather filled with the divine presence, the presence of the Holy Spirit, that divine presence which is transforming of the universe according to the reign of God. That's the field of spirituality.

It involves the whole of reality and, for the human person, it involves the whole person – head, heart and gut. All three dimensions are involved. It's not just a matter of thinking, theory, work of the head. It involves the heart, our attitudes, how we relate to people, our willingness to forgive, to be available to people, to become fully human, develop all our capacities, express ourselves as part of God's creative mission, co-creators with God. And it involves the body, action, actually doing work to transform our world by physical as well as mental labour – the total involvement of one's entire self, putting the body on the line for the reign of God.

There has to be some kind of support group for one's spirituality. For some this may mean one's spouse or other family members. We see this support now in prayer groups, faith and sharing groups, and others. The spread of these groups is clearly a sign of the Spirit at work, overcoming the forces in modern industrial culture that pull us apart from one another. More advanced science now tells us that all particles of matter are in constant relationships. Similarly, we humans need the support and energy we get from friends and neighbours. This need is what makes us social beings. So spiritual support groups are becoming fairly common. Families, couples and parents all need to meet regularly in small groups formed specifically to share experiences, to discuss how to respond as the Spirit enters our lives through daily events, and to pray. Priests also need to meet in small groups to discuss their spirituality. They still do not do this enough. It is not the sort of thing the bishop can tell them they have to do. Everyone has to realize for themselves that they need such groups, and organize them for themselves. It appears that the most successful prayer groups are generally those organized by the laity themselves.

What is holiness?

Holiness, then, is not something added from outside to the lives of a few special people. It is not primarily something that we plead for, by prayers and special intercessions to the saints. It is not simply a question of adding devotions, such as First Friday practices. Holiness is a matter of allowing the Spirit of Jesus, which is within us from baptism, to express itself. We can allow the Spirit to be expressed through our prayers, but also in all our temporal work.

This is not a case of Jesus walking beside us, or of the Spirit influencing us at the intercession of the Blessed Virgin or some other saints, from outside, as it were. Rather, it is the Spirit of Jesus inside us acting. Romans 5 and 8 are very important texts on this matter. We do not know how to pray, but the living Spirit of Jesus within us knows how to talk to God and, possibly beyond our understanding, says "Abba, Father."

The council's definition of holiness is so simple, even if it takes perseverance to achieve. It called holiness "the perfection of love": "Be perfect, therefore, as your heavenly Father is perfect" (Matthew 5:48). The ultimate degree of holiness, then, is to be in that "Abba" stance at all times, and not just when we are praying.

Holiness in our work is a matter of trying every day to do our best. That applies to every task, whether helping people or trying to transform nature into life-giving, life-serving goods and services. Even mourning a personal loss is transformative, in that it brings to deeper consciousness our need for conversion and redirection. That is part of our groaning with creation seeking deliverance.

So, everything we do has meaning and is part of holiness, from the person suffering in bed, to the one who has just had a car accident, to the one going through a marriage breakdown, and to all who hurt. They are realizing, living out, our imperfection. Our relationships break down and we have quarrels. We can recognize that this is all part of our redemption, provided that we accept our sufferings and struggles as the Spirit working within us, to bring us gradually to perfection.

Add to this what we learn from Paul's letter to the Hebrews (2:10): that Jesus himself is made perfect through suffering. It is in his obedience to the plan of his Father, and his acceptance of all that was involved, that he learned from his suffering and was made perfect. So it is with us, and Paul speaks of this: "On my own behalf I will not boast, except of my weaknesses" (2 Corinthians 12:5). If I see all that as being part of the divine purpose, then it is life-giving because it is helping to restore right relationships. It is bringing us towards the righteousness of God.

Holiness involves the work of raising our awareness of the divine presence within us. It calls us to recognize the divine, and to strive to make the Holy One present in all things.

The work of the Father

In Holy Scripture, what is the righteousness of God? It is not the idea of an angry God who punishes evil, and so on. It is the concept of God who has created the universe and will bring it into its right order, which is the reign of God. That is God's righteousness. It is the idea that ultimately God will triumph even over the designs of the evil one, and the right way will prevail because God has determined that it will.

That is the work of which Jesus speaks. It is interesting to follow the references in Luke's Gospel to Jesus doing God's work. As a child, when his parents find him in the temple, he asks: Didn't you know I had to be doing my job? I have work to do, my father's business (Luke 2:49). So it is all through his life. He is baptized, and God says, Here is my beloved son. The Spirit leads him into the desert to confront evil. He comes back to Nazareth and is invited to read in the temple. He reads from Isaiah's prophecy and says, This is being done right now; I am at work (Luke 4:21). My father is working all the time and so am I working (John 5:17). This is the work of the Father, to establish right relationships. Jesus shows this all through his life. The plan of God must be carried out. We participate in this work in all kinds of ways: by playing music, baking, washing, writing, making things, by getting involved in political struggles for justice and truth – it is all part of the work of God. That to me is what holiness is all about in the concrete.

We are called to act

If we draw back and say, well, God will look after everything, it's all in God's hands, we fall short of what we are called to do. Not only do we fall short, we falsify the whole doctrine of the incarnation and the sending of the Holy Spirit. God wants us to act in the power of the Spirit. The Scriptures are very clear on that point. We are not to sit back and wait. We are not to look upon God as some foreigner or outsider to whom we pray. We have the Spirit of God in our hearts. Romans 5 clearly states that the power is in us and we are called to act. Romans 8 makes clear that the whole of creation waits for us to help liberate it. We're responsible. We're committed. We have to act. We can't just wait. To sit passively praying and waiting for God is a misunderstanding. Hebrews is clear that Jesus learned through suffering. We are to join in and make up what is lacking in the suffering of Christ. We join in, we do not wait for God to do it.

Since Genesis, the Garden of Eden and all that, the human race alienated itself from God by wanting to make itself the centre of reference. In a sense, the whole of creation has been alienated from God, and our struggle is to bring it back. That's the fundamental repentance or conversion: turning back once again, to apply God's saving power to all of creation. Also, the other deeper dimension: Since we are creatures, we are of necessity imperfect. We're not God, and consequently we all need conversion and perfecting to achieve eventually the fullness of the reign of God.

It is not a question of appeasing an angry God for Adam's sin and for ours. That language of making retribution is one school of theology which came to us through Thomas Aquinas. Today we've outgrown the limitations of that school of thought, and we're more in line with that promoted by John Duns Scotus and the Franciscans. It says, basically, that God's creative purpose is also God's redemptive purpose. God's gracious purpose runs through the whole thing, through everything. It is not a question of making retribution; it's a question of receiving the Spirit of Jesus and continuing that saving purpose.

It started with creation but has an element of alienation in it because human freedom has sinned. We're not making retribution but in a sense restoring or remedying that alienation. It is a matter of relationship: putting all things into right relationship with God, rather than repaying a debt.

It is hard to get the right language for this, even for the idea of a continuum for God's saving purpose from creation to redemption. That is because the gift of God's love is so great that it cannot possibly be grasped by a human creature. Our human limitations, by the mere fact that we are human, prevent us from being totally faithful to the gift from God. At the same time, God wants us to become nothing less than divine. So that's where the mystery and the crisis are: That the creator wants the created to become more and more fully divine. That's the struggle. But it's in a positive, not negative, sense. There's a mystery there, the mystery of freedom. It's a matter of our hearts responding to God's call to covenant. This invitation has been repeated many times, from the days of Abraham and Sarah to the proclamation of the fullness of the covenant at Pentecost.

We are called to love

God's love is so perfect and powerful. Ours is shot through with self-love, interruptions, distractions. We are called to love as perfectly as God does. As part of that, just as God's is a creative love, we too are called to love creatively. We are creators, makers, builders, as we show through our culture, our arts, our technological achievements.

If we are to approach the divine, our creative love must have something of the quality of God's love. That is part of the crisis we see now, with environmental degradation, massive poverty, widespread violence. The way we create social systems and business plans and industrial complexes does not measure up to God's way at all. Called, as John Paul II keeps saying, to build a civilization of love, we produce instead a culture of greed and violence and death.

Obviously, some of what we do and plan and build is noble and even great and marvellous. Medicine and communications are but two areas of great human accomplishments. However, even our most wonderful achievements are blemished by the imperfections which distort our love. We are too much caught up in the vainglorious misconception that we should have full credit for the wonders we have achieved. Gifted by God to do marvellous things, we go on to claim that it was all our doing, and even go so far as to say that we can know and do it all without God, even denying that God exists at all.

At best, we are co-creators. Everything we make is touched by God's gift of energy and matter. Our brain-power and creativity are not entirely self-made. Everything we do or make is also part of God's creative love, part of God's mysterious, loving work.

+Remi

Dear Remi,

Isn't there a huge cultural problem blocking us from moving easily or readily into the kind of holiness that you described in your latest letter? That problem was well stated in an article we read about the difficulties of bringing peace to Northern Ireland. Probably the same could be said about Bosnia or

Nigeria or Afghanistan or Cambodia or Palestine or any Latin American country wracked by years of violence. And it could be said, in a sense, about our own lives.

Long periods of armed hostilities result in the development of a culture of *violence as heroism*, the writer affirmed. Especially for young people in such situations, the most evident way to be a hero, a "somebody," is to take up arms, to plant bombs, to take part in tit-for-tat acts of revenge. Steps towards lasting peace in such cases depend heavily on being able to inspire young people with other ways to be heroes.

You have been talking about a culture of holiness as heroism. That is even the official Catholic definition of a saint: someone who has shown heroic virtue, heroic sanctity. In Canada the culture of violence as heroism is not widespread, although some street gangs, drug dealers and other criminals live that way. We are much more caught up in a culture of conspicuous consumption as heroism, self-indulgence as heroism. Wealthy pop stars are portrayed as heroes. Absurdly-overpaid athletes are heroes. Super-rich but unscrupulous business leaders are heroes. Our heroes, overwhelmingly, are those who "made something of themselves" and can live flashy lives, surrounded by every toy they want. Granted, it may seem better to have a Céline Dion or Jacques Villeneuve for a hero than some masked car-bomber. But we are a long way from a culture of holiness as heroism.

Gospel values and the Catholic school

When our kids were teenagers, we were invited to speak as parents of senior teenagers in one of a series of workshops at a catechetical conference sponsored by the Ontario English Catholic Teachers Association. Participants circulated among workshops, choosing one or another according to the age group that interested them. That way, we shared our ideas with three different sets of parents and teachers that afternoon. In each workshop, the speakers had been given the same question: As parents of (age group) children, what do you expect from the Catholic school?

We said we expected the Catholic high school to give our teenagers "a counter-cultural sense of the transcendent." That is, we expected the school to help our kids rise above or stand apart from such aspects of the school culture as pre-teen dating; the highly competitive star system in school sports which reduced all but a few to mere spectators; and the lure of pop music which discouraged the personal musical talents of many students. We explained that, to us, a genuine Catholic school culture did not encourage premature sexual mating, did not reduce athletics to competition to make the star team, and did not destroy emerging artistic talents by letting them be drowned out by noisy, mindless waves of commercial music.

We argued that Gospel values should be reflected in a Catholic school in such ways, among others. We said that the examples we cited were the kind of things "the world" does, and that we expected our teenagers in a Catholic school to receive another culture, a counter-culture, which transcended the ways of the world – sexual play, competition, commercialization, and so on.

We had three kinds of reactions from each group to whom we spoke. Some said they could not understand at all what we were trying to say. In each group there were a few nuns who rebuked us because we "never mentioned Christ even once." Mostly, we were roundly scolded for "being so negative about our Catholic schools." The day ended with the participants marking evaluation sheets for the workshops and other parts of the program. The workshop given the lowest mark was ours.

That was quite a few years ago, soon after Vatican II. We had expected our viewpoint to be a tough sell. The reaction demonstrated exactly what we were trying to point out. Many Catholic parents and teachers have been assimilated into a culture that is alien to Gospel values. In some Catholic schools, some insightful teachers do give their students "a counter-cultural sense of the transcendent." We were not denying that. We were describing what we expected to happen in every Catholic classroom. We expected Catholic schools to cultivate a culture of holiness as heroism. And not just schools but also homes and parishes and dioceses and all the other institutions that call themselves Catholic.

We thought that then, and we still do.

Mae and Bernard

Dear Mae and Bernard,

You reminded me of a problem we have in the Western church about saints. When we think of the church we start with Christ and then all the people of God. To start with the hierarchy is a distortion of the rich way the gifts of the Spirit are distributed. That brings us to the fact that all the baptized are called to holiness, and to the matter of the saints.

In the Western church we tend to think of saints as outstanding people who, once they are canonized, can receive our prayers and help us get whatever we are trying to get. We can hardly wait until Mother Teresa is canonized so we can pray to her to help us with things like our hospital work. That view ignores the Eastern tradition. According to it, saints are exemplars or models who, moved by the Spirit, did things to transform the universe and, by the way they lived, show us what we can do.

Who are the saints?

We have tended to look on saints as people to whom you pray, or who help you get favours from God. We do this instead of recognizing saints as truly prophetic persons who by their very lives set examples and assure us of the goodness of God and of the possibility of being holy ourselves. Saints do that even if they do not speak, even in the silence of the cloisters. There is nothing more prophetic than to live like St. Francis of Assisi who embraced "Lady Poverty." Or St. Clare, who struggled to preserve the genius of true Franciscanism for a quarter century after Francis died; who went on a hunger strike until Pope Innocent III allowed her to retain her vow of owning no possessions of any kind. These are powerful, prophetic figures because they say in the face of evil, "Evil, you won't have the last word."

Thérèse of Lisieux is another. I'm happy that John Paul II has made her a doctor of the church. She lived to the age of 24 in a very restrictive Carmelite convent environment, doing menial tasks. Yet she is considered one of the greatest missionaries, one of the great prophets. She did this by her simple little way of living love to the fullest.

We must rediscover that sense of prophecy, this Eastern sense of saint as exemplar, instead of the rather individualistic and selfish sense of asking what can saints do for us. Not saint as my intercessor or heavenly errand-runner; but saint in the Eastern sense of great teacher, guru, holy person, to whom we show tremendous respect. India, a non-Christian country, less than two percent Christian, showed this kind of respect in 1964. I was at the Eucharistic Congress in Bombay when Paul VI came to preside at it. A parliamentarian who protested against the pope's visit was put under house arrest until after the visit, because Indians agreed that "we won't tolerate that you offend the guru."

The power of example

I'm not saying our tradition has no validity – for instance, now I have my saintly grandmother praying for me. Or Mary, Joseph or other saints interceding for us. However, we've lost a sense of the power of example. One of the most powerful forms of evangelization is the example of the saints – the saints in the biblical sense in which Paul wrote about "the saints in Corinth," and so on. The example of Christians who are really converted in their daily lives. It is not wrong to pray to Mary and ask her to do something for us. The question is not whether she will run heavenly errands for us. The question is whether we can live as she did, in total obedience to God. Can we say with her, "do unto me according to your word"? That's what it means at the end of mass: "Go now in peace to love and serve the Lord." Go out and serve the Gospel. Can we follow the example of Mary and the saints who render service to the Gospel (which I think is a better expression than ministries)? We are called to render service to the Gospel. And those who do it in extraordinary ways – here you can talk about the Vaniers and Mother Teresas and so on – have a tremendous impact, even more than many of us who are ordained and identified with the institutional church, because we are seen largely as functionaries: "The bishop has to do and say that; that is his job!"

Every lay person, having been converted to the Gospel, now is called to live an exemplary life and to work in exemplary ways – called to holiness, to sainthood. I was much impressed a few months ago when someone talked about the experience of a lay person going into the business world and doing business in an honest way with so much integrity that people sat up and asked, what's so different about this guy? Lawyers, for example, who will not tell lies under any circumstance. Business people who will always be fair. Cashiers who will never cheat. Shoppers who will not take advantage of a cashier who makes a mistake with their change. Working people who work with integrity do a good job simply because they want to make a thing of beauty, a thing that's useful, even on the assembly line. An automobile, nothing shoddy, everything done precisely, out of a sense of respect for creation. That's a powerful example. These are the nitty-gritty aspects of holiness.

But over and above example, there is also the actual teaching and speaking to be done. That's the gift of prophecy, of teachers and prophets, who don't have to be ordained people. It's interesting to go back to Acts and especially to Paul, who gives us lists of people who were rendering service to the Gospel. They're not ordained people. Women as well, outstanding women. The women remained in relationship with Jesus in his agony while the apostles fled! That needs to be re-emphasized. There will be a few, even non-ordained, who will "get on a soap box in Hyde Park," and actually preach. Now, apply that in the professions – radio, television, writers, musicians, singers, who will perform their work with complete integrity. These are examples of prophecy that need to be re-emphasized.

What is the kingdom, the reign, of God? It is the righteousness of God. The world was created right in the beginning. The refusal of Adam and Eve to trust God, to fit into that right way of being, caused the fundamental alienation we refer to as original sin. Salvation and liberation mean precisely that God will intervene, the divine purpose will set everything right.

To me, holiness is righteousness, which means everything in its proper place, in proper relationship with everything else. Liberation from sin is restoring things once again to their right order. Behind all this lies the divine purpose. That purpose is being pursued by the Spirit of God. This Spirit, not yet identified as a person, is seen hovering over the original chaos, bringing order out of chaos. Similarly, now when we work at restoring the temporal order, bringing order out of chaos, that is holiness. So to be holy is to be profoundly committed to restoring right order, not only in creation but in our own lives.

Holiness is linked to the reign of God. This is shown in Genesis by the Spirit bringing order out of chaos. Now we, by our baptism made members of the body of Christ, receiving the power of the Spirit, are responsible to bring right relationships and order into all things at every level. Economically, to bring right relationships in the exchange of commodities and so on. Politically, to respect other nations for their destinies and purpose. As human beings, to treat one another with dignity and respect, to work together in solidarity, to bring about the right conditions for full human development. And at the level of all creation, that we not destroy creation but help it to develop in harmony.

Putting things right: a mark of holiness

We talk of the capital sins: pride, covetousness, lust, envy, anger, gluttony and sloth. Each one speaks of a condition that is disordered. Action to put things right, to end the conditions of such sins, would indeed be a mark of holiness. Those who in conscious, persistent, systematic ways work to eliminate such sins in their own lives and the lives of those around them are indeed holy.

It is important always to remember that these actions to restore order are not possible by our own efforts alone. In every case where people try to restore right order by human effort alone, you end up with some kind of dictatorship or tyranny. To bring about right order you have to have transcendence. If that transcendence is only human, you have a dictator. When the principle of transcendence is divine, you have the Holy Spirit. That's where discernment has to come in. When dictators are not filled with and subordinate to the Holy Spirit, they become mean and unjust.

Justice is tied to righteousness. These two words really touch the same mystery. Justice is the science of right relationships. Distributive justice is about proper sharing of common goods, economic or otherwise. Commutative justice calls for human dealings to be in the right order. You can go on to legal justice and the newer concept of social justice; and modern science invites us to be concerned with cosmic justice as well – that is, with the right order beyond us human beings, in the universe unfolding as it should. If we do not respect right order in that regard, then the human race may very well wipe itself out and the universe will continue without us.

One of the most difficult challenges for us today is how to overcome our pessimism. It is hard to see that it is possible to move from where we are. We are so imbued with a sense of inevitability that most people think nothing better is possible. This is because social change is portrayed as part of natural evolution, not something caused by humans. We are not sufficiently aware of the negative impact of social Darwinism in our lives. That set of ideas that became pervasive in the nineteenth century dominates our thinking about society. Social Darwinism tells those who make it to the top in business or politics that they are the fittest humans. The poor are simply forgotten as losers in the struggle. We really haven't come a long way from the days of slavery. Slaves were thought of as a lower, even separate class, who worked for the rich and powerful, and we still have that mentality today. Child labour in some countries is just one example.

This is exactly the opposite of the biblical understanding. What is the kingdom, the reign, of God? It is the righteousness of God. The world was established in harmony in the beginning. The refusal of Adam and Eve to trust God, to fit into that right way of being, caused the fundamental alienation we refer to as original sin. Salvation and liberation come through believing that God will intervene, the divine purpose will set everything right. The council's idea is founded especially on what Paul, in his epistle to the Romans, says about the gifts of the Holy Spirit.

+*Remi*

Dear Remi,

So far in discussing holiness we have not talked much about prayer. After I took some courses in liturgy and Scripture, I got us started saying the Divine Office, especially morning prayer, and we have been doing that for a number of years. It is a marvellous new experience, all those beautiful prayers from the Scriptures. It sets up your whole day. Lay people are also using Holy Scripture in other ways in prayer groups.

But to come back to my earlier point, I think kids can be turned off by being too religious at home. Ours hated to kneel down every night and say the rosary. Maybe they're great people now because they knelt down, but they don't see it that way. I suspect they were influenced as much or more when we took them for walks, admiring flowers and birds and things like that – all of

God's creation. I have trouble seeing that it is going to be a great help to you rattling off Hail Marys and not really thinking about what you are doing, or not liking it. To me that's not praying, whereas you could be doing things together, like all the camping we did, and praying before those meals together. I am not saying this to dwell on the past, but to wonder how families could do things together that would bring an awareness of God being in their presence.

To me, being present to God is what prayer is really about.

Mae

Dear Mae and Bernard,

What to do about prayer? Laity are not alone in finding prayer difficult at times. A key point is that praying is not mainly a matter of doing or saying something. It is about being still, to listen to God. That should not be difficult for anyone who believes in God, who loves God. Still, some how-to-do-it suggestions can be helpful. John Shea, in *The Challenge of Jesus*, about 25 years ago, suggested five steps.

Five steps to spiritual growth

1 – About face. Turn around, refocus, redirect. That's the call of Matthew (Chapter 3). Repent. *Metanoia,* in the Greek sense, not the guilt-trip sense. Look in a new direction. Something new has happened. Christ came into our world. That's the first step.

2 – Celebrate. If you are lost and disoriented, and someone redirects you and puts you on the right road, you rejoice, you celebrate. There is greater joy if one lost sheep is found. I've been found, I've discovered a new direction.

3 – Trust. Trust in that new direction. Trust it will work out because God is in charge. Trust means that inner ability to remain creative in the midst of an unmanageable world. There are problems everywhere, beyond us. We will not change overnight, despite what the activists are screaming about. But can I continue to remain creative in the midst of all that confusion?

4 – Forgiveness. As I need to turn around, so others can do the same. I must be willing to let others turn around, refocus. I need to forgive as I want to be forgiven.

5 – Love. Self-gift. Give of yourself. Let yourself be nibbled to death, 24 hours a day. This is what eucharist is all about. It's bread to be broken, wine to be poured out. Bread and wine, body and blood. Jesus said: Here am I, body broken for you, blood poured out for you. Go you and do the same. That's eucharist, self-gift, in union with the sacrifice of Jesus!

Being present to God

These five steps are very helpful as a basis for spirituality. Where to begin? The first step is one I've learned to appreciate better through the Enneagram. To be present to myself, to my true inner self, to my "essence." By that, to be present to God. And in that two-fold presence to self and God, I'll become present to others, and to nature. So presence is the key. As Jesus so often said, stay awake, watch and pray. Then compassion. The willingness to suffer with others. Hang in there. Faith like Sarah and Abraham. The willingness to go into the darkness, into the desert, knowing we're on the way to the promised land, not because we can see it but because God has said so. Believe. These are very basic elements on which to build a spirituality of everyday life. The key idea, being present. Present to the new reality, open to any new discoveries, development, potential. Present to it and in communion with it. And seeing it all in the context of the divine plan. There is a plan entrusted to us by the Risen Lord when he sent his Spirit to teach us all things. The universe is unfolding as it should. I am part of that. I am the most glorified form of carbon. The universe has been raised to the conscious level in us humans. It is my job to be present to that, in whatsoever way, by doing the best possible work, whatever I am doing – dishes, housework, office job. Jean Vanier has a good point. L'Arche has a special thing about washing dishes – being present to what I am doing. Thich Nhat Hahn in his pearls of wisdom has a lot to say about really being present to what I am doing.

But we always have to come back to what Vatican II said about the ultimate prayer – the point that Congar was so delighted to see included in the council text. The ultimate prayer is the spiritual offering of the totality of who we are. Who I am (meditation, contemplation) and what I do (which is secondary because, ultimately, it is God's work). In the text from Romans, meditating, contemplating who I am is more important than what I do, because ultimately it is all God's work (Romans 1:1-4). All through Holy Scripture, we see Jesus doing his Father's work, doing the will of the one who sent him; blessed are they who believe in the word and do it. Who work at God's work. This is Mary, blessed because she worked, did God's will. It's all in John's Gospel.

Getting on with it

This is where lay people come in. Having been consecrated in baptism, we must get on with God's work. Jesus is consecrated in the flesh at his baptism, and immediately sets out to do his work, confronting evil and saying no to the evil one's triple temptation, and going on to do his real work. It is interesting to note that Jesus pays very little attention to the devil after that. Once he has cleaned up on the devil in the desert, that's accomplished, as it were. He is busy doing his work. Luke's Gospel suggests that the devil's out of the picture for Jesus until the final confrontation at Calvary. That's why one of the great sins of the Catholic church is fear. "Do not worry about anything," the Lord says (Philippians 4:6). This is an important issue. If we fear, we don't really believe! We have no real faith! But if we truly believe, as Hebrews Chapter 11 says of our ancestors, we walk into the unknown as if we know where we are going.

As John Shea says, Jesus triumphed because he went through his suffering without fear. Jesus in the garden could say, Father, if possible let this cup pass. That means he knew it was possible that it would not pass. He faced that clearly. Hebrews is very clear about this: It is through his pain and suffering, in the midst of his anguish, that Jesus is made perfect (Hebrews 2:10). And now (Romans 8) the whole universe is groaning in its turn, is in the travail of birthing, waiting for liberation by the children of God. That's us. All of us need to suffer. That is the work. That was what Jesus was saying to those who said he should not work on the Sabbath. They had a good point, but he had a greater point: My Father is working all the time, so I continue to do my Father's work even on the Sabbath. That brings us to John, constantly repeating about work and saying we will "do even greater work" because we are the members of Christ extending on in time. We are celebrating God's work. And that leads into the whole question of how we worship in the diocese, parish, home and so on.

It comes together there. Even non-believers – Gentiles in the scriptural context – become a spiritual sacrifice to God through my sharing the word of God with them. Their whole lives may be transformed by the good things that I say, by the story that I tell. By the good news, their lives are changed and thereby are directed to God and to God's saving plan, directed back to right relationships, and they are thereby made holy and sanctified (Romans 15:16).

+*Remi*

For Discussion

1. Discuss how to pursue holiness when one spends most of the day in secular settings and temporal occupations.

2. How might a modern Christian balance meditation on God's word, and action to bring God's word to life in the world?

3. Whom do you and your friends regard as today's heroes? What place do you give to holiness in the person you call your hero?

4. Discuss what you think about saints. Are they heavenly messengers to whom you pray for divine favours for yourself? Or do you regard them mostly as challenging models for your own life?

5. What do you think it means to do "God's work" in the world?

For Action

1. Read Chapter 5 of the Vatican II *Constitution on the Church,* about the call of the whole church to holiness. Talk to your children or other young people about what you read.

2. Study the life of one of the Canadians who might be declared a saint.

3. Read a modern book about prayer and meditation. Let it challenge how you pray.

Further Reading

Au, Wilkie. *By Way of the Heart: Towards a Holistic Christian Spirituality.* Mahwah, NJ: Paulist Press, 1989.

Cobb, Jennifer. *Cybergrace: The Search for God in the Digital World.* New York: Crown, 1998.

Conn, Joan Wolski. *Spirituality and Personal Maturity.* Mahwah, NJ: Paulist Press, 1989.

Downey, Michael, ed. *New Dictionary of Catholic Spirituality.* Collegeville, MN: Liturgical Press, 1993.

Jager, Willigis. *Search for the Meaning of Life: Essays and Reflections on the Mystical Experience.* Ligouri, MO: Triumph Books, 1995.

Johnson, Elizabeth A. *Friends of God and Prophets: A Feminist Theological Reading of the Communion of Saints.* New York: Continuum, 1998.

Keating, Thomas. *Open Mind ,Open Heart: The Contemplative Dimension of the Gospel.* New York: Continuum, 1998.

9

Together We Remember
Who We Are

Changes in the Catholic liturgy from Latin to the use of local languages are thought by some people to be the main result of Vatican II. This chapter studies the liturgy with emphasis on other, deeper changes brought about by the council. It recalls how the bishops debated these changes, and discusses the insights and arguments that were accepted. It shows that many of the changes were in fact a return to original forms of worship, including a rediscovery of the Jewish roots of Christian prayer. A renewed appreciation of the divine presence in the word and in the eucharist, in the priest and in the people, is noted. The possibilities for continuing renewal of parish liturgical celebrations are explored, with particular emphasis on how the insights and talents of young people might be more appreciated and encouraged.

Dear Mae and Bernard,

I would suggest that one of our biggest problems about prayer and the liturgy is that we are activists. Vatican II heard in part a very powerful message from the Eastern church. It has yet to be worked out fully, but we are beginning to sense it. That message is that salvation is a gift more than it is the result of our work. All is grace. And, to the extent that there is work – something that someone *does* – it is God's work more than it is our work; it is the Spirit of Jesus living and working in us; it is our response to God's prompting.

We live in a world that is filled with things made by us humans. Every day, as we mentioned before, we hear of new, more fascinating inventions – faster computers, new products from genetic engineering, all created by *our* work. We're proud of them. We are always boasting about our work; it's difficult to appreciate what God's work really means.

The first step is to go back to Genesis. On the seventh day, God rested. What does that mean to us? The triune God created this fantastic universe that we are only beginning to explore. Then God contemplated the explosion of riches and said it was good, indeed very good. God said, this work of mine, this magnificent expression of divine love, is good. I will set an example by just contemplating it. And what does this tell us? We are told that every seventh day we will stop, and contemplate, and give thanks to God. And in the process of doing so, we will realize who we are: that we are nothing less than divine. We will contemplate and celebrate what God has done; and we will also contemplate and celebrate what we have done. We will contemplate the presence of the divine in our humanity, and in all our human accomplishments. We will contemplate how everything we do is always really co-creation with God.

Keeping the Sabbath

The Jewish people have kept that heritage in the shabbat shalom. In Jerusalem, all commercial activity ceases for the Sabbath. Shops and businesses are closed. Traffic disappears. The city is quiet. We need to rediscover Sabbath. Rabbi Heschel's powerful book on the Jewish Sabbath would be a big help to all of us. The protection of the Sunday as a sacred time is important. It must be more than just a day free for a shopping spree. Sunday must be a statement of principle about who we are. Also, in our private lives, all the time, we need to bring the sense of the Sabbath back in. Not necessarily just on Sundays. We need to find time to do nothing, *no thing*, except to freshen, clarify, strengthen our relationship with God. This is the important thing.

That comes before any expression of prayer, before *saying* prayers in the Western activist sense. In the Western world, too many people still think that if we get down on our knees, and pray hard enough, that is going to change the world. It is not. The universe is unfolding as it should. In other words, God is in charge of the way it is unfolding. The really important question is:

Are we part of that unfolding? Or do we just say, Stop the train, I want to get off?

There is a kind of double tension here. We are supposed to be on the train, in the sense of doing God's work in the temporal order. That is the special lay vocation, as we have said a number of times. So we have to stay on that train, and not leave the building of the world to others who ignore God altogether. At the same time, we have to be a people who get off the train, to contemplate, do nothing, especially on Sundays. That day we recognize that everything we've done during the past week was really thanks to God's previous initiative. That day, we offer God all our week's work as our sacrifice offering.

That brings us back once more to Father Congar at the council. He was so delighted the day the drafting committee agreed with him to include the teaching, from Romans 12:1, that the ultimate prayer is the spiritual offering of the totality of who we are. Look at your Vatican II texts, and you'll see it near the beginning of Article 10 of the *Constitution on the Church*. The section goes like this: Christ, the high priest taken from among us humans, made us, the new people, a sovereign people. The baptized, by regeneration and the anointing of the Holy Spirit, are consecrated to be a spiritual house and a holy priesthood, so that through all the works of Christian people they may offer spiritual sacrifices and proclaim the perfection of him who has called them out of darkness into his marvellous light. And then comes the phrase Congar persuaded them to include: "Therefore all the disciples of Christ, persevering in prayer and praising God, should present themselves as a sacrifice, living, holy and pleasing to God."

Offering our living bodies as a holy sacrifice

The council text paraphrases St. Paul on the point. The actual scriptural text is perhaps more dramatic: "I appeal to you therefore, brothers and sisters, by the mercies of God, to present your bodies as a living sacrifice, holy and acceptable to God, which is your spiritual worship" (Romans 12: 1). That is really dramatic teaching: that we should worship God by offering our living bodies as a holy sacrifice.

When we tease it out like this, we see that Vatican II is saying something dramatic and profound. We read in the Hebrew Scriptures that people offered live animals as sacrifice. We know that Abraham and Sarah were asked to offer even their only son, Isaac. We know that Jesus offered his living body. But as we go to church Saturday or Sunday, how many of us go to worship God "by offering our living bodies as a holy sacrifice?" We usually say we go to church to offer our intentions, our prayers. But that's mostly head stuff. Vatican II teaches we should offer our living bodies. And, make no mistake, this is not just a figure of speech!

But whoa! Just a minute! What have we been doing in the flesh, with our bodies, this past week? We can offer pious thoughts and prayers and a little money in the collection envelope, okay. But all the rest of that stuff that we thought and said and felt and did, all that heart and body stuff, around the house, at the office, around the rectory, in the schoolyard, watching TV, at the dance, in the bar? Is my entire self, my entire living body, ready to be presented to God this week as a worthy sacrifice?

Of course, before we get too depressed, we have to remember that God loves and accepts each one of us as we are. Like the woman taken in adultery, he does not condemn us, but he does challenge us to "go your way, and from now on do not sin again" (John 8:11). That is always the challenge until next weekend. But this weekend, the challenge always is to present our living selves.

But, now, I have to cut this off here, and get ready myself for a eucharist – and for the same challenge that every other Christian faces: Am I worthy to present myself . . . ?

+Remi

Dear Remi,

Your latest letter got us thinking how sad it is that some people are hooked on the notion that switching to vernacular languages was the biggest liturgical reform at Vatican II. The main thing about continuing debate over the Latin mass, as far as we're concerned, is that it distracts people from learning about more important aspects of liturgical renewal. Such as offering our bodies, our entire life, as sacrifice, as you mentioned. Or greater use of Holy Scripture in our prayer life. It is a remarkable experience, to listen to God's word each day by praying the Divine Office. Before the council, the breviary was regarded as the private prayer of priests. Strictly speaking, it wasn't, but use of it by the laity began to be encouraged only after the council. How wonderful that change is!

Christ present in the congregation

The council teaching about the liturgy that we find ourselves mentioning most frequently is found at the beginning of Article 7 of the *Constitution on the Liturgy*. We think of it especially when we hear people say they don't like people talking in church, or shaking hands or exchanging some other sign of peace after the Lord's Prayer. The council text says simply that there are four ways in which Christ is really present at the liturgy: in the eucharist, in the presiding priest, in the Scripture readings, and in the congregation. Some people complain that there has been "a loss of reverence" for the eucharist since the council. That is sad where it happens. But we see more of a new reverence for other "presences," without loss of respect for the eucharist. We find that we grow especially in our awareness of Christ's presence in the Scripture readings. More and more, the Scriptures are being surrounded with the respect they deserve as the word of God. The book is carried in procession to its ambo in the sanctuary; the readers are well prepared to proclaim the word; the psalm is chanted beautifully. We know of one church where this is not so – no procession; the first two readings and the psalm read from a music stand on the floor of the church outside the altar rail – but that sort of thing is the exception now, in our experience.

It is the fourth "real presence," in the people, that we think is still least appreciated. As we mentioned before, Father Ron Rolheiser wrote an interesting column about this. He noted that we have become accustomed to hearing the people, the baptized, described as the Mystical Body of Christ. This language was popularized by Pius XI and Pius XII and is retained by Vatican II. Unfortunately, the word "mystical" can convey the impression that the way we are in Christ and he in us is not truly "real," Rolheiser noted. When the council says Christ "is present when the church prays and sings," it means he is *really* present. Still, we tend to reserve the term "real presence" for the eucharist and use "mystical" to refer to his presence in us as people.

Well, the question is not whether we agree with Rolheiser's analysis. The important fact is that we are slow to recognize that by our baptism the Spirit of Jesus *really* comes to dwell in us. At church, as at all other times, we should recognize this wonderful *mystical* fact. When we greet a friend or neighbour inside the church, therefore, we are not being "disrespectful" of the real presence in the tabernacle. We are also *respecting* the real presence of Christ in that other person. Not to recognize Christ's presence in this way is to act like the woman who was told in a dream that Christ would come to her house the next day. She woke up early and scoured and dusted. Her day was blissful except for the three occasions when neighbours interrupted her to ask for favours. But she was happy that, each time, she was able to get rid of the unwelcome caller and carry on getting ready for the Lord's visit. Except, he never came. That night he talked to her in her sleep again, and she scolded him for not coming. But I did come, he replied. Three times, in fact. I was those bothersome neighbours you shooed away! That story helps us to reflect on the four ways Christ is present at every liturgy, as Vatican II teaches.

Texts in the language of the people: meeting a pastoral need

Coming back to the matter of using local languages instead of Latin, some suggest this was an error foisted on the council by a few irresponsible "modernizers." That's not the way it came about. One of Bernard's memories of the Vatican II debate on the liturgy is a press conference by a bishop from the Philippines. Bishop William Duschak, a German-born missionary, argued in the council that local languages should replace Latin; and he explained to journalists why he took that stand. He said his 30 years as "a practical missionary" in the Calapan region of the Philippines had convinced him that an unfamiliar language such as Latin "deprives the people of their right to participate in the Mass." He argued that Latin was not a symbol of unity but a cause of disunity. The apostle Paul, he recalled, spoke of one body, one spirit, one lord, one faith, one baptism, one God (Ephesians 4: 4), but not one language.

Duschak proposed at that time, in just the second week of the council, that a new ecumenical or world mass should be created. It would be in the common language of the people wherever it was celebrated. As much as possible, its texts would be the words of Christ from Holy Scripture. It would be based on the first mass, the Last Supper. Therefore, Duschak argued, the priest must face the people. "Nobody who invites guests to a supper turns their back on them." The priest should speak in an audible voice and, like Christ at the Last Supper, should speak in the language of those present.

Those who criticize changes in the church after Vatican II often argue that these reforms were promoted by left-leaning experts who somehow hoodwinked or stampeded the bishops. Duschak's argument shows how mistaken this criticism is. He was a bishop speaking about the pastoral needs of his people. His intervention is an example of the practical arguments that shaped the final council votes. (And we need to remember that the council moved forward by voting, as a political convention would do. A text had to receive a simple majority to get on the council agenda for further discussion, and a two-thirds-plus-one vote to get final approval.) Duschak's proposal for one new ecumenical rite did not materialize, but we can see many of his ideas in our reformed liturgy. For example, we have a variety of eucharistic prayers, written to suit various occasions. Latin continues to be used, but it is sad that some who prefer that language also go to the extreme of claiming that theirs is the only valid mass. Usually, the person they insult by this false claim is Paul VI, since he is the pope who presided over the implementation of the major liturgical changes after Vatican II. It is hard to imagine a more meticulous chief pastor, or one less deserving of being slandered in this way.

Mae and Bernard

Dear Mae and Bernard,

There is no doubt that a renewed appreciation of the word of God is one of our greatest gains from Vatican II. That is true for every aspect of our lives as Christians, and especially in our liturgy, which we have been discussing. Regarding our participation in Christ's three-fold mission as prophet, priest and sovereign, the primary aspect is prophecy, proclaiming, preaching the word. I am very impressed by the concept, brought to our attention by Congar, that proclaiming the word of God is my fundamental priestly role. This is true for all of us. Go out and *teach* all the nations, Christ told us. Tell the good news.

It is especially important that parents and teachers grasp this. Children, from birth and as they grow up through the school years, should hear stories and songs about God who always loves them, Jesus who died for them, and the Spirit who is always with them. Unless the story is told, people can't take any meaning from it. The heart of our religion is telling the story of the marvellous things God has done, is doing and will do.

Our Sunday liturgy is storytelling in a more formal setting, with more sacramental linkages. The readings are faith stories. So is the eucharistic prayer and other parts of the mass. That's pretty obvious, I suppose. But everything about our churches – the buildings and grounds, the access ramps, the welcome that people get at the door, the fixtures and decorations, the music – tells some story. Or they should do so. This is probably the one yardstick that priests and people should use when planning and organizing everything that enters into the Sunday liturgy, from parking lot to altar: Does it tell people the good news that God loves them, that Jesus died for their sake, and that his Spirit dwells in each one of them?

Here and there we have small churches, especially in rural areas, but in the cities we need to have rather large churches. We shouldn't build luxurious big churches but, thank God, we still have a lot of people coming to church, even if many don't do so regularly. Small basic Christian communities are wonderful. But we can't be a eucharistic community with enough priests for every 10 or 20 families. We can't go in the direction of a congregationalist church, where anyone can be designated to preside. So we have rather large parishes with rather large buildings for rather large Sunday gatherings.

Celebrating Sunday

Sunday mass is about bringing the whole past week's adventure to the celebration as an offering. It's about each of us bringing our living body there to be offered as sacrifice. Everyone in each Christian community, not just the priest and liturgy committee, must struggle to make each weekend gathering truly part of the Lord's day of rest, when we do nothing but contemplate God's love and our response. This cannot happen if Sunday mass is not welcoming, if it is not telling good news, as too many people find nowadays. The ideal would be if people could get together after mass, to continue their fellowship in Christ. Ideally, Sunday masses should be about two hours apart, to allow for time together after mass. To allow for a peaceful time, just to be together, to do nothing but be friends together, to overcome the individualism we have absorbed from the secular culture around us.

When you think of the Sabbath as a time for contemplation rather than activity, the very rigid laws in the Hebrew Scriptures make sense. One could walk only 2000 steps on the Sabbath. As a result, there were little synagogues all over the place. Even today in Jerusalem, all over the place, there are synagogues, little holes in the walls in some places. They can't be more than 4000 steps apart – roughly every two miles.

Our typical Canadian parish must serve people from a lot of different backgrounds, and not just different languages. It would be a wonderful thing if each parish could have a varied program of weekend masses to meet the cultural and spiritual needs of people in various stages of Christian growth and development. People will get them if they demand them and help to create them. Right now, people of the old school from the days when there was one mass throughout the Latin church, deplore even minor changes in the liturgy, and often prevent changes that are badly needed by others. It shouldn't be only what the pastor, or some dominant clique, prefers. Let the people who think differently be heard! Vatican II makes plain that people have the right to claim the pastoral services they need. Article 37 of the *Constitution on the Church* enshrines their right to speak up to their pastor and make their needs known. Don't just complain behind the backs of the clergy. That's part of the old paternalism – the childish attitude of complaining behind Daddy's back. So what if you're going to get criticized? Since when is God's reign going to come about without criticism? Since when did Jesus not get criticized?

What I'm talking about is not some kind of pandering to novelty. The point is to try to make the Sunday liturgy an occasion that "tells the story" to *everyone.* I liked your story about the missionary bishop at Vatican II who wanted the vernacular. Christ not only turned his face to the apostles at the Last Supper. He talked the language, and used the signs and symbols, that they knew and understood. Take music, for example. If some people prefer a choir with organ and others prefer guitar-led singing or something else, the various styles of celebrations must be developed, as is happening all over the place. Does the music tell the story of God's love? Does it invite us to meditate on who we are as Christ-bearers? There is still lots of room for improvement in the storytelling aspect of our liturgies. Our celebrations are too formal and dry, much of the time, and could be much more lively.

Nurturing the seeds of the word

Vatican II talked about the presence of God in foreign lands – the *semina verbi,* seeds of the word. To me, that is a key phrase in Vatican II – like the word "subsists," to describe how the fullness of truth is present in the church. But it is not just in mission lands that there are different seeds of the word. Everywhere, the seeds are there. The word has been planted. It is all over the universe. But we need to be attentive to those seeds, to nurture them, let them grow, tend them, as a garden. So, in that sense, liturgy is gardening. Let there be seeds and plants of all kinds. Organ music, solos, choirs. Let each be tended as needed for what it is, so that you have variety in the garden, to encourage full participation.

The Greek origin of "liturgy" is "the work of the people." One reason we need periods of silence throughout our Sunday liturgies is so that the divine work can go on in the people. We have to take time; that is part of the gardening. We made the point earlier, that salvation is more reception than performance. It's a gift. We need silence, quiet, to allow "the work" to go deep into our hearts, God's favourite garden. To make the soil receptive, to let the word sink in and bear fruit.

Having been baptized, Christians begin as a group, as a community, to undertake the work of the reign of God. They begin to celebrate liturgy. Here is where the primary role of the church comes in, particularly from an institutional point of view. The assembled community, around their bishop and pastors who represent the bishop, gather on the Day of the Lord to bring the totality of their life experience into public witness and to do eucharist. And that doing of eucharist, which is basically the liturgy, consists primarily in the telling of the story. In the telling of the story we actualize the mystery of the redemption. We bring it consciously to apply to our lives, to raise it to the level of alert awareness, and to share it with others. That's why the church can say that each time we celebrate these mysteries, the work of our redemption is being accomplished, here and now. I sometimes say to people in church: "We are gathered, we are telling the story, we are celebrating, we are redeeming the world right here, right now. This is it. This is our primary work." The relation to the temporal is by extension, to continue bringing the universe into that work. But the work begins in our hearts.

We go out into the temporal realm as prophet, priest and sovereign, to transform society and all creation, so that all is spiritualized, in the true sense of the word, fit to be returned to the Father. At the end of time – that is the recapitulation – Christ will come and will return everything to the Father, and God will be all in all. So, we're part of that drama. Having come from the Father, we return to God in the power of the Spirit. It's important to say that. That's why we must gather for liturgy on Sunday. If we do not gather, we are not doing our part, our share in this work. It is not a case of me as individual having a pipeline to God and doing my own thing. That misses the whole point: that we are members of Christ. It's the whole Christ, not an atomized Christ. Not a collection of individuals. Vatican II again: God has willed to make people holy and save them, "not as individuals without any bond or link between them, but rather to make them into a people who might acknowledge him and serve him in holiness." That's Article 9 of the *Constitution on the Church*.

The central importance of the Sunday eucharist on the day of the Lord's rest is brought out more clearly, perhaps, if we think of what is different about weekday masses. Sunday masses date from the Last Supper. When did we start the weekday mass? It began much later, with monasticism. It was more a private devotion than a public celebration by the whole community. The monasteries always also had a main Sunday liturgy for the whole community. Weekday masses were less formal, and did not necessarily involve everyone. Today, some people are real contemplatives in the world. As part of that way of life, they begin each day with mass. Not everyone can join them, but Sundays are for the whole community.

+Remi

Dear Remi,

Reading what you were saying about bringing our bodies to mass as sacrifices to be offered started us thinking about young people the ages of our grandchildren – toddlers to twenties. They can't feel the same about bringing their young bodies as we do, creaking and groaning a bit. We have seen at least two parishes, one in Italy, the other in Canada, where people seem really to understand positive aspects of the age difference. They let the "generation gap" help to shape the liturgy so that young people are enthusiastic to take part.

Overall, they have normal Sunday liturgies. Inside that traditional framework, however, they create more than the usual amount of space for young people to "do their things." Particularly around special occasions, such as Holy Week and Christmas or feast days. Some obvious things, such as having young people well trained as readers, or as ministers of hospitality. Or letting even toddlers carry up something at the preparation of the gifts. Also, seeking out young people studying music, and fitting their instruments and voices into the celebration. Even letting a youth group work out a major part of the liturgy, such as a drama or mime to illustrate the story of the passion or nativity.

Young people: bringing the Sunday liturgy to life in new ways

Kids like to dress up and pretend, to play roles. When they do, they also want the elders in the family to "come and see." Given a chance to bring their bodies to church their own way, they can dream up deeply moving ways of telling the faith story and offering their gifts to the Lord. We're not talking here about what would be a youth mass at a school or a retreat or some other special occasion mainly for young people. We're referring to how Sunday liturgies can come alive in new ways when pastors and people make a point of regularly having occasions for young people to "do their thing" – to bring *their* living bodies – as part of the weekend liturgy.

It even helps solve that hoary old pastoral problem: Why is it always the same people who get stuck doing everything?

Mae and Bernard

Dear Mae and Bernard,

Your letter came when I was reading something about the question of ritual and the use of symbols. We have to work out a balance between keeping good old symbols and discovering helpful new ones. The older generation helps to preserve the old ones and the younger folk help to find new ones. Ritual is part of celebrating the life of the Spirit and our membership in Christ. Ritual has to do with becoming part of Christ, and coming to church on Sunday to do the work of God.

Ritual and symbols

How do we do this work of God, the mysterious work of the reign of divine life? We do it by ritual, which means using the deepest symbols of human-kind that are in the sub-conscious – fire, water, light, earth (for which our Native people have great respect). We relate these basic symbols to the reign of God. We apply and relate them to the revealed word. This is how we shape our liturgy. We bring together the word of God and our lived experience on the basis of deeper symbols.

An example: The symbolism of the love of God. God's love is total. God is willing to give without limit. The total self-giving love of God is symbolized in Isaac with Sarah and Abraham. They are invited to offer their only son. Then their action becomes a symbol of the ultimate gift of God's only Son at the crucifixion, the sacrifice of the mass, and so on. So there you see a symbol emerging.

Another symbol is in Genesis when God separates the water from the dry land. The water which can be a source of death by flood also becomes a source of life. Baptism expresses that symbol as the source of life. Water is a symbol of death when we talk about being baptized into the death of Christ, so that we can rise again. Obviously, it is the power of the Spirit that makes these symbols life-giving. So, the acting out of this as a community together, according to certain prescribed patterns that, in turn, reflect our history, is what you call ritual.

For instance, the sacrifice of the mass. The eucharist can be studied in terms of the forms of worship that evolved through the Jewish experience. Before the council, we tended to forget or suppress our Jewish roots. Then this connection began to be made clearer just before Vatican II. Now this is part of the Vatican II renewal. For example, we now use very ancient Hebrew prayers to ask God to bless our gifts of bread and wine. The Vatican II liturgical renewal started in the great Benedictine monasteries where they began avant-garde liturgies that were frowned upon and discouraged by the Vatican at that time. What they were doing in these monasteries was really the result of what they were discovering, or rediscovering, through renewed studies of Holy Scripture. Prayers and practices from our earliest liturgy, often taken from the Jewish people, were reintegrated into the liturgy in these monasteries. So our renewed ritual began to emerge, and Vatican II confirmed this process.

I have been looking at what *The Collegeville Pastoral Dictionary of Biblical Theology* says about signs and symbols. It says: "Modern liturgical scholarship suggests that liturgical symbolism includes more than the established objects the Christian community has customarily associated with specific sacrament. All words and actions said and performed by the liturgical assembly during the ritual expression are inherently symbolic. This expands the notion of liturgical symbol to include the entire composite of various rites. Hence the very participation of the community has symbolic import. Every aspect of liturgical celebration co-operates in the integrity of the rite that is symbolic as a whole. As such, the entire rite and all that takes place, not just the hallowed objects, discloses the salvific activity of the divine presence, and transforms the assembly more perfectly into God's holy people."

New signs and symbols

That's it! That's the point! Before Vatican II we focused particularly on the hallowed objects. For instance, the definition of ordination: When exactly does the person being ordained become a priest? Pius XII said, when the bishop hands him the chalice and paten, when he receives the hallowed objects. Now we say, no, it's when, through the imposition of hands, the Holy Spirit comes upon the person. It's the Spirit who has the power, not the hallowed objects. That's a very concrete example of a shift in our understanding of church since the council.

The dictionary article goes on to say: "Not to be forgotten nor undermined is the liturgical assembly itself as symbol of the risen Christ." You made this point earlier – that Christ is *really* present in assembly. What are the new signs or symbols that will help us see and express this presence?

This is an important addition to the older liturgical tradition whereby the priest, as the other Christ, mediated God's presence for the assembly and represented Christ ritually. We do forget – indeed it is almost never mentioned from the pulpit – that the assembled congregation also represents Christ through their baptism. That is why the Vatican II document about the liturgy teaches that at a eucharistic celebration Christ is present in four ways – the congregation, the priest, the readings and the eucharist.

+Remi

For Discussion

1. Discuss what you think are the most important changes in the Catholic liturgy resulting from Vatican II.

2. What do you think were the main reasons for the bishops' decisions at Vatican II for changes in the liturgy?

3. How well do you think people understand that at church on Sunday we should worship God "by offering our living bodies as a holy sacrifice"?

4. Discuss the implications for a parish of the Vatican II teaching that God willed to make people holy and save them "not as individuals without any bond or link between them, but rather to make them into a people who might acknowledge him and serve him in holiness"?

5. Discuss the Jewish roots of Christian prayer, starting with the Sunday liturgy.

6. What might be done in your community to make Sunday a day more dedicated to contemplating God's good works?

For Action

1. Read a modern history of the Catholic liturgy.
2. Research what mass was like in the 1950s, and compare it with today's liturgy in your parish.
3. Study the increased attention and respect given to Holy Scripture in today's liturgy, and the greater use made of the Scriptures in personal prayer.
4. Research what further adaptations in your parish liturgy might make it more appealing, meaningful and prayerful for various groups, such as young people or recent immigrants.
5. Attend a meeting of your parish pastoral council or similar group and suggest ways to help everyone entering your church feel more welcome.

Further Reading

Cabie, Robert. *History of the Mass.* Trans. by Lawrence J. Johnson. Washington, D.C.: The Pastoral Press, 1992.

Deiss, Lucien. *The Mass.* Collegeville, MN: Liturgical Press, 1989.

Foley, Edward. *From Age to Age: How Christians Celebrated the Eucharist.* Chicago: Liturgical Training Publications, 1991.

Guzie, Tad. *The Book of Sacramental Basics.* New York: Paulist Press, 1981.

Hellwig, Monika. *The Meaning of Sacraments.* Dayton: Pflaum-Standard, 1972.

_____. *The Eucharist and the Hunger of the World.* New York: Paulist Press, 1976.

Heschel, Joshua Abraham. *The Sabbath.* New York: The Noonday Press, 1951.

Gifts Come Before Laws:
Structuring the Church

The possible future church is further explored in this chapter. It continues ear-lier reflections on the role of the Spirit, and in particular the relation of the church's institutional leadership to the gifts which the Spirit gives to all mem-bers. The role of pastors in giving order to the Spirit's abundant gifts is outlined. This leads into a discussion of Vatican II insights about the relation of the col-lege of bishops, as successors of the apostles, to the pope, as Peter's successor. Unresolved issues concerning relations between bishops and the pope are explored. So are the rights and roles of laity in the church. Pope John Paul II's 1995 encyclical on Christian unity is studied, especially for what it says about the possibilities of changes in the way the primacy of the pope is exercised. Some examples of tensions between individual dioceses and the Vatican are examined, as are relations between the Canadian bishops and Rome. Differ-ences between church procedures and political processes are noted.

Dear Mae and Bernard,

We were talking the other day about what church structures might look like in the future. There are going to be a lot of changes. We may not see them before we die, but they're coming – if only as our church becomes less and less white and European, as is happening. The Asian bishops at their early-1998 Synod gave lots of signals about the changes they want, to appeal to Asian ways, and those changes *will* happen eventually.

In a sense, the church has only two basic permanent elements: it is divine, and it is human. It is formed, composed, structured – whatever word you like – by the Holy Spirit and by us people. At Pentecost, the Holy Spirit, the divine, came upon and into the disciples, human beings, and the church began. We can use lots of other words, but they always amount to the same thing: the church is divine and human – divine gift and human response.

The church, we can also say, has two expressions: the charismatic and the institutional, Spirit and organization, divine and human. Immediately after Pentecost, that same day, you could say, the church needed order, governance, so the Spirit and the first Christians began to give it a form of human government. As church history unfolded, there emerged what we have come to call the three-fold order of bishop, priest and deacon. Edward Schillebeeckx illustrates in his book *Ministry: Leadership in the Community of Jesus Christ* how this development took centuries to achieve. The Spirit was with the whole community, the whole church; from among them certain ones were called to serve in special ways. The Acts of the Apostles relate the steps, how it all began. I find it fascinating to follow the development of ministry from the time of the apostles to our era. It is important to remember that order (from which the word "ordination" comes) is totally at the service of the Spirit, at the service of the charismatic dimension, which extends to and includes everyone.

Vatican II made this very clear. All the baptized receive the gifts of the Holy Spirit. All are equal in dignity and capacity to serve. Because all those gifts and services must have order so that they will bear maximum fruit, you have a sacrament called ordination. It is a service of order. Those called to this special service are called in this way to serve the plurality of ministries or services in the whole church. Using the term "institution" to designate us who are called to the service of orders, we must say that the institution is always at the service of the *charismatic* dimension of the church, which is the Holy Spirit dwelling in all the baptized (including those who are ordained).

Church structures: a means to facilitate the advent of the reign of God

As the pilgrim people of God in history, we are called to listen to the Spirit and to follow the guidance of the Risen Lord as we fashion the institutions we need to serve the world more effectively. Church structures are not an end in themselves. They are a means to facilitate the advent of the reign of God. When we listen carefully to the Spirit and discern the directions in which we need to move, the required variety of structures will emerge. Eminent scholars, such as the late Raymond Brown or Edward Schillebeeckx, have amply illustrated how the external forms of the local churches evolved over the centuries. The Acts of the Apostles and the four Gospels bear witness to the creativity of the Spirit of Christ guiding the apostles and disciples. In today's rapidly evolving world, are we not called to a similar discernment about the forms that ministry will take in our church as we move into the future?

As a result, the primary responsibility of those in the service of order is to listen to what the Spirit is saying in the diversity of ministries throughout the church, without thinking that they will ever exhaust what the Spirit is doing, because the Spirit does the work of the reign of God. If the church and the institutions of the church are Spirit-filled and faithful to the Spirit, then the charismatic dimension will relate to that. But if the institution is less faithful, as it has been at certain times in history, the Spirit will continue to work, but will bypass the institution. As Cardinal Newman stressed, that's what happened at the time of the Aryan heresy in the fourth century. Many bishops failed the test but the people were faithful. The institution can never control the Spirit. See 1 Thessalonians 5:12-22 about weighing all things, retaining what is good and never quenching the Spirit.

The role of the bishop

One of the shifts of Vatican II is that it deliberately spoke of the entire people of God and their place in the church before it spoke of the hierarchy. We shouldn't start a discussion about the church with a distinction between the ordained and the non-ordained. We should start with the idea of the people of God, and the equality of everyone on the basis of faith, baptism and confirmation, and the gifts of the Spirit. Equality in dignity and capacity to serve is the starting point. After that ordination comes in, as a special sacramental gift to put order into what otherwise could become chaos. In the Acts, we see how Paul and the others had to go from church to church to keep order. Ordination is at the service of the church and of all the gifts of the Spirit.

I have never seen myself as basically different from a lay person. I've said so time and time again. I have all the responsibilities of every baptized person. I have lost none of that. I have the added responsibility of a bishop, to provide a kind of order and guidance. One of my main responsibilities as bishop is to try to listen to what the Spirit is saying through all the people in this local church. I am to facilitate their gifts, and keep them united if possible, and help them to flower.

One main function of a bishop, of the magisterium, is discernment of the continuous promptings of the Spirit. Discernment is done in the light of Scripture, tradition, theological research, and so on. The vast majority of the laity, precisely because they are engrossed in temporal affairs as their primary responsibility, do not have the background or time to keep up with studies of Scripture, theology, church history and all that. Part of my job is to see to it that they are not without this service of discernment.

There have been plenty of examples throughout church history of how problems can develop. Sometimes the institutional or structural side of the church fails to listen faithfully to the Spirit. They may be paying more attention to canon law, or whatever, than to what the people are trying to tell them. Then some people, on the other side, become a sect of *illuminati*, enlightened fanatics. Then, like all fanatics, they reduce the totality of truth to their opinion, conditioned as it may be by culture, a narrow theology, human advantage, ideology or whatever. Then in the name of truth or God or whatever, they pursue their thing. They are no longer members of Christ guided by the Spirit and living the life of the Spirit.

That is why the gifts of discernment and order have their places, along with all the other gifts the Spirit gives to the church. More on this later.

+Remi

Dear Remi,

Your letter reminded us of Raymond Brown's little book, *The Churches the Apostles Left Behind*. Using New Testament data, he shows that the churches formed by the various apostles quickly developed distinctive and varying features and styles. He outlines the differences between John's more charis-matic communities, Paul's missionary ones, Matthew's more structured and long-lasting churches, and so on. Every one of those Christian communities, it seems, had some of these differing models or characteristics within it. As we understand it, this is how the different Eastern and Western rites devel-oped (some 20 in the Catholic church now), and the five great patriarchates, and so on.

Exploring different models of church

We wonder how that will work out in the future. We know that Vatican II talks (LG, 37) about the right of the laity to ask for the pastoral services they think they need. Since different communities have different needs, the exercise of that right would mean that local churches, dioceses or parishes, would not all develop in the same way. And, we suppose, that is what does happen. Media reports about the early-1998 Synod for Asia showed that bishops at that Synod raised our question in a more serious way. "A plea for more trust and diversity was the common thread in the interventions of many of the first 100 bishops to speak at the Synod," *The Tablet* reported (May 2, 1998, page 565). Canadian bishops serving Native communities have raised similar points several times. For example, we remember that you have called for the right to ordain married men as priests. Similarly, the Asian bishops at their synod were calling on Rome to give the local churches authority to decide issues directly related to local situations, and to allow the church in Asia to preach the Gospel in a truly Asian way. In counterpoint, we were also told by media reports, came the insistence by bishops of the Roman Curia that Christian truth must never be sacrificed.

That seems to us to be a good example of the tension you mentioned in your letter between the charismatic and institutional aspects in the church. In this case, we are identifying the Asian bishops with the charismatic, and the Vatican officials with the institutional. However, we'd agree that the power of the Spirit and institutional concerns are involved on both sides. So how does discernment work in such cases? We gather from Acts that Peter and

Paul had an all-out debate before Peter conceded that Gentile converts did not need to follow Jewish rules about circumcision and so on.

On a more local point, we see the Spirit involved in what we were discussing earlier about a parish having different kinds of eucharistic celebrations to suit the needs and tastes of different groups. This would be a good example of the charismatic taking precedence over the institutional.

Mae and Bernard

Dear Mae and Bernard,

Variety and differences from one church to another is as important, I think, as basic unity among Christian churches. Diversity goes with the apostolic and catholic nature of the church. That's what the Asian bishops are saying. To evangelize, to be apostolic, they need to be more Asian and less European. To be a church for all peoples, a truly catholic church, necessarily means to allow for this kind of diversity.

Changing the structure of the church

How will change come about? Well, by discernment, in the end. We have an example, as you noted, in the story of how Paul finally persuaded Peter that the church had to open up to the uncircumcised. They discussed, argued, prayed – and eventually the Spirit showed the way. That's how change came in the Vatican Council. If and when the changes wanted by the Asian bishops come about, that's how they will happen. Over all, the Spirit will see to it that the church always has diversity in unity, as well as unity in diversity.

The point is that we have four Gospels, telling one story. The Good News is one and also multiple. There is only one God and Father of all, one Lord, one eucharist, and only one story of salvation. But there are different story-tellers, and different listeners.

The structure of the church was initially given by the risen Christ, as a mandate, not a blueprint. It shows there is divine inspiration in its fundamental structure; and that there has been divine guidance down through the ages. The authority of the church rests on the Spirit of Christ. Authority is necessary and therefore must be respected. However, all that having been accepted, there are further questions. Jesus did not give a detailed blueprint of the church, as Schillebeeckx, the late Raymond Brown and other scholars have amply illustrated. Rather, Jesus gave the gift of the Spirit, to help us elaborate the structure. Of necessity, being human, and also accepting the presence of the Spirit in the temporal order, over the centuries we borrowed all kinds of structural details from the temporal order. For example, in today's diocese, the bishop's title and authority and much else have been shown to be largely borrowed from the Roman Empire. Constantine had a big influence, not all positive. Our history explains why you and I grew up in a white, European, even Mediterranean, church, a church that followed the expansion of military and commercial empires. World demographics explain why the church of the future will be mostly non-white and very different from today's, but only the Spirit knows its exact appearance or shape.

Because church structures evolve in response to the Spirit, looking into the future we can see that these structures are still capable of changing. The perfect church structure has not been given. There is none. So today there are some questions in the church which never before have been raised. Some of the questions raised by the Asian bishops, for example, about how to reach out to peoples of other world religions in those countries, have not been raised in that way before.

That's where I place the issues emerging today around ministry or even the possible ordination of women. Such questions were never before brought up in a formal way to the level of the consciousness of the entire church. They are on the verge of reaching that level. Ordination is blocked officially now because we are not ready to look at it, but you can sense that the question is growing, taking on greater importance. The more church authority says you can't talk about it, the more it will be talked about. In today's culture, people don't accept that an authority says you can't talk about something. As parents you know what the kids really think when Dad or Mom says, "Don't even mention it!"

We have borrowed from the movement called democracy, starting with Magna Carta – the movement of citizens to challenge the king. All that is part of our heritage and it continues to develop. So I think we have to be respectful of the fact that final answers have not yet been given on certain questions.

+Remi

Dear Mae and Bernard,

I meant to raise this point in my previous letter. It is about synods. The holding of synods is a major shift as a result of Vatican II. The synodal principle is restored, even if some questions remain about the constitution of the Synod in Rome, and so on. Previously, what was being followed in our church governance was basically the model of monarchy. The synodal principle implies changes in the whole organization of the church. This is very important for the future. People here on Vancouver Island now recognize that ours is a synodal church.

When we celebrated our diocesan synod from 1986 to 1991, I had a wonderful experience of how lay people contribute to the development of doctrine. A bishop can invite to a synod other people besides the clergy who are the usual participants. We gathered close to 100 representatives of all parishes and organizations. Before this group met, all the people in the diocese were asked to meet in groups to share their faith stories, relate them to church tradition, and make proposals for the future of the diocese. Thus the synod topics came from real faith experiences. I found the agenda to be far richer than if it had been prepared by a few designated specialists. This showed me that the experience people have of living our faith is indeed a reliable source of insight in matters of doctrine.

One approach is to see a synod from the point of view of authority and canon law, as something given or allowed by the bishop. According to another view, that's not where a synod starts. It starts with baptism and the other sacraments, and the gifts of the Spirit. It is not a bishop's function to delegate powers to the laity. They have responsibilities and rights in the church stemming from their baptism. There's a good tradition behind that view.

The Spirit: extending beyond the institution of the church

At one time in the early church there was no opposition between clergy and laity. There was a diversity of services to the Gospel, both charismatic and institutional. Sometimes we say a diversity of ministries, but services is a better term. What has happened over time is that the institutional side of the church has, in a sense, overwhelmed the charismatic side. The charismatic side proceeds out of faith and baptism, and continues as the Spirit wills. The influence of the Spirit is broader than the institution and extends beyond it. The Spirit keeps moving. If the institution is not fully sensitive to the Spirit, the Spirit moves without the institution.

So I don't accept the thesis that the bishop gives authority to the laity. No. Christ, by the gifts of the Holy Spirit, gives authority to everyone to perform services in the name of the Gospel. Laity have their responsibilities, regardless of what the bishop says or does. From their baptism, laity carry responsibilities for the church. Marriage gives couples another and very particular set of rights and duties, including the right and duty as parents to teach the faith – something the formal magisterium does not properly recognize these days. Obviously, laity need to remain in communion with their bishop, so they don't just go off on tangents, and also so that the bishop in turn can bring in the larger perspective. The local church, the diocese, with its own culture and focus, could lean too far in one direction or get distorted by some local preoccupation, and the common good of the whole church could be affected. To guarantee the communion of the totality, you need that relationship with the centre.

However, it should not be a relationship of domination by the centre – either by the parish priest or bishop locally, or by the pope at the universal level. This brings up the whole question of the authority of the pope. Right now, the authority of the pope is exercised too unilaterally. The pope must be there, presiding over the communion in charity, but not imposing central authority. This situation is further aggravated by the fact that right now Rome, one of the five patriarchates of the broader church, is pulling too much weight by itself. Jerusalem, Alexandria, Antioch and Constantinople are overshadowed by Rome, for historical reasons. In his book *What Is Orthodoxy?*

Peter A. Botsis observes that the Orthodox consider Rome to be in heresy for having made unilateral decisions not in conformity with the first seven ecumenical councils. The Orthodox are not going to just submit and come under Latin domination. They would be willing to recognize the primacy of one who guarantees their unity in charity, but they are not about to let the bishop of Rome meddle in how they run their churches. In theory, this relationship has been recognized, including by Vatican II. In fact, serious tensions remain.

For the ordering of a diocesan synod, I like the approach that starts with the Gospel, then the people, and then the magisterium. The church is basically off-balance now because the people are largely ignored. The Gospel has been proclaimed. Here are the people who receive it and live it. And here is the teaching side, the magisterium. These three – Gospel, people and magisterium – have to challenge one another constantly, in creative and wholesome ways. The problem is that most people have been pressed into passivity and we have an unhealthy church.

The church says revelation is complete, "that no new public revelation is to be expected" (DV, 4). However, this is not to be understood in a literalist or fundamentalist fashion. The Gospel and tradition are living realities. Their full meaning is not given once and for all. Each people, and every generation of the various peoples, lives the Gospel with the Spirit at work in their midst. New insights are given by the Spirit, coming from the one unchanging word. The living experience of the people should therefore constantly challenge the tradition, so that it can in a sense be updated and kept relevant, because it is a living reality.

And, yes, the magisterial, teaching side (bishop and theologians together, and not really separately) has responsibility for interpreting the Gospel and tradition to the people. This service is not to be diminished. But the people also have responsibility, out of their lived experience with the Spirit, to challenge the magisterium and its teaching. That's where the whole question of reception of teaching comes in. We have many examples where the magisterium has taught something officially and the people have not received it, because it did not correspond to their experience.

Finding a healthy balance

I like the tripod model for a healthy church: Spirit, people, magisterium. We have to reinvigorate the people, the second leg. The problem in the church right now is that the lived experience of the people – their culture and all that – is largely ignored. Vatican II implies this kind of tripod model. Even to say that in the end the bishop or pastor must decide is to some extent monarchical. Bishops or other pastors should never discern alone. The bishop must be doing his discerning from within the communion. And, yes, he will ultimately speak, but not from outside the communion.

That is part of the problem right now with Rome and the bishops. There are difficulties the moment the pope takes it upon himself to declare alone the mind of the church, instead of doing so with the bishops. Vatican II is significant for the way Paul VI promulgated its teachings. He recalled ancient tradition, going back to the Acts of the Apostles. After noting that a text had been approved by the bishops, he too approved it, saying: "We, too, by the apostolic authority conferred on us by Christ, join with the Venerable Fathers in approving, decreeing, and establishing these things in the Holy Spirit, and we direct that what has thus been enacted in synod be published to God's glory." These are very important words! They need to be raised up in our consciousness. This was the first time in modern times that a pope used this formula, so much in keeping with tradition, to promulgate a text. Note how he stressed solidarity of the pope *with* the bishops *in synod*, and centred everything in Christ and the Holy Spirit. We can assume that John XXIII would have used some similar formula but he did not live to promulgate any Vatican II teaching. John XXIII had the genius to call the council. Paul VI had the genius to recognize that John XXIII had done the right thing. Paul VI had the political capacity and sensitivity to make it all happen.

But, you might ask, what if for some reason the people in a diocese split over an issue: for instance, about property, using diocesan lands for a shelter for the poor, former prisoners, or people living with AIDS. Imagine all the wealthy neighbours being against this project and the majority in the diocese agreeing with them. Would the bishop not be called to intervene in the name of the biblical "preferential option for the poor"? The numbers involved would not be the basis for deciding right or wrong. It would be a question of discerning which opinions are in accord with Gospel values. The entire believing community would normally be responsible for resolving the matter. However, the bishop could be called to take the lead by challenging the opposing majority. He could try to use his authority to influence the parties concerned. He could even block certain initiatives or speed up decisions because he is sensitive to the higher light of the Gospel and sees that the majority view is unacceptable. So he might call people to take another look at the Scriptures and at church tradition and teaching about social justice. He might keep everyone studying, praying and discerning as a community. He would be careful about the process for reaching the final decision. He would not just come out, high handed, and impose his own view. This to me would be an illustration of the model that places Divine Revelation first, moves through the people, and finally involves the official magisterium.

I fear we are starting to slide back into the pre-Vatican II mentality, which I knew in the seminary in the 1940s. You started with church discipline, then explained theologically why this discipline was the way it was, and then used the Scriptures to justify your theological conclusions. That method became so ingrained over several centuries that it is very hard to reverse the process. So we must deliberately recognize and name this approach as wrong, and come back to an ecclesiology based on the gifts of the Holy Spirit. Spirit, people, magisterium!

The heart of revelation is our relation with the Spirit of the Risen Lord living within us. It's an affair of the heart, charismatic. It is only at a second level that we come to head stuff – that is, reflection on revelation in the light of experience. This we call theology and teaching. Then, only at a third level, looking at the church from the point of view of structure and its institutional side, do we get into canon law – what to do, body stuff.

Now I have to do some body stuff – get some sleep!

+*Remi*

Dear Remi,

Your recent letters have challenged us to think about questions that we usually don't consider very much. We like the models of church that you are presenting. Charismatic before institutional, for example. That makes obvious good sense. Also the tripod – Gospel, people, magisterium.

However, as we see it, the right ordering of the church in this sense is not a primary concern for lay people. At least, that is how we interpret what Vatican II said about the particular and primary vocation of the laity. Paul VI emphasized the same point, and it was also stressed by the 1987 Synod on the laity, and by *Christifideles Laici,* John Paul II's report on that synod.

Our point, as Paul VI put it, is that the laity's "principal and primary function is not to establish or promote ecclesial communities, which is the special function of pastors, but to develop and make effective all those latent Christian and evangelical possibilities which already exist and operate in the world" (EN, 70). John Paul II has put it even more bluntly, calling it a temptation for us lay folk to get so involved in church affairs that we neglect our proper work in the world (CL, 2). Both popes were, of course, building on the Vatican II teaching, that "by reason of their special vocation it belongs to the laity to seek the kingdom of God by engaging in temporal affairs and directing them according to God's will" (LG, 31).

It's not that we don't care how the church is perceived and organized. For example, we think that pastors and faith educators should be giving laity a lot more of the council and papal teaching that we just sketched, about the laity's secular vocation. Also, it is clear that what is going on in the church can have an impact on the effectiveness of lay church members in their secular work. A lay person struggling for human rights in the world is handicapped if the pastor is dragging his feet about human rights inside the church. Thus, it is more difficult for a Catholic to promote respect for women in secular situations when women are not respected inside the church. In other words, the laity can't be indifferent to relationships and structures in the church. It's just that we don't see that as our main concern as laity.

For our work of ordering temporal affairs according to the plan of God, as the council said, we need models. We think we should be able to look to the church and find in its structures and operations the models we need for building up the world according to the plan of God. In your outline for the church – Gospel, people, magisterium – we see important values for society at large: Authority as service, respect for each person, special concern for the poorest, openness and transparency in all relationships, respect for cultural diversity, and so on.

We agree with what you are outlining as the way things should be organized in the church. It's just that we think that it is more the business of pastors than of laity to get things right in the church. It's our main job to get relationships right in the world.

Does that make sense?

Mae and Bernard

Dear Mae and Bernard,

I agree with your point in your last letter and . . . and yet, there is more to it than that. We must not fall into new dichotomies just when we are leaving some old ones behind. It's a case of both/and, not either/or. I agree that you laity should not have church structures as your main concerns. However, the church needs to learn from the world, and you who are in the world have to bring good ideas from the world to the church. Here's one example. Many secular organizations have developed excellent procedures for settling personnel disputes. Disputes arise in dioceses and parishes, and the church can use, and should be able to count on, the help of its lay members who have dispute settlement skills.

Families: the domestic church

However, there is another more basic point, and I might have overlooked it if you hadn't raised your point. This applies especially to parents, but also to teachers and the like. Family life is an area that we should think of as both secular, in the world and, at the same time, part of the structure of the church. The phrase "domestic church" catches the second aspect. When we talk about the church being Spirit, people, magisterium, we should list parents (and by extension, teachers) with both people and magisterium. You parents are the first teachers of the faith to your children. Everything that I said earlier about the magisterium discerning spirits, not snuffing out the Spirit, and so on, applies to parents with regard to their children, or to classroom teachers, not unlike the role of pastors with regard to the people of God at large. So, in these ways, lay people are as much "part of the structure" as bishops or priests are. You have to make the charism-institution or the tripod model work in your family life or in your classroom; and you should try to make it work in your parish, as well as at your office or factory, and so on. In other words, having made a great step forward at Vatican II by clarifying that you laity are fully part of the church, we have to make sure you are not marginalized again by turning the council's teaching on your secular vocation into a rigid church-secular dichotomy.

I am going back here to what you said earlier about the importance of having couples teach about the full Christian meaning of marital intimacy. As you said, our church teaching about marital intimacy cannot be authentically based on experience unless married laity are involved in doing that teaching. This is partly a matter of clergy-lay relations. There are centuries of distrust, stereotypes and taken-for-granteds behind the notion that ordinary wives and husbands cannot hand on teaching about married love in and for the church. Surely one of the crucial problems for the church in this whole area of sexual morality is a kind of clerical distrust and fear that lay people will get it wrong.

Putting the head first

What we see here is partly the fallout from the Enlightenment. The use of reason was exalted at that time. This same approach spread into the church. We began to intellectualize and rationalize everything and, as a result, gradually reduced magisterium to the promulgation of a body of doctrine. Catechetics became a matter of questions and answers to be memorized, all very intellectual and dry. Catholic living became the practice of following a set of rules. In the process we forgot that human beings are not just heads, but also hearts and bodies.

Earlier, Christians were known as "followers of the way," which implies the dynamism of walking and moving, putting your body on the line, facing martyrdom by the way you lived and died. Christians were known for how they loved one another, not for having the right answers.

The moment you put the head first, you get into dividing things. The intellect is the faculty that makes distinctions. Thus the basic scientific method is analysis, breaking things down into components, measurable and manageable parts, for the purpose of control and mastery. In contrast, the heart unites, seeks harmony and solidarity, as well as a synthesis, putting things together. The body is where dynamism, motion and life come in.

Having reduced Catholicism to memorizing the catechism, we then further narrowed the teaching role to what I would call the formal magisterium – bishops and theologians. The role of an informal magisterium was neglected, forgotten. However, the classic example of the informal magisterium is that of baptized and believing parents teaching their children. In a sense, that is the most important teaching of all, because that is where the faith is transmitted – in the family. This most important magisterium was downplayed or ignored, and we shifted all attention to the formal magisterium, bishops, priests and theologians.

The role of the theologian

Now, we do have to recognize the role of the formal magisterium. Revelation is a gift. It was given by formal mandate by Jesus to the Twelve and was codified in the writing of Holy Scripture. Therefore, there is a mission in the church whereby those who have expertise and scholarship and who are designated publicly by ordination are the ones entrusted with safeguarding that revelation. They are to be public witnesses and the ultimate reference point. They are to make sure that what is being passed on is indeed authentic. Theirs is like the role of elders in aboriginal communities, to keep the tradition alive and pass on the story. The formal magisterium also keeps the message universal. Individual local churches can have their own little story, but they get caught up in a certain culture, and somewhere there must be a point of reference that is more universal. This is officially done by the bishops and the successor of Peter.

However, we have so over-emphasized this formal dimension that we've lost sight of any magisterium except that one aspect of it. That's one of our big problems today. We need to re-situate the informal magisterium in its proper place. This informal magisterium is basically the telling of the story by all believers, based on their experience of having received the Holy Spirit. And, yes, the reference point of the formal magisterium remains, and is important. But it has to be seen as the reference point, and not the beginning and end of it all.

Over the years, we've turned things upside down, as if teaching of the faith begins with the formal magisterium. It doesn't. The beginning is from Christ. Christ is teaching, through all Christ's members, through the gift of the Spirit. Maybe the best way to see this is to stress the theology of the Spirit which was developed in Vatican II but not fully. This stresses the importance of the baptism of Jesus when he received the Spirit and, in turn, our baptism, giving us the Spirit, so that we are called to be saints by example, by action and by word.

The role of the Spirit

We are looking here at the whole charismatic side of the church. This means in the broadest sense the giftedness of all members. As Vatican II emphasized, all members through the power of the Spirit are equal in dignity and capacity to serve. All are instructed by the Spirit. We are all empowered by the Spirit. That is a dimension of church life that too readily escapes the institution. It is recognized more in the Eastern church.

This is the role of the saints in the broad sense Paul uses when he speaks of the saints in Corinth, Jerusalem or elsewhere. All those incorporated into Christ through the power of the Spirit are empowered by the Spirit to do whatever needs to be done to advance God's reign. This is our daily work throughout the whole created universe. The institution has nothing to say to this directly, except inasmuch as the gifts of ministry, of service to the Gospel, may need co-ordination. But we have over-emphasized this ordering or co-ordinating function. It is best not to oppose the charismatic and the institutional aspects, for in the church all is grace, all is gift.

At one of the Sunday morning lectures that Canadian bishops organized in Rome during the council, Congar reminded us that until Vatican II we did not have an ecclesiology, a full theology or understanding of the church. We had instead a hierarchology – the idea that the church is the hierarchy. Too many people still think the church belongs to the pope, bishops and priests, and the laity are to help them do their job – to help the priest run his parish, help the bishop run his diocese. As someone said, before Vatican II we had fallen into the habit of thinking of the church as pope, bishops and priests, with the people somehow attached. Vatican II again put the people squarely into the church, as it was in the beginning.

What and who is the church?

Vatican II was the first council ever to give us an ecclesiology – a theology of the whole church. It addressed these question: Church, who are you? What do you say of yourself? Look at Vatican II's *Constitution on the Church* and you will see how the answer to these questions was organized. It begins by emphasizing that the church is a mystery, the mystery of God's reign in the world. Then it speaks of the church as the whole people of God – all Catholics, all other Christians and, in some way, through the power of the Spirit, all religions and all people of good will. It speaks of the hierarchy in a third chapter, followed by one on the laity. Concluding chapters deal with the universal call to holiness, the role of religious women and men, how the pilgrim church on earth is called to unity with the heavenly church, and the place of the Blessed Virgin in the church. This order of chapters is very important. Few questions at Vatican II were debated more vigorously than what the church would say about itself, and in what order the ideas would be presented.

We all still have a lot to learn about what Vatican II said.

+Remi

Dear Remi,

Your letter reminded us that since John Paul II's encyclical on Christian unity was published in May 1995, we Catholics seem to be ignoring something very important that he said. He admitted that the pope needs conversion, because he makes mistakes, commits sins, or whatever. Also, he asked Christians to help the pope exercise his office of primacy in ways that will better serve the cause of Christian unity. We don't often hear the pope talk about the need for personal conversion and a change of job description. At least, that's how we read his letter.

The pope asks for our prayers and help

The first point about conversion is the less dramatic for us. We know that the pope goes to confession, just as cardinals, bishops, priests, religious women and other Catholics do. We don't know if the pope, like many of the rest of us, now seeks the graces of the sacrament of reconciliation less frequently than he used to. And, of course, we don't have any idea what he discusses with his confessor. He does have a confessor, though; and what he said about the pope needing conversion is very important, we think.

Rather pointedly, he centred his remark around Christ's words to Peter. Christ commissioned Peter to unite and strengthen the disciples. But Christ also made clear to Peter that he had human weakness and a special need of conversion, the pope noted, quoting Luke 22:32. "The Bishop of Rome," he added, "himself must fervently make his own Christ's prayer for that conversion which is indispensable for 'Peter' to be able to serve his brethren. I earnestly invite the faithful of the Catholic Church and all Christians to share in this prayer. May all join me in praying for this conversion" (UUS, 4).

When will we hear it? Yet we should hear it. In parish and personal prayers everywhere: "Let us pray for the pope. May he receive the grace to turn away from whatever personal sins make him less able to serve the cause of Christian unity as he should." He asked us to pray that way.

Later in the same encyclical, the pope also asked us to help him respond to "the request of me to find a way of exercising the primacy that, while in no way renouncing what is essential to its mission, is nonetheless open to a new situation. . . . I insistently pray the Holy Spirit to shine his light upon us, enlightening all the Pastors and theologians of our churches, that we may seek – together, of course – the forms in which this ministry may accomplish a service of love recognized by all concerned. This is an immense task, which we cannot refuse and which I cannot carry out by myself" (UUS, 95-6).

Powerful stuff! Now, we're not going to quibble because he said he was asking all the pastors and theologians for help, but not ordinary folk. We suppose he'll accept any help he can get. The main thing is that the pope says he wants to find a new way of exercising the primacy – a new way of being pope. Since one of the stumbling blocks on the path to Christian unity is that some do not accept the role of the papacy, he wants to look for ways of being pope acceptable to all – "the forms in which this ministry may accomplish a service of love recognized by all concerned" (UUS, 96).

Why aren't Christians taking the pope's plea for help as seriously as we should? Or are we, but our efforts just aren't making the headlines?

Mae and Bernard

Dear Mae and Bernard,

You're right. The pope has admitted his need for personal conversion and asked for help with discovering a new way of exercising the primacy – "a new job description," as you put it. And this is big news, even if it's not hitting the headlines as it should. However, in an April 8, 1998 editorial, the *Prairie Messenger* noted that John Paul II has apologized 94 times, 25 times saying expressly, "I ask forgiveness." This is recorded in Luigi Accattoli's book, *When a Pope Asks Forgiveness: The* Mea Culpas *of John Paul II*. Sadly, minor Vatican officials have not followed the pope's lead in this regard.

In fact, so far as we know, this is the first time in history that the Roman pontiff has said words like that, about his own constant need for conversion. It certainly is a sign of great hope. Very few people have picked that up. And, as you noted, it ties in with the remarkable later statement in the same encyclical, where he says: "When the Catholic church affirms that the office of the Bishop of Rome corresponds to the will of Christ, she does not separate this office from the mission entrusted to the whole body of bishops, who are also 'vicars and ambassadors of Christ.' The Bishop of Rome is a member of the 'college,' and the bishops are his brothers in the ministry. Whatever relates to the unity of all Christian communities clearly forms part of the concerns of the primacy" (UUS, 95). He went on to speak about his responsibility to seek a new way of exercising the primacy. You quoted that part.

Renewing the papacy

The pope is talking here about searching for a new way to be primate. Similarly, all of us must think of new ways to be bishop, priest, religious, laity. The struggle for conversion, for turning in a new direction, must go on constantly.

I admit that I can and do make mistakes and that I am in need of conversion as much as anyone else. All of us, bishops and heads of Roman congregations and so on, must take to heart what John Paul II says about himself in this encyclical. This shows the pope as being open to the future, which is so different from the stance of the Vatican in other cases, which wants to call us back to yesterday.

There is a lot of background to any question about renewing the papacy, and touching the relative authority of the pope and the college or council. Down through the centuries, in sometimes acrimonious debate, at times the pope was declared superior to the council and at times, vice versa. Early in the fifteenth century, it was a council that brought three contenders for the papacy into line and decided who was really pope. Subsequent popes, who accepted the decision of that council, later refused to follow the recommendations of other councils.

There is an open, unresolved question between conciliarism and monarchy regarding the office of Peter and the Twelve (now all the other bishops). This is because there is an unresolved question as to whether Jesus called the Twelve first and from among them picked Peter as their leader, or picked Peter first, before the Twelve and over them. That is an open question.

Vatican II, for all its great achievements, left some such questions with unresolved ambiguities. The matter of authority in the church was one of these. The council teaches both that the pope has full authority by himself, and that full authority rests with the pope and all the bishops as a college. In the council debate, these two views emerged and, as a kind of compromise for the sake of moving on, both views ended up in the document. This, then, is an area in which we can expect further doctrinal development some day. There are other such examples, such as the way the council cautiously promoted the role of women in the church but did not discuss the ordination of women. For now, there are some open questions. The encouraging thing is that the Spirit keeps moving and can't be repressed. And the Spirit does not call us to move backward.

Moreover, ambiguity in the church did not end with Vatican II. An example of continuing ambiguity in the exercise of authority is the Instruction on the liturgy issued by eight Vatican offices late in 1997. On the face of it, it was intended to correct abuses said to exist in some churches as more and more lay members assist in liturgical functions, such as readers and eucharistic ministers. This Instruction could also be used, however, to discourage lay people from coming forward to aid their pastors, as they have a right and duty to do, according to Vatican II teaching and canon law provisions. This is a clear example of how a universal instruction must be interpreted by the local churches if it is to serve the church well.

Focusing on goodness

In this regard, I think the hierarchy has some lessons to learn from what St. Paul has to say in beautiful passages about giving greater respect to weaker members, and not crushing their spirits. To call forth the gifts people have is more life-giving than to lay down laws for them to follow. We ought not to be always calling people to order and repressing those who think somewhat differently. We would do better to pursue the truth in its fullness than to pounce on every half-truth and try to suppress the error that goes along with it. John Shea speaks of that when he says we focus too much on sin and too little on the goodness within us. As good parents and teachers know, it is much more productive to call forth the goodness in a child, to say to the less gifted, "I believe you can do better. Let me help you to prove to yourself that you can do better." If you say, "you nit-wit," you only confirm the child's low self-esteem and leave the child trapped.

I am pleased that many people in the Victoria diocese seem to have noticed and appreciated my efforts to empower the laity and set them free to become who they are meant to be in the church. That is one of the goals I set as a result of Vatican II – to encourage people to discover their gifts. I concentrated on encouraging all the people, instead of spending my time repressing the mavericks. I think that is a very important aspect of my ministry. It has led to occasional misunderstandings. For example, a few of the clergy have complained that the bishop cares only for the laity.

Some priests are living a complex – a kind of passive-aggressiveness that indicates they are suffering some form of collective depression. I would like to see more parishioners expressing their understanding and showing compassion towards priests in these situations. After the council, the media carried the message that the bishops had talked only about themselves and had neglected the priests. Yet there is a full council document about priests with beautiful stuff in it, as well as many other important references to priests. With many priests, that has not registered. Nor has it made a difference with some in the Victoria diocese that we have regular clergy meetings. I know every priest by his first name and have visited every parish more often than any bishop before me. There is something deeper. What is this complex that causes what I am trying to do to be perceived in this negative way?

And priests are not alone in this. There are some people who also question what I do, oppose change and want things to stand still or even move backward. The questioning of Vatican II and the attempts to undo the council go to the very heart of our concept of church. The oft-repeated debate, about whether pastoral councils and synods have decision-making status or are only advisory, is a classic example of the narrowing of ecclesiology into its third dimension, which is canon law.

Three levels of revelation

This is to forget that revelation is a person. The heart of revelation is our relation with Jesus, the Spirit of Jesus living within us. This is the charismatic level. It is only at a second level that we meet reflection on that revelation in the light of experience. This is what we call theology and doctrine. Only at the third level do we look at the church from the point of view of structure and its institutional side and get into canon law. Until Vatican II, our whole approach to ecclesiology was upside down. Vatican II made the correction of giving first place to revelation, to the Spirit.

Bishops and the church

For the record, sections 23 to 27 in *Lumen Gentium* are where the problem of the role of the bishop in the local church emerges. The beginning of no. 27 needs to be quoted: "The bishops, as vicars and legates of Christ, govern the particular churches assigned to them." (They are not vicars and legates of the pope; that is the point here.) "This power which they exercise personally in the name of Christ, is proper, ordinary and immediate, although its exercise is ultimately controlled by the supreme authority of the church and can be confined within certain limits," if the good of the church requires that.

That's the point: Is it really in the interest of the church to restrain the power of the bishops? And, if so, when, where and how? Is it in the interest of the church that there be a set of bodies in Rome, called congregations, which, whatever their administrative usefulness to the pope for the governance of the church, are basically a policing agency, overseeing the bishops and interfering in dioceses over issues that are not necessarily of interest to the church universal? If, for example, some theologian gets out of line, does there have to be interference in that diocese by a Roman congregation? This is where the question of subsidiarity comes in – the idea of not doing at a higher level what can be done at a lower one. That principle should apply in the church.

The other key point concerns the local church. The total reality of the church is in the local church. That's why the local church should seek to be as complete as possible an expression of church, and in each local church we should have a diversity of ministries. A very concrete case is the way the hermitical discipline, the tradition of having hermits, was restored to the church universal by what we did in the diocese of Victoria. I presented the documents to the Vatican asking for restoration of hermits in the Latin church. A priest here, a hermit, asked recently to be publicly recognized. I agreed to receive his vows according to Canon 603, so that he would in a sense be protected for the future. Another bishop cannot come along and tell him to look after a parish. With the shortage of clergy, people could say, "Why's this hermit, an ordained priest, sitting there? He should be running a parish." He doesn't want to, that's not his vocation, and now his canonical mission (you have to give a priest a mission) is to bring that gift to the diocese, by preaching retreats, by spiritual direction, by the example of his life as a hermit.

I hope I don't sound like I am sounding off too much. More later.

+*Remi*

Dear Remi,

The more we think of it, the more we see the importance for the future of the church of what Vatican II said (LG, 37) about the right of the laity to ask for the kind of pastoral service we think we need. This comes into play at every level. We can and should speak out about the primacy, synods, curia, and canon law. We can talk about what kind of bishops' conference we want and need, and what kind of bishop and pastor. When the pope says, in his encyclical on Christian unity, that he wants help rethinking how primacy might be exercised, we should take him at his word.

Let the laity speak up, then, and say, this is the type of church structure that we feel is really needed, on the basis of our experience amid the temporal realities we are supposed to influence, so that the all-saving purpose of God, under the guidance of the Holy Spirit, can be fulfilled. Perhaps we cannot give specific proposals, but we can do it by questions. What would it be like if . . . ? Could we envisage the possibility that . . . ? Put it right out and open up the dialogue. Not for John Paul II, perhaps, but for his successor.

Another point. We have been reading about how the Asian bishops at their Synod asked for many changes to suit Asian cultures. Why did Canadian bishops seem less outspoken during the Synod for the Americas just a few months earlier?

Synods: time for renewal?

The Asian bishops asked for less central control in the church. This complaint could also be made about preparations for the Americas synod in the fall of 1997, in which Canadians participated. The Working Paper prepared for it was a clear example of the excessively centralizing mentality in the Vatican at present. This 64-page document purported to be a summary of replies sent to the Vatican by bishops from Latin America, the U.S. and Canada in response to questions – *lineamenta* – sent to them earlier about possible topics for the Synod. The Working Paper did summarize their replies, and each reply mentioned was footnoted. However, not a single footnote indicated the country from which the suggestion came. A reader could not tell which idea came from Brazil or Mexico or Canada or any other country. Instead, every footnote referred either to Vatican II texts or to earlier teachings of the papal magisterium – a pope or a Vatican office. For example, a suggestion from Canada was not credited directly to the bishops of this country; its footnote only showed that their suggestion related in some way to some earlier text from the Vatican. From the Working Paper, one has the impression that nothing could be discussed that had not already been affirmed or approved in some earlier Vatican publication, as footnoted. As a document purporting to record the result of a hemispheric survey, that Working Paper is truly remarkable. It totally hides the sources of the ideas presented. Of course, at the synod itself a bishop in his oral or written intervention might say something novel, but no new suggestions from the bishops were given credit in the Working Paper.

This is an example of how the synod might be reformed or renewed. During the first synods during the late 1960s and early 1970s, the Canadian bishops always made suggestions for synod reform. Inspired by Archeparch Hermaniuk of Winnipeg, they asked over and over again that the synod should have decision-making powers with the pope, and that Vatican offices should be limited to essential executive functions. We don't hear of the Canadian bishops doing that any more. Is there a reason for this?

Mae and Bernard

Dear Mae and Bernard,

You ask what the Canadian bishops are doing about changing some things around the Vatican. Why don't we complain and protest more? The Canadian bishops are not just "sitting there taking it." However, we have learned that confrontation gets us nowhere. The Canadian bishops' attitude now is one of peacefully and repeatedly telling Rome how we feel about things. But at a given moment, if what we say is not being heard and is becoming counter-productive, we stop knocking on one door and try another, to try to make our point.

But we're on the record. For example, Cardinal Flahiff and Bishop Alex Carter as CCCB presidents, and other CCCB executive committee members over the years, have consistently spoken out. On that point I support the Canadian bishops. That we may be perceived as doing nothing in a world that's used to confrontation, by media who think that the truth comes out of conflict: that we have to live with. And that the messages of the Canadian bishops are not being sufficiently heard at the church grassroots, that's a reality, too. In general, I agree with what you said earlier about it.

Political processes and church life are two different things. By temperament, I'm not a confronting bishop. I never have been. Some people reproach me for "not giving leadership in the diocese." They say that out of a model of church that wants the bishop to be laying down the law, "telling it like it is," so that people can then resist and say they are not going to obey. Instead, I appeal to people's better judgment and wait for things to happen. The Spirit will win in the end. I am happy to see that this is being picked up after 36 years: that I have respected people.

At the same time, to get back to the solidarity of the Canadian bishops, I want to say this to their credit. In some media I have been selectively perceived as a maverick. Although I know from a variety of sources that some of the things I've said and done have scared some bishops, several have spoken to me in practically these words: "You know I'm not necessarily in agreement with you, and I certainly wouldn't say or do it your way, but I respect the fact you're doing it." And this is to the honour of Cardinal Emmett Carter. You know we have disagreed openly on the floor of CCCB meetings, and also in public over things like the 1983 CCCB statement on the Canadian economy. Yet, despite those and other cases, Emmett Carter always was a personal friend. I've gone out of my way to visit with him in Toronto.

At a given moment after the 1983 statement, I realized that there was a danger of this becoming a personal issue around me, so I said to myself, I'm going to look for another approach. At a following bishops' meeting I wasn't speaking up. Several bishops wondered why, so I told them. Emmett Carter came over to see me and we went for a walk. He, too, was wondering why I was silent and I told him the same thing. He said: "I respect that. But I want you to know this, Remi. You and I don't always agree on a number of things. Yet I respect and admire what you are doing. If ever you're in trouble, let me know, because I'll be there for you." You've got to give credit for that.

Despite solidarity at the conference level, bishops are very vulnerable at the level of their own diocese. I've been called on the carpet more than once. Some of it is cheap politics. A Victoria priest wrote a two-page, single-spaced letter of complaint to the pope via the papal nuncio in Ottawa about all the things I was doing wrong. Nasty stuff. The nuncio sent me the letter. He took pains when it was photocopied to blank out the letterhead and signature. All I got was the body of the letter. As I was sitting looking at it, the light from the sun fell across the paper at an angle that revealed the shadow of the letterhead, and I knew who had written it.

I went to see the nuncio. He asked me to explain, and I said I would not. "You blanked it out," I said, "but I know who wrote this. I'm asking you to tell this priest to come to the next Victoria clergy meeting, repeat all this to the rest of the priests, and see what happens." Well, the nuncio was upset. "I will not reply to this letter," I explained, "because that would imply that I accept the complaints as true. I reject that. At the same time, I know you have a job to do, and if you have to report something to Rome, ask me some questions and take notes of my replies. What's more, I'd also like you to tell Rome that if you keep on treating bishops like this, don't be too surprised if you have trouble finding candidates for the job." Well, eventually I got a letter from the nuncio saying that everything was fine. And the priest never read his letter at a priests' meeting! And I never spoke to him about it! He is still a friend of mine. I understand.

Vatican II recognized (LG, 23; CD, 11) the local church as the gathering of people around their bishop. In this local church, the fullness of the Catholic church is present. However, that teaching has yet to be fully applied. For reasons of weakness, unresolved problems and so on, the church has not yet given itself some of the structures needed to bring certain aspects of Vatican II to life in the church. This is a major problem. The Vatican II renewal is unfinished at the level of church structures.

Some say that in the new global market situation, national states are obsolete. However, a national state has identity through a people with their language, history, culture, the right to self-determination and much else. Nations may benefit from doing some things jointly, for example, through trade alliances, but the identity of each state is also important to its people.

Bishops: working together nationally

Similarly, local churches need, and in fact have, their own identity. At the same time, in an increasingly interconnected, complex world, bishops of local churches, especially smaller dioceses, find it impossible to deal all alone with significant issues of policy. For the well-being of the church, bishops of a country need to be able to meet, in discernment, in concert, to talk and learn, reading the signs of the times and gradually figuring out what is the best policy to follow. So, for example, in Canada we have the Canadian Conference of Catholic Bishops (CCCB). Technically, we do not meet as a church. There is no Canadian church. The church is in each diocese, and is universal, but not national. But the CCCB is the beginning of a new structure by which we bind ourselves regarding some policies, regarding the liturgy, for example. More and more, the conference is adopting policies for this country which are distinctly Canadian. This is necessary, because the Vatican cannot be present to all these realities.

In its turn, the diocese of Victoria needs to learn from these broader realities. The local church, which is subject to pressures to go it alone with its local culture and does not have distance to see the broader picture, needs the guidance of the centre of unity in Rome. The pope, presiding in charity and fraternity, has a legitimate and necessary role. But given the complexity and growth of the world – and this is new – somewhere between the local church and the church universal we need to build secondary, intermediary structures in a new form of broader council, such as the CCCB. It would be interesting to explore how an episcopal conference could fulfill a role similar to that of an ancient patriarchate.

Paul VI recognized this when he restored the conciliar, synodal principle and called for synods at all levels. And not just general or special synods in Rome, of which there have been some 50 since Vatican II. That's where bishops' conferences fit in. They are new entities in some ways, slowly emerging. There are some parallels with the early church, when synods or councils were held for local areas. These were not necessarily ecumenical, for the whole church. This distinction was already made in our earliest memory and tradition. Councils and synods were recognized by popes, emperors or other rulers as valid and having authority.

Pope and bishops working together

As far as theologians like Archeparch Hermaniuk of Winnipeg were concerned, Paul VI left the synod with an incomplete constitution. At Vatican II, Hermaniuk was the first to call for a new "council" made up of the pope and representatives of the diocesan bishops, to meet every few years to make pastoral decisions for the universal church. The synod that Paul VI set up in the fall of 1965 just before the final session of Vatican II only partly satisfied bishops like Hermaniuk. Its constitution makes it totally dependent on the pope for all details of timing, agenda and outcome. The question of bishops at a synod having decision-making power with the pope was left in abeyance. The synod's constitution is a papal *motu proprio* so the pope could change it easily enough. As it is now, the synod is another example of tension between conciliarity and primacy. At all the early synods in Rome, the Canadian bishops always included a strong intervention about reform of the synod itself, along with the other things they had to say about each specific synod topic. They advanced the Hermaniuk thesis that the pope and bishops at the synod should be decision-making, and the curial congregations should be just for follow-up and administration.

In this context, I subscribe fully to Tillard's paper on the office of Peter in the future. It's all there. Tillard makes the point that when the pope alone unilaterally convenes synods and makes all decisions about the agenda, he is not acting as he should be. He is taking something away from the bishops. It is not helpful or healthy. Two more personal stories may help to show how things go now. You have mentioned how we have supported the wish of bishops of northern Canadian dioceses to ordain married men as priests. I was president of the western Canadian bishops' conference on one occasion when we made this request. As usual during such visits, John Paul II invited our group to a working lunch. As president, I was seated at his right hand and was expected to begin by reviewing what we were discussing with curial offices. When I mentioned the need to ordain married men because we risked losing the eucharist in the north, the pope banged the table with his knife handle in his fist and said in Latin, "God will provide!" End of discussion on that point! So he has been closed on some issues. But another story shows there isn't solid unity around the Vatican at other times. I was called on the carpet a few years ago because I dared to say, at an international women's rally in Washington, that discussion should continue about the role of women and their ministries. I was told by Cardinal Ratzinger that all I should do was read what the pope had said and tell people it was wrong to think in any other way. Some time later, when our Canadian group was visiting the Vatican secretariat of state, I asked whether it was the pope's intention to end debate on that subject completely. The answer came that the pope has strong personal views and wants to make them clear on the record, but knows quite well that this will continue to be debated. And they made it clear that the congregation for the doctrine of the faith has special competence in matters of doctrine, but when it comes to interpreting the mind of the pope concerning policy, discipline or strategies, the secretariat of state has competence. In fact, it was Paul VI's reform of the curia right after Vatican II that made the secretariat the lead curial office, in place of the former Holy Office. It is good to remember that. My experience has shown, time and time again, that the Vatican is not a monolith. People there support various schools of thought and there are legitimate divergences of opinion about policy matters.

One final note about the future of the church. In our new world, one question is whether there could be a Vatican III made up only of Roman Catholics on the same model as Vatican II. So there is talk of a future Council of Jerusalem. I did a paper on that once. It is intriguing to think of the three great families of the faith of Sarah and Abraham – Jewish, Christian and Islamic – all coming together, and to speculate on what they would say and do.

+Remi

For Discussion

1. Discuss what signs you see of gifts being given by the Holy Spirit to everyone in your community.

2. In general, in your home, school and parish, which approach is emphasized: Encouraging the free gifts of the Spirit, or keeping a close eye on good order? What are the merits and shortcomings of each approach?
3. Discuss why Vatican II did not settle all church issues, such as all questions about relations between the college of bishops and the pope.
4. What are some of the foreseeable changes in the world that might call for further updating of church practices?
5. Discuss why the pope (and other church leaders) might need to pray for conversion in order to serve the church better.
6. What signs do you see in your parish community of tension between the gifts of the Spirit and the need for order in the church?

For Action

1. Read John Paul II's 1995 encyclical, *Ut Unum Sint,* about unity in the church. Invite friends who are not Catholic to discuss it.
2. Study Chapter 4 of the Vatican II *Constitution on the Church,* with particular attention to what it says about the rights and duties of the laity.
3. Read a church history about the development of the modern papacy and the question of the pope's relations with the bishops.
4. Read a book or article about the development and role of synods, and the different models of governance in the Western and Eastern churches.
5. Promote the synodal principle in any church group you belong to as a sign of democracy in action.

Further Reading

Brown, Raymond. *The Churches the Apostles Left Behind.* New York: Paulist Press, 1984.

Brown, Raymond, Karl Donfried, and John Reuman, eds. *Peter in the New Testament.* Minneapolis: Augsburg Publishing, 1973.

Gervais, Pearl, and Grant Maxwell, eds. *Forward in the Spirit: Challenge of the People's Synod.* Victoria, BC: Diocese of Victoria, 1991.

Hillman, Eugene. *Toward an African Christianity, Inculturation Applied.* New York/Mahwah: Paulist Press, 1993.

Hughes, John Jay. *Pontiffs: Popes Who Shaped History.* Huntingdon, IA: Our Sunday Visitor Publications, 1994.

John Paul II. Christifideles Laici: *Vocation and Mission of the Lay Faithful.* Post-synodal apostolic exhortation. Sherbrooke, Que.: Editions Paulines, 1989.

Tillard, J. M. R. *The Bishop of Rome.* Wilmington, DE: Michael Glazier Inc., 1983.

The Reach of the Spirit:
Uniting Christians and All Peoples

In his 1995 encyclical, Ut Unum Sint, *John Paul II stressed that at Vatican II "the Catholic church committed herself irrevocably to following the path of the ecumenical venture." This chapter reviews some of the interventions of Canadian bishops at the council regarding work for Christian unity. It also recalls ecumenical developments in Canada since the close of the council in 1965. Continuing difficult pastoral questions, including the sharing of communion, are discussed. Council teaching about how the Spirit works in all peoples is noted. This leads into a discussion of Christian appreciation of other world religions, with particular attention to insights shared by Asian Catholic bishops during the 1998 Synod on Asia. The progress of interfaith co-operation in Canada is noted. Changes in the church's approach to work in mission lands as a result of Vatican II are discussed briefly.*

Dear Mae and Bernard,

When we look for signs of the work of the Spirit, the most evident may be what has been happening in ecumenism. I say this despite the fact that many people have the impression that progress towards Christian unity is slow, if not stalled. I agree that developments in some churches, such as the ordination of women, loom as large roadblocks for others, notably the Orthodox and us Catholics. However, the important thing is that difficulties have not ended all efforts for greater unity.

John Paul II has been very strong and clear in insisting that work for Christian unity is a necessity, not an option. He stressed in his 1995 encyclical on Christian unity that at Vatican II "the Catholic church committed herself irrevocably to following the path of the ecumenical venture, thus heeding the Spirit of the Lord." As one practical dimension of this, the Vatican recently issued an instruction making ecumenical education obligatory for seminarians and others preparing for pastoral ministry.

Catholics working for Christian unity

In Canada we have a long history of ecumenical developments. Some of them may seem small in themselves. Many have been largely ignored by the general public but, added up, they have changed how Christian churches in this country relate to one another.

When our bishops' conference (the Canadian Conference of Catholic Bishops, or CCCB) became a full member of the Canadian Council of Churches (CCC) in the fall of 1997, it marked the climax of a movement that began among non-Catholic churches when the CCC was formed in 1944. Catholics were not involved in that initiative but, looking back, we can see that the Spirit was. Dialogue to overcome denominational differences had begun. Gradually, things began to happen locally. Individual Catholic priests got involved here and there in local ministerial associations, as they were then called. They discussed shared pastoral problems, such as helping mixed-marriage couples. Some priests, including Jesuit Irenée Beaubien in Montreal and the Paulists in Toronto, began to attract attention as Catholic ecumenists.

Then came Vatican II, with John XXIII's insistence that it would be about church renewal, Christian unity and dialogue with the modern world. You'll recall that Father Peter Nearing was named director of the bishops' social action office in Ottawa soon after John XXIII announced the council in 1959. Nearing began co-operating on social justice issues with his counterparts in the national offices of the other churches. That collaboration continues to this day. You will probably want to say something about your own part in this. My social justice work with the CCCB social affairs commission was always in an ecumenical context.

When the Canadian bishops sent John XXIII their suggestions for Vatican II topics, none mentioned ecumenism as such. However, once the council began, several Canadians made suggestions which found their way into final texts. Archbishop Baudoux of St. Boniface called (October 4, 1963) for specific mention of non-Catholic churches and communities. There could be no doubt, he argued, that souls are saved through their work. If this is God's work, the council should acknowledge it; and it did. Baudoux also regretted that the shortcomings of some Catholics were not admitted more courageously. The council, he said, must be ready to acknowledge that many sad events in the history of the church had been due to the failings of its members. Both of these ideas were retained by the council.

Similarly, the council took to heart the advice of Cardinal Léger of Montreal. The text on ecumenism, he argued, should not try to describe all the Christians separated from Catholicism since the sixteenth century. The "authentic treasures of truth and spiritual life" of separated Christians needed to be understood and honoured, he agreed; but they represented such a variety, and had such different backgrounds, that any summary description would be unsatisfactory, and the risk of over-simplification should be avoided in a council text.

Baudoux later made the further point that ecumenical dialogue was not merely a human initiative but was a genuinely supernatural conversation under the guidance of the Holy Spirit. The chief means of promoting understanding, he urged, were mutual pardon, friendship and trust. He welcomed the fact that the text on ecumenism then being discussed recognized the real though imperfect communion of other Christians because of their incorporation into Christ through baptism and their profession of Christ's name. As president of the Canadian bishops' conference, he told the council of a letter from the general synod of the Anglican Church in Canada, and called it a sign that other Christians were expecting great things of the council.

In a second intervention on ecumenism (November 28, 1963), Léger urged that care should be taken to show that the unity desired by the council was compatible with great diversity. Perfect obedience in the church is matched by supreme freedom, he argued. In the past, the church frequently had somewhat neglected "certain legitimate demands of freedom and diversity within the bounds of unity." He added that well-ordered missionary work and ecumenical activity both called for "a strong statement saying that unity in the church of Christ can never stand in the way of legitimate liberty and diversity."

Léger also wanted something said about the need for humility in ecumenical work. The council had already stressed the importance of the church confessing its human shortcomings. It was often affirmed, he noted, that the Catholic church possesses the full truth revealed by Christ. Given the necessary distinctions, such a statement could be correctly understood. There was reason to fear, however, that for many people such an affirmation hid the fact that while on earth nobody was capable of understanding fully and exhaustively the truth that Christ came to reveal. A reminder of human weakness in the face of the transcendence of God completed rather than contradicted the church's belief in its infallibility. God's transcendence made intellectual immobilism "completely impossible for Christians," he said. The search for a deeper, fuller understanding of God must go on constantly. This was the true way to overcome doctrinal difficulties.

The ecumenical movement: work of the Spirit

At about the same time, Archbishop Flahiff submitted written comments about Christian divisions. There should be more emphasis, he thought, on the historical aspect of the very fact that there is an "unhappy division among Christians." What is the significance of divisions in the history of the church? Since "the Lord of all history" allowed these divisions, Christians must search for their meaning. Divisions are the result of sin, he affirmed. Therefore, "these terrible schisms" should always remind the church that it is not yet as holy as it should be, nor obedient enough to its call to be truly universal. He called attention to "another still more positive aspect of our divisions." He was fully convinced, he said, that the ecumenical movement is the work of the Holy Spirit through which, out of the effort to overcome divisions, "all churches profit immensely, are challenged to renewal, find new ways of acting in love, and come to a deeper understanding of the Gospel." In this movement, for the first time in history, all church and ecclesiastical communities "witness together to Jesus Christ the Saviour, thus giving new vigour to the proclamation of the Gospel in the world." He thought this historical and dynamic aspect of ecumenism should be explained in the text. It would then be more evident that what was said about ecumenism was not a final judgment but only "the beginning of an action or development whose author is the Spirit of God himself."

I recall the words of Baudoux, Léger and Flahiff for several reasons. In themselves, they are thought-provoking. They also help us to understand how the texts of Vatican II were built up from the prayerful wishes and insights of pastors who loved the church. John Paul II has stressed that we should celebrate the council's teaching on unity and what has taken place since its close. "I thank the Lord," he said in his 1995 encyclical, *Ut Unum Sint,* "that he has led us to make progress along the path of unity and communion between Christians, a path difficult but so full of joy." He praised the interconfessional dialogues aimed at resolving doctrinal differences. But more than that is needed, he added. "Christians cannot underestimate the burden of long-standing misgivings inherited from the past, and of mutual misunderstandings and prejudices," as well as complacency, indifference and insufficient knowledge of one another. The commitment to ecumenism must be based on conversion of hearts and prayer, leading to a "purification of past memories" (UUS, 2). Ecumenism is not just some sort of "appendix" added on to the church's traditional activity, the pope stressed. Ecumenism is "an organic part of her life and work, and consequently must pervade all that she is and does" (UUS, 20). "The quest for Christian unity is not a matter of choice or expediency, but a duty which springs from the very nature of the Christian community" (UUS, 49).

One of the most remarkable things in John Paul II's encyclical is the way that he applies to himself Christ's words to Peter: "And you, when once you have turned back, strengthen your brothers" (Luke 22: 32). He said that he "must make his own Christ's prayer for that conversion which is indispensable for 'Peter' to be able to serve his brethren." He asked Catholics and all Christians to pray for his own conversion! We discussed earlier what this means for new ways of organizing the church. It also has profound implications for ecumenism.

Later on, I want to return to this dramatic notion, particularly in the light of the fact that I once gave a talk in Washington state on authority and the magisterium. I talked basically about that text: "And you Peter, once converted, confirm your sisters and brothers in faith out of your experience of conversion." My interpretation was not exactly the Vatican interpretation, and I got called on the carpet for that one, too. Rather interesting, to see the pope now saying basically the same thing that was frowned on a few years ago. Things move, even if only a little, and very slowly. . . . So, as the saying goes, "Hope springs eternal in the human breast."

+*Remi*

Dear Remi,

There is no doubt that great progress towards Christian unity has been made since Vatican II. Mae remembers that before the council Bishop Pocock in Saskatoon refused her permission to sing at a wedding in an Anglican church! There is much more ecumenical hospitality now. Still, one of the difficulties is maintaining day-to-day local interest. We have the impression that even for major annual events, such as the Week of Prayer for Christian Unity, local interest has declined from what it was a few years ago.

The work of ecumenical coalitions

We have not managed to *popularize* the ecumenical movement. This is a problem that the various interchurch social justice groups in Canada have not resolved. As you mentioned, from the early 1960s and well before the close of Vatican II, Catholics were working at the national level with Anglican, Lutheran, Presbyterian, United Church and other colleagues on social problems of the day. They organized a National Committee on Church and Industrial Society. They linked up with the Toronto-based Religion-Labour Council. They were leaders in the 1965 national conference in support of the Emmett Hall Commission report, which led to Canada's national medicare program. In May 1968, some 500 people gathered in Montreal for an ecumenical conference about "Christian Conscience and Poverty." To follow up, the churches led in the organizing of a short-lived national "Coalition for

Development," teaming up with groups from labour, Native organizations, industry and commerce. In 1970, the Catholic bishops and the Canadian Council of Churches presented a joint brief to the Special Senate Committee studying poverty in Canada. In the spring of 1972, a four-member team of observers from the Canadian churches attended the United Nations Conference on Trade and Development in Chile, and noted how Canadian government representatives there voted with the rich countries against the poor ones. This awareness led to the launching, over the next few years, of 13 interchurch coalitions dedicated to making Canadians aware of the need to change government and corporate policies concerning Natives, immigrants, refugees, population and development, world trade, sale of arms, and human rights in Africa, Asia and Latin America.

While a number of these ecumenical coalitions continue to do good work, the period of their peak activity was in the 20 years from the mid-1970s. All national church offices now have fewer resources and reduced personnel, but the social justice work goes on, especially in the struggles for human rights and against poverty. A measure of the public education job still to be done can be seen in recent Canadian elections, which brought to power governments more interested in satisfying the wealthy than doing justice for the poorest. The Canadian Catholic Organization for Development and Peace (CCODP), founded in 1967 at the height of our post-council enthusiasm, remains our church's chief means to educate people about the needs of poor people around the world. Many parishes, unfortunately, do not support CCODP enough.

The Canadian ecumenical social justice projects in which Catholics were full partners did not win enough public support. Even less attention has been paid, however, to the various theological dialogue groups. The first to be organized after Vatican II was the Joint Working Group (JWG). It was sponsored by the Canadian Council of Churches and the Catholic bishops' conference, and modelled on a similar international group formed by the World Council of Churches in Geneva and the Vatican.

The Canadian JWG was launched in 1968, soon after the close of the Christian Pavilion at the Montreal world's fair. That pavilion itself was an historic example of a new spirit of collaboration between seven Christian

216

churches in Canada. The JWG moved quickly past preliminary discussion of theological differences to launch several joint pastoral projects. One was a study that resulted in agreement to recognize each church's baptism as valid when performed with flowing water and the Father, Son and Holy Spirit formula. It also developed programs for pastoral care of mixed marriages, ecumenical education and the joint preparation of materials for the Week of Prayer for Christian Unity.

The CCCB and the Canadian Council of Churches

In 1969, the JWG members agreed in principle that Canada's Christian churches should look to a closer structural relationship. This process reached its climax in 1997, when the Catholic bishops' conference became full members of the Council of Churches. They had been accepted as associate members in 1986. What took them so long? The answer to that question reveals the delicacy and complexity of building unity after centuries of separation. The first step was a JWG study that resulted in a 1973 national consultation at which the participants agreed on the formation of a new Canadian Christian Council, including Catholics as members. The task of designing this council was given to a Wider Ecumenical Fellowship (WEF) committee set up by the JWG. It encountered two main difficulties. The easier one was getting members of the 30-year-old Council of Churches to abandon it for a new entity. More difficult was the question of how to integrate Catholic members equitably. Catholics are more than 50 percent of all Canadian Christians. Catholic members did not want to dominate every aspect of a new joint body. Moreover, the new body would need to be bilingual, paralleling national Catholic bodies such as the bishops' conference. As various proposals were studied, an interim Inter-Church Committee (ICC) was established. Then, in 1983, the bishops' conference proposed a second look at simply modifying the existing Council of Churches. The CCC therefore revised its constitution to admit the bishops as associate members in 1986, and as full members 10 years later.

Meanwhile, bilateral dialogue groups have been carrying on quiet discussions of theological topics: Anglican-Catholic, Catholic-United Church, Catholic-Lutheran, Catholic-Evangelical Fellowship. Main topics have been baptism, the eucharist and ministry. Progress has been made in mutual understanding on such matters, despite new disagreements about some questions of sexual morality and the ordination of women.

We think it is important to keep in mind these stories about the progress made since the 1940s. This is part of the storytelling that keeps faith alive. Our human efforts may seem not to thrive, but the Spirit is alive. We notice that Archbishop Carey of Canterbury has called on Catholics to share Holy Communion as a "bold sign" for the Year 2000, but England's Cardinal Hume has replied that such sharing could not take place without agreement on belief in the real presence and on the theology of the church. What are your thoughts about this?

Mae and Bernard

Dear Mae and Bernard,

To start with the question that ended your latest letter, Cardinal Hume has raised the important questions. However, I am sure he would agree that while you can name the key questions, the answers to them are all over the place. I mean this in the sense that there is no official Anglican-Catholic agreement about the eucharist and the church, but I can find individual Anglicans who do agree with me about such things. This is where the tough pastoral decisions and the personal pain come in. At an Anglican-Catholic wedding, for example, you may know from experience that some people present agree fully about the eucharist and related realities, and others do not. How do you draw the line between being too rigorist in refusing to share communion, and too casual in sharing it with no questions asked?

Intercommunion: recognizing restrictions

Casual intercommunion is a problem. It all depends on how people understand the eucharist. It depends on our faith. If we really believe that the Holy Spirit through the eucharist is making us one in Christ, then it is very important to be able to show that we share that faith. But it is not good enough to see it as just a social gesture, and say: "Let's all be friends together, and have an open table." That attitude ignores the deeper reality and bypasses the whole struggle for unity. Unity has not been achieved, and we need to struggle for it. That's an unresolved tension. It will always be there. A whole wing of the church, particularly the Orthodox wing, has a very powerful and well-developed theology of the Holy Spirit. They are absolutely against inter-communion. That may be an extreme position, and there is a tendency to go to the other extreme. That, to me, is a painful problem, especially where it touches very local situations.

While I do not accept a come-one-come-all open table, and while I recognize that for the common good there have to be restrictions, at the same time my position as a pastor is to see the importance of meeting individual needs. I would be very broad and flexible in interpreting what needing the eucharist means. Take the case of a non-Catholic who truly believes in the eucharist and wants to receive communion, but cannot readily do so, in a mixed marriage situation, for example. I would say, let that person come forward and receive. That is a question of hospitality towards a person you know well who has faith. To me the difference is there: I would practise hospitality but I can't authorize an open table. In the latter case the eucharist loses its meaning and we stop struggling. We say in effect: "Let's all go to church together; we have no more problems." That's not realistic. And we can defeat the very purpose of ecumenism by assuming that unity is easy and avoiding the struggle.

Unity and diversity in church structures

Another side of the problem is that the structures get in the way. That's why I think that we'll never see full structural unity of the churches. Structures are deeply embedded in a variety of cultures. Those cultures simply may not relate to one another. They have no common language. Language is a big issue here. You can't really have worship together in the full sense of the word if you don't speak the same language. You can't bring together two communities who speak totally different languages and have them celebrate in one communion. Individuals can cross linguistic and cultural lines, but entire communities cannot. Unity will come. The Spirit will see to that, helping us overcome the human sinfulness that keeps us divided now. But I believe that after our unity in faith is achieved we will still have structural diversity, something like the various rites we have now. Unity in faith, but diversity in liturgies, theologies, traditions, languages, and so on. John Paul II talked about the importance of this kind of diversity in the church during his 1984 visit to the Ukrainian Catholic cathedral in Winnipeg.

If we remember that there are two principles, as it were, in the church – the charismatic and the institutional – we will be less perturbed when we see that it will be very difficult to bring the churches all into one church in a structured way. The structured, institutional side, by its very nature, is going to be much more difficult to bring together than the charismatic side, what the Spirit says in people's hearts. When we spoke about unity at Vatican II and right after, a lot of people thought the goal was structural unity. Now I think we are seeing more that it's going to be a charismatic unity in the Spirit. Not without some structural unity, but less of that comprehensive unity, embracing all the churches, which was the early concept.

+*Remi*

Dear Remi,

Did you notice in news from the Synod for Asia what some of the bishops said they had learned from non-Christian religions? Apart from the actual values listed, we found it striking to learn of the growing openness of Asian Catholics. This clearly reflects a Vatican II theme, that the church on earth is not already perfect and needs to be open, learning from others, including other religions.

What the church can learn

The account we saw said the bishops of Malaysia, Singapore and Brunei had listed what the Catholic church could learn from other religions, as follows:

"From Muslims the church can learn about prayer, fasting, and almsgiving.

"From Hindus the church can learn about meditation and contemplation.

"From Buddhists the church can learn about detachment from material goods and respect for life.

"From Confucianism the church can learn about filial piety and respect for elders.

"From Taoism the church can learn about simplicity and humility.

"From animists the church can learn about reverence and respect for nature and gratitude for harvests.

"The church can learn from the rich symbolism and rites existing in their diversity of worship.

"The church can, like the Asian religions, learn to be more open, receptive, sensitive, tolerant, and forgiving in the midst of a plurality of religions."

From stories we've heard you tell, we know you could add things we could learn from Native Canadian religions.

Very interesting. *Semina verbi*, the seeds of the word, scattered and coming to life everywhere, did you say?

Mae and Bernard

Dear Mae and Bernard,

Thank you for the list from the Asian bishops. I hadn't noticed that news item. While we in Canada do not have the same experiences as Asian Catholics, here too ecumenism has progressed well beyond what Vatican II anticipated. Now it is basically interfaith. Ecumenism's focus on Christ and Christian unity remains important. But with the shift of emphasis now more to the Spirit of Christ, I think we are less narrow in our definition of unity around Christ. We recognize more readily now that the Spirit is everywhere, and Christ is Lord of the cosmos. So I think we have broadened and made the interfaith dimension more flexible. Even regarding ecumenism we use a broader sense of the word.

While we are sharing news, I want to mention an article by Thomas Michel SJ. He wrote it while he was at the Vatican Secretariat for Interreligious Dialogue, before taking up another assignment. Michel's encounters with Muslims have brought him more and more into dialogue with Jews, Hindus, Buddhists, Taoists and followers of indigenous religions, both African and American. "The same Holy Spirit who has been active in my own life," he says, "is also at work in the lives of my friends of other faiths, using our encounters to touch them too and transform their lives. Most of the time we do not see evidence of this. We work in hope, which is, after all, trusting that God is invisibly active in this world. But God knows that we need encouragement from time to time and gives us 'feedback' to keep our hopes alive."

The evangelizing mission

Dialogue and proclamation of the Gospel are two distinct aspects of the evangelizing mission that Christ gave his disciples, Michel says. Neither can replace the other. God's grace, he notes, "produces anyplace in the world people of great holiness, generosity, and love. God carries out this saving work among people of other faiths through the Holy Spirit, who makes use of the religious traditions that people follow to lead them farther and farther along the path of true holiness." Sometimes a person's knowledge of God's saving work in Jesus Christ comes first and the person is baptized. More often, "the Holy Spirit precedes people's knowledge of Christ. There is no contradiction here: it is the One God who is at work, whether in Christ or in the Spirit."

Being open to dialogue

The deepest motivation for dialogue is to recognize the Spirit of God wherever the Spirit is at work, Michel says. "Time spent with sincere believers of other faiths is time spent in discovery of the many and varied fruits – love, joy, peace, patience, goodness, kindness, gentleness, faithfulness, self-control – that the Spirit continues to produce in the lives of other believers." In his view, one of the great causes of failure in dialogue is lack of patience. He links this to "the modern business ethic of quick and concrete results" and the philosophy of history which holds that "humankind, through education and technology, is continually evolving towards greater maturity, openness, and well-being," and ignorance and violence are bound to be superseded. Against this optimism, Michel believes that sin is a part of who we are as human beings and, where there is sin, there will be suspicion, hatred and conflict. Therefore, dialogue will not solve all the religious conflicts in the world, just as the struggle for justice will never put an end to all forms of injustice and oppression. Indeed, it is for this reason that dialogue is something that must be carried on in every society, in every age. Understanding and respect must be built anew in every generation.

Michel speaks of dialogue of life (the goal is living together in peace); dialogue of action (working together to oppose whatever enslaves and degrades people); dialogue of religious experience (opening fully to God so the Spirit can touch and transform); and dialogue of theological exchange (to overcome ignorance and achieve greater appreciation). Each type, he stresses, is to be conducted in patience and hope.

I find his insights very helpful. Michel warns that the church can fall into a naive humanism that says human beings will eventually bring perfection to this world, that it is just a matter of time. According to that view, all that is wrong with the world is behind us. We are now going to have a new paradise on earth, an idea which animates some of the New Age religions also. In the sense that we have been discussing it, historicity moves us away from the image of the church as a static reality, a perfect society, one monolithic body. It opens us to a more dynamic type of church, carrying its mission into the future, constantly renewed by struggle, in the continuity of its apostolic mission, but never completely fulfilled on earth.

A broader sense of ecumenism is to be linked with the faith of Sarah and Abraham, and the promise God made to them. God said, "I will make your offspring as numerous as the stars of heaven and as the sand that is on the seashore" (Genesis 22:17). Not long ago, I was privileged to serve as a chaplain for a pilgrim group travelling through the Holy Land. In Jerusalem we were greeted by Steve Langfur, an exceptionally competent Jewish guide. At a stop on Mount Olive overlooking the city and the temple foundations, he read from Romans 11, about the conversion of the Jews and the restoration of Israel. He invited us to be sensitive to our own calling as children of Abraham and Sarah. I experienced at that moment a profound conversion, with a deepening insight that has guided me ever since.

Among my favourite books is David H. Stern's *Jewish New Testament and Commentary*. I also recommend his *Restoring the Jewishness of the Gospel: A Message for Christians*. I have learned that I cannot plumb the depths of Revelation, as found in the Christian Scriptures, if I do not plant myself firmly in the Hebrew Scriptures. Part of the difficulty between Jews and Christians is that too many of us Catholics do not appreciate the various theologies that condition our attitudes towards our Jewish sisters and brothers. I favour what is sometimes called "Olive Tree theology" (see page 17 in Stern's *Restoring*). It reminds us that God's covenant holds for everyone, and that the separation between the church and the followers of Sarah and Abraham is a disastrous and scandalous wound which we are all called to heal by conversion, compassion and solidarity. Jesus was quick to recognize the faith of Abraham when he saw it even in Samaritans, centurions, sinners, prostitutes. When the root of a tree is holy, so are the trunk and branches. We remain grafted on the tree of the faith of Abraham and Sarah by living saintly lives and helping to hasten the coming of the "day of the Lord" (see 2 Peter 3:12).

It was a great loss to me when the Jewish rabbi, his wife and family left Victoria for a new assignment. Victor Reinstein, Susan Berrin and their three children were close friends. I miss sharing their Jewish feasts, and the warm hugs with which they always greeted me. Victor's inspired reflections nourished me spiritually. The book Susan edited, *Celebrating the New Moon: A Rosh Chodesh Anthology,* heightened my appreciation of the deep cultural and religious roots of the Jewish holidays on which some of our Christian rituals are modelled. It also clarified some feminist schools of thought.

Being open to the pursuit of truth

The fullness of truth is basic to working for life, justice, peace, love. When we limit ourselves to our Roman Catholic perception of truth, we do so at our own expense. We have to be open, both ecumenically and on an interfaith basis, to the pursuit of truth. This is an area of tremendous growth since Vatican II. The seeds were planted during the council. There was that famous statement that God's Spirit is present in all peoples and cultures. This was distinct from the view many Catholics had before Vatican II, when Protestants were seen as being saved despite being Protestants. Anyone beyond the church was seen in the same way. One of the major shifts since Vatican II has been the growth of the interfaith dimension, going beyond Christians.

Symbolic of this is what happened on the University of Victoria campus. We started with an ecumenical Christian chaplaincy some 16 years ago. Now it is an interfaith chaplaincy. When the old St. Ann's chapel in Victoria was rededicated, there were representatives of 10 world faiths present. Vanier's

L'Arche movement is increasingly non-Catholic. That's something to be recognized and heralded. The expression *semina verbi* (AG, 11), seeds of the word, and the presence of the Spirit, come in here.

From Catholic to Christian to Interfaith

Ecumenical change – for example, being able to sing at an Anglican wedding – is an area where we can rejoice. We must recognize the tremendous growth that has taken place. In the field of social justice, for example, one of the points of some contention was whether the diocese of Victoria would have its own social justice office. There is now more energy going into interfaith justice work than into Catholic work as such. We still have a commission, with a part-time person in charge, but most Catholics are involved in a wide variety of groups dealing with social justice. I meet them all over the place. At meetings I recognize that the majority are Catholics, but they are not identified as Catholics. They are active as concerned, humanitarian citizens. They go out and work with other people of a variety of faiths, or no particular faith. I had the same experience in human rights work, when I was chair of the B.C. Human Rights Commission from 1974 to 1977. Some people belonging to no particular church were among the most dedicated.

I have seen it shift significantly here in the diocese, from things we used to do as Catholic social justice, to a Christian ecumenical label, to now basically interfaith. There is relatively little left that is exclusively Catholic. I come under some criticism because some people thought the Victoria diocese had somehow backed off on social justice. That hasn't happened. It is just that we're spread out into broader teamwork and networking. And as a result we get less Catholic press coverage. But I go to all kinds of organizations and meetings and find a very substantial number of Catholics. They are present in social justice work well beyond their proportion in the total population.

The Spirit: moving beyond the institutional church

We are recognizing more and more all the time that, ultimately, the Holy Spirit is bringing about the reign of God. The Spirit works even beyond the institutional church. We see what may be a crumbling of the institutional church to a certain extent, but no slackening of the Spirit's work. It is sure that the European and Italian-centred christendom, which once even dictated to kings and emperors, is gone. Those days will never come back. But that is not the end.

Vatican II noted that the Holy Spirit spreads gifts throughout the church and even beyond. That is said delicately, but deliberately nonetheless. By baptism all members become equal in dignity and the capacity to serve. That implies more than institutional authority. It means giving far more care and attention to the charismatic gifts of various members. Once we had Francis and Clare; now we have Jean Vanier and Mother Teresa and other "gurus," saints, who are recognized as holy people with tremendous influence.

Some bypass the institutional church. The Spirit moves beyond the institution and is not restricted by it. The Spirit cannot be identified just with the authority of the magisterium. And the magisterium – here's where synodality comes in – is much more conscious of having to listen to what the Holy Spirit is saying to the whole people. This is what Cardinal Newman was getting at in his book *On Consulting the Faithful in Matters of Doctrine.*

Even the protection of the faith comes not simply from the magisterium. Yes, the episcopal magisterium aided by theologians has a special role, to verify and confirm the truth of what is being said. However, what we call the consensus of the faithful (*sensus fidelium*) has to be, as Vatican II said, more than just a consensus of the pope and all the bishops. It calls for a consensus of everybody under the guidance of the Holy Spirit. The interpenetration of the charismatic element and the institutional element has to be like two wings of a bird, if you will.

The influence of the Spirit extends in this way beyond us Catholics. Vatican II recognized that while the fullness of the faith subsists in the Catholic church, other Christian churches also are sources of salvation. As well, the "seeds of the word" are to be found in the other religions. The faith of Sarah and Abraham is to be found in the Jewish religion. The other world religions also have manifestations of the Holy Spirit in them.

Catholic missionaries are supposed to be trained today to look for signs of the Spirit among the people they serve, as well as to bring them the word. Similarly, Christians working in the world must not only "impress the divine law on the affairs of the earthly city" (GS, 43), but also discern or discover how and where the Spirit is already at work throughout the entire universe.

+Remi

Dear Remi,

We want to come back to one point in your latest letter. There is no doubt that the progress toward Christian unity is the will and the work of the Spirit. But we cannot just sit back and let the Spirit do the work, as if ecumenism is on automatic pilot. Father Bernard de Margarie, the Saskatoon Catholic ecumenist, made this point in an important talk reported in the November 12, 1997 *Prairie Messenger.* Church unity will come only with human effort, he stressed. Christians have been divinely equipped with gifts to enable them to live in a harmonious unity with each other, but unity does not come automatically.

Striving for Christian unity

Although "our calling in one baptism is the first gift of unity," he said, "those who want to heal the divisions of Christianity must work hard for it." He stressed that people, especially those who are impatient to reach full unity, must "invest themselves and the energy" to overcome the divisions and achieve healing among Christians. He said it is imperative that "the healing of the body of Christ be done first before we go out to heal the world. If we ignore the problems within the body, we won't have a body, just a bunch of legs." It is easy, de Margarie added, for one denomination to blame another; but all churches must acknowledge their own sins that have contributed to division. Each church must look over the past thousand years and acknowledge any sinfulness that they needed to repent of, on behalf of their church. Greater solidarity would follow. "We belong together, each part of us is weakened by the absence of the other." The Irish theologian Enda McDonagh made a similar point in an Ottawa lecture we attended: That to achieve reconciliation, individuals or churches or races need to see and appreciate that "the other" has qualities that they themselves lack and need to make their own.

We would leave open the question you raised, whether Christian unity will be institutional or mainly spiritual. Our point is that we must work at unity, in whatever form, in the conviction that we are called to do so by the Spirit who also gives us the gifts we need to move forward. In ecumenism as in any matter of justice or peace, we resist the idea that mysterious, evolving currents or forces are emerging which promise a new day – and make it less necessary for us to do justice and actively love God and neighbour. What we have to count on is the eternal Spirit and our efforts.

Mae and Bernard

For Discussion

1. Discuss and assess developments in your local church community towards greater Christian unity.
2. Do you think there might be more need today than 50 years ago for dialogue and co-operation between Christians and members of other religions?
3. How do you understand the Vatican II idea that the presence of the Holy Spirit might be found in all peoples?
4. Do you agree that it might be easier to achieve spiritual understanding among Christians than institutional union? What experiences shape your opinion?
5. What is your understanding of John Paul II's statement that the Catholic church is "irrevocably committed" to the ecumenical venture?

For Action

1. Interview the leaders of efforts among churches in your area to move towards greater Christian unity. Discuss what facilitates and hampers their progress.
2. Research what the Canadian bishops have done and are doing to promote Christian unity.

3. Study how immigration is changing the relations in your community and in the country generally between Christians and members of other world religions.

4. Interview the spiritual leader of a prominent non-Christian group in your community, to learn about their beliefs and practices and about their experience in your midst.

Further Reading

Berrin, Susan. *Celebrating the New Moon: A Rosh Chodesh Anthology.* Northvale, NJ: Jason Aronson, 1996.

Botsis, Peter A. *What is Orthodoxy?* Athens/Meteora: Monastery of Varlaam, 1997 edition.

Congar, Yves. *Diversity and Communion.* Mystic, CT: Twenty-Third Publications, 1985.

Dessaux, Jacques. *Twenty Centuries of Ecumenism.* New York/Ramsey, NJ: Paulist Press, 1984.

Fries, H., and Karl Rahner. *Unity of the Churches, an Actual Possibility.* Philadelphia: Fortress Press, 1985.

Ware, Timothy. *The Orthodox Church.* New York: Penguin Books, 1983.

Epilogue

Dear Remi,

In one of your earlier letters you pointed out that no new divine revelation will be added to what is now recorded in the Bible. However, God's word in Holy Scripture continues to speak in new ways to each generation and, indeed, each person. The Holy Spirit is constantly showering God's people with gifts of new understanding, wisdom and knowledge, as well as the courage to pursue new insights. For example, when we were just married and you newly ordained, we could not have written the kinds of letters we have been exchanging; and we can reasonably expect to live long enough to look back on what we have written here and see it as somewhat outdated. Change in the church and the world will continue from new sources, such as the insights of women theologians.

We often talk together about what we call the "miracles" which we have experienced as a couple. We learned in catechism when we were children that each sacrament is accompanied by its own "actual graces." When we were married a priest pointed out that the actual graces of the sacrament of marriage include "gifts" dealing with "worldly" stuff, the concrete, nitty-gritty things of marriage and family life – jobs, housing, food, medical care, and so on. We have found this to be so. Many times, facing family problems that seemed to be beyond our ability to cope, we have found ourselves blessed with "miracles" that carried us on to the next stage of life. Apparently apart from our own planning or praying, out of the blue, so to speak, a child escaped injury, a house sale went through against all odds, a family quarrel resolved itself. Each such miracle came just when our own efforts seemed doomed. Or sometimes we experienced a "miracle" that we did not even realize we needed! We believe the Spirit works in such concrete ways for every family, as well as for the entire human family. Thanks be to God!

Looking ahead with hope

Everything we have written here is prompted by our conviction that God's work done by Christ is continuing in the church Christ left behind. Everything we know of God's plan for creation prompts us to believe that the church is much closer to the beginning of its work than to the end of its mission. True, we do not know what tomorrow will bring for each one of us or for the whole of creation. We believe, however, that there will be many more tomorrows, and we know that belief sets us apart from those who look ahead with fear and no hope.

One of the greatest gifts of Vatican II was to acknowledge that the church must constantly undergo renewal and change. This is because the church is both divine and human. One thing we have experienced all through life is that God is as much Lord of change as of permanence. The sun rises every day as a sign of God's constancy, but the time it rises changes each morning. As for God's people, day by day and generation after generation we make mistakes and inflict pain, so we constantly face the need to change direction and open ourselves to new beginnings. And when we look beyond our own lives, to reach out to the needs of others, and to help "cultivate and tend" the whole of creation, we know that we as church must change and renew, in order to do God's work day by day in a rapidly changing world.

What changes will occur in the church? As our previous letters show, we emphasize changes introduced and foreshadowed by Vatican II. We think in particular of the power of the Spirit waiting to be awakened in us lay members of the church. In summing up the 1987 Synod on the laity, John Paul II spelled out a vision which we share: "The eyes of faith behold a wonderful scene: that of a countless number of lay people, both women and men, busy at work in their daily life and activity, oftentimes far from view and quite unacclaimed by the world, unknown to the world's great personages but nonetheless looked upon in love by the Father, untiring labourers who work in the Lord's vineyard. Confident and steadfast through the power of God's grace, these are the humble yet great builders of the kingdom of God in history" (CL, 17). There are a billion of us Catholic laity. Our particular task is "to restore to creation all of its original value" (CL, 14). The face of the earth will indeed be renewed when we really wake up to the power we have in the Spirit.

Mae and Bernard

Dear Mae and Bernard,

It has been said that one of the greatest forces in history is an idea that has come of age. Vatican II opened the church to new ideas whose time had come. We are changing from a church of culture, doing things because they were "always done that way." We are becoming a church of choice, each member responding personally to the person of Christ alive among us members of his body, who are the church, through the gift of the Holy Spirit which Christ sent from the Godhead. Every human being stands ultimately under the authority of truth. Our faith is challenged to become a mature and active personal relationship with God. No longer can our faith be mostly a matter of memorized answers to a few catechism questions.

We take seriously now what Pius XII said about the need for public opinion in the church itself; what John XXIII said with his heart, about being brothers and sisters seeking peace through compassion and solidarity; what Paul VI said about dialogue, respect for the other as other, and about solidarity among nations; what John Paul II says about our vocation to build a civilization of love.

A new image of church

A quiet revolution is going on, a revolution of values. The fulminations of some in authority cannot stop it because it affects more than the structures over which they have control – but no longer perfect or fully effective control.

I welcomed Vatican II because I had been prepared for it by a number things. My personal experience has been positive since the council. I have been awakening to the increasing significance and value of what was happening there. Chief among all these influences has been that of key lay people. I have worked and associated personally with them, and learned to listen to them with deep respect sometimes tinged with awe.

Pat Brady did a doctoral dissertation in philosophy on what Vatican II achieved in the diocese of Victoria. She summed it up by saying that the circle had replaced the pyramid as image of church, and that a new mystical dimension was emerging in lay spirituality and social action.

Quebec had its own "quiet revolution," shaped to an important extent by the lay people who had experienced Cardijn's Catholic Action pedagogy – "see – judge – act" – for mature lay Christianity. That movement has since become significantly politicized, and the bishops in Quebec have had the prophetic prudence and wisdom to dialogue with it instead of seeking to repress it.

The people of the Philippines also showed the world the power of massive popular, peaceful resistance, also guided by lay people trained in Catholic Action. It developed according to their own local style and culture, with the backing of their cardinal and their bishops. I witnessed the results when I attended the 1996 World Youth Conference in Manila.

Leading women theologians and Scripture scholars are helping me understand more fully the significance of new ideas summed up in the term feminism, in the sense in which Joan Chittister presents it in *Heart of Flesh: A Feminist Spirituality for Women and Men.* Elizabeth Schüssler-Fiorenza's *In Memory of Her,* and other works, taught me how to be intellectually critical about the systems that govern our ways of thinking. Elizabeth Johnson has summed up cogently what several scholars have said about God from this new perspective. I find her books *She Who Is* and *Friends of God and Prophets* truly inspiring. Other women ministering to the poor and marginalized helped me appreciate the "quiet revolution" of the heart. Men and women, who each day dance and move through the world's mess and marvel, have helped me to appreciate how our bodies are having an impact on creation, as David Suzuki, with Amanda McConnell, remind us in the book, *The Sacred Balance: Rediscovering our Place in Nature.* All this is part of the spiritual sacrifice we offer to God when we bring our bodies, our total selves, to celebrate the liturgy.

Gustavo Gutiérrez and other Latin American scholars introduced me to the biblical and intellectual foundations of what is now called liberation theology. I recognized there forces similar to those which animated Cardijn and others in Catholic Action. Canadian pioneers in this latter domain laid solid foundations for what eventually became our own version of liberation theology, as expressed in the social teachings and initiatives of the Canadian Conference of Catholic Bishops.

I must also mention the theological giants who helped to shape Vatican II. They nurtured the many bishops who arrived at the council as "substantialists" and left it as "existentialists." They enriched me, and helped to formulate the insights that were growing in my heart as well as my mind.

Add to all this my discovery of the ancient "wisdom of the heart," which emerges fully from the example of Jesus, as in the Sermon on the Mount, but which had atrophied in most parts of the church. Researching with Enneagram leaders and reading scholars such as Robin Amis (*A Different Christianity*) have led me to appreciate how the rift between the Eastern and Western parts of Christianity can be described as a split between the heart and the head.

In its turn, the Enlightenment enriched us by opening the doors to modern scientific and technological achievements. It also impoverished us, however, because of its focus on rationality. It reduced the three centres of intelligence – body, heart and head – almost exclusively to the head. It viewed the world as a machine. The determinism which accompanied that vision made for a concept of our universe that was centred on the human as dominating exploiter instead of compassionate partner. Modern science has a severely reduced notion of the human being. The global market economy, propelled by science and technology, rides rough-shod over people and cultures, marginalizing them as people and despising their cherished values and centuries-old forms of wisdom. The results are all too obvious in the arms race, the chemical poisoning of our environment, and economism as the dominant ideology or religion. Rediscovering the true nature of the *humanum* now comes into focus. Anthropology is central today.

The quiet revolution now affecting our church needs to take all this into account. *Aggiornamento*, renewal, conversion, and new structures must continue to grow. So must pneumatology (our study of the ways of the Spirit) and ecclesiology (our study of the nature of the church). All this is challenged by the depth of the transformation now affecting us all in irreversible ways.

Hope remains, however, because we believe all of this is part of the unfolding of the reign of God through the power of the Spirit of the Risen Lord. So we remain as confident as we are realistic.

What we have written here is one small effort to enrich the dialogue going on in the church, by adding the voices of a couple and their bishop-friend sharing insights from their pastoral experiences across the 36 years since the close of Vatican II.

+ *Remi*

Notes

Chapter 1

For knowledge of Vatican II, the 16 texts promulgated by the council are essential reading. Most important are the four *constitutions* – the church, the church in the modern world, revelation, and the liturgy. The nine *decrees* deal with the media of communication, the office of bishops, the renewal of religious orders, the training of priests, the ministry and life of priests, the lay apostolate, missionary activity, the Catholic Eastern churches, and ecumenism. There are also three *declarations*, about religious freedom, Christian education, and relations with non-Christian religions.

The earliest English edition of the texts is *The Documents of Vatican II,* with notes and commentaries by Catholic, Protestant and Orthodox authorities, Walter M. Abbott SJ, general editor, co-published by Guild Press, America Press, and Association Press, 1966. The commentaries make this book particularly helpful. For our quotations from council texts, we used the more recent two-volume *Vatican Council II: Conciliar and Post Conciliar Documents,* edited by Austin Flannery OP, 1988 revised edition, published by Eerdmans, 1988. In this edition, each of the 16 Vatican II texts is accompanied by a large collection of post-council instructions, decrees and statements from Vatican offices concerning the implementation of Vatican II. This edition is available on CD ROM, (IBM 386SX or equivalent), by Dominican Publications, Dublin; Costello Publishing, Northport, Long Island; and Liturgical Press, Collegeville, Minnesota. There is also a 1998 edition of *Vatican II: Conciliar and Post Conciliar Documents.* A 1998 enlarged edition of *Vatican II:*

More Post Conciliar Documents was being prepared as we wrote these notes. There is also a 1996 inclusive-language edition of the 16 council documents: *Vatican Council II: Constitutions, Decrees, Declarations,* Northport, Costello and Dublin, Dominican Publications, 1996. The council texts are also on the Vatican website: http://www.vatican.va

There are by now hundreds of other books and articles about Vatican II, including the diaries and memoirs of many participants. The most recent extensive review of how the council was organized and conducted, including details of debates and votes, is the five-volume *History of Vatican II,* edited by G. Alberigo and J. A. Komonchak, co-published in the U.S. and Belgium by Orbis/Peeters. Volume 1 on the preparatory period appeared in 1995, and Volume 2 on the 1962 opening session in 1997. Volumes 3 to 5, dealing with the council's second, third and fourth sessions, are in preparation. We have used Volumes 1 and 2 for checking our own recollections and files. The quotation from the Tardini letter comes from page 94 of Volume 1.

For the work of Cardinal Suenens, including his recollections of John XXIII, we depended on *Memories & Hopes,* by L.-J. Cardinal Suenens, Veritas, Dublin, 1992. Our direct borrowings, in the order used, come from pages 152, 112, 65, and 106-107 in Suenens' book. The Cardinal Hume quotation comes from page 427 in *Restoration and Renewal: The Church in the Third Millennium,* by Joseph F. Eagan, Sheed and Ward, 1995. Eagan's book is especially useful for its study of what has happened to Vatican II decisions and what new issues have arisen since the council.

For English and French essays about Canadian participation in Vatican II, see *L'Eglise canadienne et Vatican II,* Gilles Routhier, editor, Fides, 1997. It includes a review in English by Michael A. Fahey of the suggestions for Vatican II's agenda made by English-speaking bishops, and members of Catholic theology schools in Canada, in reply to John XXIII's request for their ideas. Routhier's French essay reviews the suggestions by bishops in Quebec dioceses.

The quotation from John Paul II about celebrating the millennium is from No. 20 of his apostolic letter, *Tertio Millennio, Adveniente,* in *Origins,* CNS documentary Service, Nov. 24, 1994, p. 407.

Chapter 2

The Avery Dulles checklist of Vatican II accomplishments is summarized by Eagan on pages 38-40 in *Restoration and Renewal* (see Chapter 1 notes). See also: Avery Dulles, *The Reshaping of Catholicism: Current Challenges in the Theology of the Church*, San Francisco, Harper & Row, 1988.

The standard English reference for laws of the Western church is *The Code of Canon Law*, new revised English edition, HarperCollins, London, 1997.

Chapter 3

The impact of modern technology on people has been a concern of all three of us throughout our adult lives. The results of our reading, study and reflection are spread throughout this chapter. We also borrow from the work of others. A good account of the continuing debate about Stephen Hawking's "big bang" theory of the origin of the universe appeared in *The Guardian Weekly*, March 1,1998, pages 9 and 12. The Toronto *Globe & Mail* reported January 9, 1998 on the 1997 reports to the American Astronomical Society that the universe may expand forever. Our borrowings in this chapter from Diarmuid O'Murchu appear on pages 95, 28, and 179 of his book *Quantum Theology*, Crossroad, New York, 1997.

A feature in *The Guardian Weekly* for April 26, 1998, page 31, alerted us to Stephen Hawking's March 1998 White House talk, as well as to Michio Kaku's book, *Visions*, Oxford Press, 1998, and Edward O. Wilson's book, *Consilience*, Little, Brown, 1998. The same source introduced the differing opinions of Lee Silver, and his book, *Remaking Eden*, Toronto, Hearst Book Group, 1998. We cite Christopher Dewdney's views from his April 1998 *Saturday Night* magazine article, "after deep blue," page 27, adapted from his book, *Last Flesh*, HarperCollins, 1998.

Michael Barber's pessimistic view of religion was reported in *The Tablet*, London, March 28, 1998, page 425. We borrow extensively from *The Biotech Century*, by Jeremy Rifkin, Tarcher/Putnam, New York, 1998, including: page 170, about Francis Bacon; page 236, about the kind of debate about science needed today; page 117, about Theodore Roosevelt's views on eugenics; page 127, about Paul Popenoe's article, "The German Sterilization Law," in the July 1934 issue of the *Journal of Heredity*.

We note the views of U.S. theologian George H. Tavard about Teilhard de Chardin, page 251, and about the future of the church, page 249, in his book, *The Church, Community of Salvation*, Collegeville, Liturgical Press, 1992. For more on the views of Thomas Berry and Brian Swimme, see their book, *The Universe Story*, San Francisco, Harper, 1992. We refer to Jennifer Cobb, *Cybergrace: The Search for God in the Digital World*, New York, Crown, 1998; and to Ken Wilber, *The Marriage of Sense and Soul: Integrating Science and Religion*, New York, Random House, 1998. John Paul II's quotation about science and religion is found on page M13 in Rober John Russell, William R. Stoeger and George V. Coyne, editors, *Physics, Philosophy and Theology: A Common Quest for Understanding*. Vatican/Notre Dame, IA, Notre Dame University Press, 1988.

Chapter 4

As in Chapter Three, our own files and recollections provide the bulk of the information in this chapter. Our attention was drawn to new biographical information about Alfred Kinsey by James H. Jones' article, "Dr. Yes," in *The New Yorker* magazine, August 25 & September 1, 1997, pages 99-113. Our analysis of the development of advertising, marketing and consumerism depends for many of its details on *The End of Work*, by Jeremy Rifkin, New York, Tarcher/Putnam, 1995. In this chapter our borrowings are from his book at page 42, about utopian visions in our past; page 55, about our new cyberspace visions; pages 19-21, about the engineering of consumption, including Hazel Kyrk's arguments (cited by Rifkin from her own book, *A Theory of Consumption*, Boston, 1923, p. 278), and page 19, about post-war consumption levels.

The quotation from *The Guardian Weekly* about the growing poverty gap is from the issue for July 28, 1996. The quotation from *When Corporations*

Rule the World, by David C. Kortens, West Hartford, Kumarian, 1995, is from pages 11-12.

Pope John Paul II's apostolic letter *Christifideles Laici,* summing up the 1987 synod on the laity, is cited extensively, as in (CL, 2), and so on. Similarly, Paul VI's apostolic letter, *Evangelii Nuntiandi* (EN), reviewing the results of the 1974 synod on evangelization, is referenced here as (EN). In the *Catechism of the Catholic Church,* New York, Doubleday Image Book, 1995, the three references to *Christifideles Laici* are footnotes 304 and 305 in Article 828 about canonization, and footnote 432 in Article 899, where John Paul II quotes Pius XII about the role of the laity.

The quotation we use describing the church as a "God-given, Christ-centred, Spirit-empowered community of salvation" is from page 258 of Tavard's book described in our Chapter 3 notes. The quotation by Clare Short is from her article "Why I take heart," in *The Tablet,* London, September 6 , 1997, page 1119. Our borrowings from *Culture, Spirituality and Economic Development,* by William F. Ryan SJ, International Development Research Centre, Ottawa, 1995, come, in turn, from his pages 41-42, 42, 44, 45 and 15-16. The quotation from Archbishop Orlando Quevedo also was reported in *The Tablet,* May 30, 1998, page 696.

Anne Alexander's book, *The Antigonish Movement: Moses Coady and Adult Education Today,* was published in 1997 in Toronto by Thompson Educational Publishing, Inc.

Chapter 5

The quotation from *The Luck of Ginger Coffey,* by Brian Moore, McClelland and Stewart, Toronto, 1972, is on pages 43-44.

We refer to the collection of John Paul II's Wednesday audience talks about marriage and family life. They are now published in one book, John Paul II. *Theology of the Body: Human Love in the Divine Plan,* Boston, Pauline Books, 1997. The reference to a husband committing adultery with his own wife is on page 157, from his October 1, 1980 audience talk.

Regarding how animals are "programmed" by sexual instincts and humans are not, Sociologist Peter Berger has written: "The ethnological evidence shows that, in sexual matters, man is capable of almost anything." See *The Social Construction of Reality,* by Peter Berger, Doubleday, 1967, page 49.

Chapter 6

Much of the background material for this chapter comes from our personal files, recollections and reflections. For the full text of Grisewood's historical review of church views about sexuality, see "On human sexuality," by Harman Grisewood, *The Tablet,* London, March 1, 1997, pages 286- 287.

Because the archives of Paul VI's birth-control commission are still closed, secondary sources must be depended on for information about its work. We start with Cardinal Suenens, who was involved with the commission at all stages of its work. In his *Memories and Hopes,* Suenens recalls on page 145 that the history of this commission and of its debates has been revealed in detail by Robert Blair Kaiser in his book, *The Encyclical Which Never Was,* Sheed and Ward, London, 1987. "His facts are historically correct; his book is largely based on the personal papers provided by one of the commission members, Mgr. Ruess, auxiliary bishop of Mayence," Suenens affirms. Kaiser also has an earlier book about the commission: *The Politics of Sex and Religion,* Leaven Press, Kansas City, 1985. The latter work is used as background for *Turning Point* by Robert McClory, Crossroad, New York, 1995, which updates Kaiser's work by adding details supplied by Patty Crowley of Chicago. She and her late husband were one of the three couples added to the commission for the latter stages of its work. The quotations we use from McClory appear on pages 105, 105-106, 105, and 181-2 in his book.

For more scientific details about the SERENA natural family planning method, see *Planning Your Family the S-T Way,* by Suzanne Parenteau-Carreau MD, SERENA-Canada, Ottawa, 1987; and *Love and Life,* fourth edition, SERENA-Canada, Ottawa, 1989.

The quotation from McKeen and Wong appears on page 154 in their book, *The Relationship Garden.*

Chapter 7

All material in this chapter is drawn from our personal files, recollections and reflections.

Chapter 8

Bernard Daly's articles from the four sessions of Vatican II can be found in the *Canadian Catholic Conference Information Service,* Volumes 8 to 11, CCCB Archives, Ottawa.

We also refer to Thich Nhat Hanh's book, *Being Peace,* by Parallax Press, Berkeley, CA, 1996.

Chapter 9

The quotation in the last letter in this chapter comes from "Liturgical Prayer," by Joyce A. Zimmerman CPPS, *The Collegeville Pastoral Dictionary of Biblical Theology,* Carroll Stuhlmueller, editor, Liturgical Press, 1996, page 915. We also refer in a general way to Rabbi Joshua Abraham Heschel's 1951 book, *The Sabbath,* published by The Noonday Press.

Chapter 10

The first letter in this chapter refers to *On Consulting the Faithful in Matters of Doctrine,* by John Henry Cardinal Newman, John Coulson, editor, Sheed and Ward, New York, 1961.

The working paper (*Instrumentum laboris*) for the 1997 Synod special assembly for America is *Encounter with the Living Jesus Christ: The Way to Conversion, Communion and Solidarity in America,* Vatican City, Libreria Editrice Vaticana, 1997. We also refer to the *Instruction on Certain Questions regarding the Collaboration of the Non-ordained Faithful in the Sacred Ministry of Priest,* Vatican City, Libreria Editrice Vaticana, 1997.

242

We also refer to Edward Schillebeeckx's *Ministry: Leadership in the Community of Jesus Christ,* New York, Crossroad, 1981; and to Raymond Brown's *The Churches the Apostles Left Behind,* New York, Paulist Press, 1984. The book by Peter A. Botsis is *What Is Orthodoxy,* Athens/Meteora, Monastery of Varlaam, 1997. The paper by J. M. R. Tillard is "The Mission of the Bishop of Rome: What is Essential, What is Expected?" *Ecumenical Trends,* January 1998, pages 1-10.

Chapter 11

Archbishop Carey's remarks about inter-communion, and Cardinal Hume's reply, are reported in *The Tablet,* London, May 2, 1998, page 570. The list of suggestions by the Asian bishops regarding values to be found in other religions is reported in *The Tablet,* May 2, 1998, page 571. Paul VI's formula for approving Vatican II texts is cited on page 96 and elsewhere in *The Documents of Vatican II,* edited by Walter M. Abbott, New York, Guild Press/American Press, 1996. "Interreligious Dialogue and the Jesuit Mission" by Thomas Michel SJ, appears in *The Review for Religious,* November/December, 1997, pages 605-613. We also refer to John Henry Newman's *On Consulting the Faithful in Matters of Doctrine,* John Coulson, editor, New York, Sheed & Ward, 1961.

Epilogue

Books mentioned in our Epilogue include Joan Chittister, *Heart of Flesh: A Feminist Theology for Women and Men,* Ottawa, Novalis, 1998; Elizabeth Schüssler-Fiorenza's *In Memory of Her;* Elizabeth A. Johnson's *She Who Is* and *Friends of Gods and Prophets: A Feminist Theological Reading of the Communion of Saints,* New York, Continuum; and Ottawa, Novalis, 1998; and the book by David Suzuki with Amanda McConnell, *The Sacred Balance: Rediscovering Our Place in Nature,* Vancouver, Greystone Books and Toronto: Douglas & McIntyre, 1997.

For the most recent statements of the Canadian bishops, contact the Canadian Conference of Catholic Bishops, 90 Parent Avenue, Ottawa, ON K1N 7B1. Earlier documents are in two volumes edited by Edward F. Sheridan: *Do Justice: The Social Teachings of the Canadian Catholic Bishops (1945-1986)*, Sherbrooke, QC, Editions Paulines; Toronto, Jesuit Centre for Social Faith and Justice, 1986; and *Love Kindness,* Montreal: Editions Paulines; Toronto, Jesuit Centre for Social Faith and Justice, 1991.

Glossary

These glossary entries are drawn when possible from Vatican II texts, *The Code of Canon Law* and the *Catechism of the Catholic Church*, and various encyclopedias and dictionaries. The Glossary in Joseph F. Eagan's *Restoration and Renewal: The Church in the Third Millennium*, Kansas City: Sheed & Ward, 1995, was helpful. The bracket after the term indicates where it first occurs in our book (introduction or chapter).

Aggiornamento (Introduction): Italian word meaning literally "bringing up to today," and usually translated as updating or renewal. *Giorno* is Italian for "day."

Archeparch (7): The title of an archbishop in the Eastern Catholic rites. *Eparch* is their term for bishop.

Bretton Woods (4): Representatives of 44 nations met in Bretton Woods, New Hampshire, July 1-22, 1944, to agree on a framework for the post-World War II global economy. The World Bank and International Monetary Fund were set up then, and the General Agreement on Tariffs and Trade (GATT) soon after.

breviary (1): Official daily prayer of the church. See "Divine Office" below.

cardinal (1): Cardinals are ordained men named by the pope to be a special small college to assist him in a variety of tasks. One of their special functions is to meet to elect a new pope from among their own members.

cassock (1): A close-fitting garment with long sleeves, fastened up to the neck and reaching to the heels. Worn at church services by clerics and sometimes by assisting laymen. Cassocks were once required daily attire for clerics in the Latin rite, but since Vatican II worn less frequently and rarely as street dress. Usually black, but white, purple, scarlet and other colours are used. Also called *soutane*.

Cathars (6): A widespread sect of the Middle Ages, who believed that Satan, the evil God, is lord of the world, especially of the outward human being and of the flesh, which holds humans captive under the law of sin and desire. Therefore, they considered everything sexually begotten to be impure.

Catholic social teaching (4): The body of teachings by Catholic church leaders about social relationships in the light of biblical principles, dealing in particular with questions such as human rights. The term is generally applied to teaching beginning with Pope Leo XIII's 1891 encyclical letter, *Rerum Novarum*, about capital and labour. It includes the writings of his successors, Vatican II texts, and statements by bishops in many countries.

celibacy (6): The renunciation of sexual contact. In the Latin or Western Catholic church, celibacy is required of candidates for the priesthood. *Permanent deacons*, reinstituted since Vatican II, may not marry after ordination; a married deacon may not remarry after the loss of his wife, and a deacon who is single at ordination must remain so. Eastern Catholics have married priests; like the Orthodox, they ordain married men as priests and deacons, but bishops must be celibate.

charismatic movement (2): A movement of church members who promote awareness of the gifts of the Holy Spirit, and who themselves may experience special gifts, such as joy in prayer and sometimes the ability to heal or to speak in tongues. The word charismatic comes from *charism*, from the Greek for gift or talent.

Christian Family Movement (CFM) (1): A movement of Catholic couples who met regularly in small groups with a chaplain to observe social conditions, judge them by gospel values, and decide on group actions. This "like-to-like" apostolate, using the see-judge-act method, was the basic form of Catholic Action movement which aimed at increasing lay involvement in church and society. CFM flourished in Canada and the U.S. especially from the mid-1950s until the mid-1970s.

Code of Canon Law (2): The collection of laws in the Western Catholic church, promulgated in 1983 after an updating of the previous 1917 code. There is a similar but separate code of laws for the Eastern Catholic churches.

collegiality (2): The teaching, highlighted by Vatican II, that the bishops are successors of the twelve apostles and as such form a *college* who, with the pope, have full authority in the Catholic church. Collegiality is fully exercised in an ecumenical or general council such as Vatican II.

cosmos (3): From the Greek for *world,* cosmos refers to the entire universe. Thus, *cosmology* is the study of the universe, its origin, history, make-up and functioning, and is sometimes used to refer to one's worldview or understanding of the whole world.

Counter-Reformation (1): The effort to reform the Catholic church that began after the Protestant Reformation, was given a framework by the Council of Trent (1545-1563), and carried out in following centuries, especially in Europe.

Cursillo (8): From the Spanish for "short course." In Catholic circles the term is applied to intensive short courses in Christian living, usually conducted over a weekend. An organization for giving these courses has grown up since Vatican II.

diocesan priests (2): Priests under the authority of the bishop of a diocese, as distinct from *religious priests* whose superior is the head of the religious community or order of which they are members.

Divine Office (8): Also called the *Liturgy of the Hours,* or the *breviary.* An official prayer of the church, consisting mainly of prayers, readings and songs from Holy Scripture. Formerly mainly the obligatory daily personal prayer in Latin for those ordained or living under religious vows. Now in the vernacular languages since Vatican II, and increasingly used also by laity for daily prayer in private or small groups.

evangelic counsels (2): Traditional name for the three vows, chastity, obedience and poverty, taken by persons entering consecrated religious life. Also sometimes called the *states of perfection*, to indicate perfect or total dedication to following Christ.

Galileo affair (3): Galileo, an Italian astronomer who died in 1642, was condemned by church authorities for teaching that the earth revolves around the sun, contrary to the interpretation of the Bible held at that time. John Paul II has formally exonerated Galileo.

genetic engineering (3): A general term for various techniques for exploring, altering and manipulating the genes as basic elements in the makeup of all living beings.

Gnostics (6): Believers in the theory, prominent the first centuries after Christ, that matter, including the human body, is both the product and source of evil. Gnostic groups were convinced that they had secret, mystical, revealed knowledge. From the third century, they were largely replaced by the closely-related *Manichaean* movement (see below).

Holy Office (10): The name formerly given to the present Vatican Congregation for the Doctrine of the Faith, the watchdog of correct teaching. Formerly also called the Inquisition.

Holy Spirit (Introduction): The name for the third person (with the Father and the Son) of the Holy Trinity. Also formerly usually called the Holy Ghost.

infallibility (1): The Catholic doctrine defined by Vatican I (1869-1870), which says that, by virtue of his office, the pope is free from error (infallible) "when, as chief shepherd and teacher of all Christ's faithful, with the duty of strengthening his [brothers and sisters] in the faith, he proclaims by definite act a doctrine to be held concerning faith or morals."

intercommunion (11) The practice of offering the eucharist, or holy communion, to persons not formally members of the host church.

intrinsic evil (6): The teaching that some acts are always gravely sinful, regardless of any circumstances.

Jansenists (6): Followers of Cornelius Jansen, who lived from 1585 to 1638 and, for a few years before his death, was bishop of Ypres, now in Belgium. As a theologian, he battled contemporary Jesuits and others whom he accused of lacking rigour in their teaching of faith and morals, and especially about sexual morality. Jansenists believed in the utter sinfulness and powerlessness of human beings. Despite loss of papal favour, their communities flourished in France, Holland, Germany and northern Italy, and had influence as harsh perfectionists even into the early twentieth century.

Kodaly (10): A philosophy of teaching music, which involves the total personality and all the senses, developed by the Hungarian composer, teacher and musicologist, Zoltan Kodaly (1882-1967).

lay auditors (1): Over the course of the four sessions of Vatican II from the fall of 1962 to the fall of 1965, some 50 lay women and men were invited to attend the council. At the daily plenary debates, they could listen but not speak; hence *auditors*, from the Latin *audire*, to hear. They could speak at meetings of the small working commissions or committees to which they were assigned.

limbo (7): In pre-Vatican II theology, the name used for a supposed region on the border of heaven and hell, the abode after death of unbaptized infants and of the just who died before Christ's coming. From *limbus*, the Latin for edge or border.

lineamenta (10): The questions sent by the Vatican secretariat for synods to all the bishops to canvass their opinions on a proposed topic for a Synod of Bishops. From the Latin for line, outline or sketch.

Loyal Orange Lodge (1): The Protestant fraternity formed in 1795 in Ireland, named after William of Orange, the late seventeenth-century king who conquered Ireland for England. Dedicated to Protestant ascendancy, Orange lodges were organized also in Canada and were active until the 1950s, mostly in Ontario cities where their annual parades were often the occasions of clashes with Catholics – as is still the case in Northern Ireland.

magisterium (2): The teaching authority or function in the Catholic church, officially the pope and bishops and theologians loyal to him. From the Latin title *magister* for master teacher or one having authority.

Manichaeans (6): Prominent towards the close of the third century, they believed in a rigid dualism, in which good is light and evil is darkness. They identified the sensual aspects of human life with evil, including every gratification of sexual desire and, hence, also marriage.

motu proprio (10): The term for an administrative act by the pope, such as his 1965 document establishing the constitution for the Synod of Bishops (see below). From the Latin, meaning literally "by his own decision."

Paraclete (2): Another name given to the Holy Spirit, third person of the divine trinity, from the Greek word for *advocate* or *intercessor.*

Patriarchates (10): The five great centres of Rome, Constantinople, Alexandria, Antioch and Jerusalem, whose bishops since the sixth century have been called *patriarch*, after the Greek word for "father who rules." The pope is the patriarch of the Western church. In the Orthodox churches today, patriarch is the usual title for the bishop with authority in the churches in a *patriarchate* made up of churches in a country or region.

principle of synodality (10): After Vatican II, Paul VI called for a variety of synods to be celebrated in the Western church. The *principle of synodality* is the theological basis for a synod, in particular the recognition that the Spirit gives to all the baptized gifts which can be expressed at a synod. This principle favours the circle as a symbol for a church in which all share, rather than a pyramid or vertical model, dominated from on top.

rites (10): The formal practice or procedure for celebrating the liturgy. In the Catholic church today, besides the Roman rite followed by the majority (now in many local languages), some 19 other rites are used. Predominant among them are the various rites of Eastern Catholics; but there are also approved local practices, such as the Ambrosian rite used in Milan, Italy, in memory of St. Ambrose.

RCIA (7): Rite of Christian Initiation for Adults. Vatican II decreed the restoration of a *catechumenate* – a period of preparation for baptism. The RCIA is the step-by-step process of this catechumenate, by which adults who wish to be baptized are accompanied in their journey towards baptism by members of a local church community. The program is also followed by some baptized people who either wish to join the Catholic church formally or to enter into its way of life more fully.

rubrics: (2): The words said by priests celebrating the eucharist and administering sacraments are printed in black, with directives in red alongside for things to be done, gestures, movements and the like. These actions and practices came to be called rubrics, from the Latin for "red," and *rubricism*, or inordinate attention to gestures and movements, indicates a preoccupation with lesser aspects of the liturgical ceremony.

"subsists" (2): This is the term settled on by Vatican II to describe how "the sole church of Christ" is to be found in the Catholic church, although "many elements of sanctification and of truth are found outside its visible confines." The Vatican II *Constitution of the Church*, Article 8, contains a full discussion of this term.

Synod of Bishops (4): Instituted by Paul VI in 1965, the Synod of Bishops is a gathering of some 300 representatives of the world's Catholic bishops, convened by the pope (usually every three years) to discuss a topic of his choice and to give him their advice on it. The name *synod*, from the Greek for "council," is also given to meetings of priests and other Catholics called by a local bishop to deal with matters in a diocese.

Theophany (7): From the Greek, meaning literally "the showing (or revealing) of God." The term is used for events, such as the baptism of Jesus, when God was directly revealed, as by a voice saying, "This is my beloved son. . . ."

Trinity (2): See *Triune God*, below.

Triune God (9): From the Latin for "three in one," another term for the doctrine of three divine persons in the one God. Three articles of the Apostles' Creed speak in turn of Father, Son and Holy Spirit. In Christian faith, God is not "a solitary entity" or "an agent acting in three episodes," and God is not "three people." God is one and God is three. In God there are three ways or modes of being, and anything said of one is said in relation to the other two. God is the mystery of relationship and communion.

Vatican (1): Vatican City is a small sovereign state located inside the city of Rome. The term *Vatican* is used in a limited sense in this book to refer to the central administrative offices of the Catholic church, also called *curial offices* or simply the *curia*, from the Latin for administrative division or court.

Bibliography

Chapters 1 and 2 on Vatican Council II

Abbott, Walter M., ed. *Documents of Vatican II: With Notes and Commentaries by Catholic, Protestant and Orthodox Authorities.* New York: America Press, 1966.

Alberigo, Guiseppe, and Joseph A. Komonchak, eds. *History of Vatican II.* Maryknoll, NY: Orbis; Leuven: Peeters, Volume 1, 1995; Volume 2, 1997.

Congar, Yves. *Lay People in the Church: A Study for a Theology of Laity.* London: Bloomsbury, 1957.

Daly, Bernard M. *Remembering for Tomorrow: A History of the Canadian Conference of Catholic Bishops, 1943-1993.* Ottawa: CCCB Publications Service, 1995.

de Chardin, Pierre Teilhard. *The Divine Milieu: An Essay of the Interior Life.* Re-issue, San Francisco: Harper Collins, 1989.

Dulles, Avery. *The Reshaping of Catholicism: Current Challenges in the Theology of the Church.* San Francisco: Harper and Row, 1988.

_____. *Models of Church.* Expanded edition, New York: Image Books, 1991.

_____. *Models of Revelation.* Maryknoll, NY: Orbis, 1994.

Eagan, Joseph F. *Restoration and Renewal: The Church in the Third Millennium.* Kansas City: Sheed and Ward, 1995.

Fagin, Gerald M., ed., with Stephen Duffy, Avery Dulles, George Lindbeck, Gregory Baum, and Francine Cardman. *Vatican II: Open Questions and New Horizons.* Wilmington, DE: Michael Glazier Inc., 1984.

Flannery, Austin, ed. *Vatican Council II: The Conciliar and Post-Conciliar Documents.* Revised edition, two volumes, Grand Rapids, Mich.: Eerdmans, 1988.

_____. *Vatican Council II: The Conciliar and Post-Conciliar Documents.* Revised edition, Northport: Costello Publishing; Collegeville: Liturgical Press, 1992. (Volume 1 available on CD-ROM, IBM 386SX or equivalent.)

_____. *Vatican II: Constitutions, Decrees, Declarations.* Inclusive language edition, Northport: Costello Publishing; Dublin: Dominican Publications, 1996.

_____. *Vatican II: Conciliar and Post-Conciliar Documents.* Northport: Costello Publishing; Dublin: Dominican Publications, 1998.

_____. *Vatican II: More Post-Conciliar Documents.* Enlarged edition, Northport: Costello Publishing; Dublin: Dominican Publications, 1998.

Hales, E. E. Y. *The Catholic Church in the Modern World: A Survey from the French Revolution to the Present.* Garden City, NY: Doubleday Image Books, 1960.

John Paul II. "On the Publication of the *Catechism of the Catholic Church*, prepared following the Second Vatican Ecumenical Council," in *Catechism of the Catholic Church.* New York: Doubleday Image Book, 1995, 1-7.

Leddy, Mary Jo, Remi J. De Roo, and Douglas Roche. *In the Eye of the Catholic Storm: The Church since Vatican II.* Toronto: Harper Perennial, 1992.

McEnroy, Carmel Elizabeth. *Guests in Their Own House: The Women of Vatican II.* New York: Crossroad, 1996.

Naud, André. *Un aggiornamento et son eclipse: La liberté de la pensée dans la foi et dans l'Eglise.* Montreal: Fides, 1996.

Newman, John Henry Cardinal. *The Idea of a University.* Garden City, NY: Image Books, 1959.

O'Malley, William J. *Why Be Catholic?* New York: Crossroad, 1993.

Roche, Douglas, and Remi J. De Roo. *Man to Man: A Frank Talk between a Layman and a Bishop.* Milwaukee: Bruce Publishing Co., 1969.

Routhier, Gilles, ed. *L'Eglise canadienne et Vatican II.* Montreal: Fides, 1997.

Suenens, Leo Joseph Cardinal. *Memories and Hopes.* Dublin: Veritas, 1992.

Tavard, George H. *The Church, Community of Salvation: An Ecumenical Ecclesiology.* Collegeville: Liturgical Press, 1992.

The Code of Canon Law. New revised English translation, London: Harper Collins, 1997.

Tillard, J. M. R. *Chair de l'Eglise, chair du Christ: Aux sources de l'ecclesiologie de communion.* Paris: Editions du Cerf, 1992.

Weakland, Rembert G. *Faith and the Human Enterprise: A Post-Vatican II Vision.* Maryknoll, NY: Orbis, 1992.

Website for Vatican: http://www.vatican.va for Documents of Vatican II

Chapter 3: New Science, New Cosmology, New Theology

Auel, Jean. *The Clan of the Cave Bear.* New York: Bantam Books, 1981.

Berry, Thomas. *The Human Presence within the Earth Community.* Sonoma, CA: Global Perspectives, 1988. (Audio series)

Boff, Leonardo. *Ecology and Liberation: A New Paradigm.* Maryknoll, NY: Orbis, 1995.

Brandt, Charles A. E. *Meditations from the Wilderness.* Toronto: Harper Collins, 1997.

Capra, Fritjof, and David Steindl-Rast. *Belonging to the Universe: Explorations on the Frontiers of Science and Spirituality.* San Francisco: Harper San Francisco, 1992.

Chabreuil, Patricia, and Fabien Chabreuil. *L'entreprise et ses collaborateurs par l'enneagramme: Guide pratique de l'enneagramme en enterprise.* Geneva: Editions Vivez Soleil SA, 1997.

Cobb, Jennifer. *Cybergrace: The Search for God in the Digital World.* New York: Crown, 1998.

Conlon, James. *Earth Story Sacred Story.* Mystic, CT: Twenty-Third Publications, 1994.

_____. *Pondering the Precipice: Soul Work for the New Millennium.* Leavington: Forest of Peace, 1998.

Dewdney, Christopher. *Last Flesh: Life in the Transhuman Era.* San Francisco: Harper Collins, 1998.

Gilmore, Robert. *Alice in Quantumland: An Allegory of Quantum Physics.* New York: Copernicus, 1995.

Gotch, Carol Ann, and David Walsh. *Soul Stuff: Reflections on Inner Work with the Enneagram.* Winnipeg: Inscape Publications, 1994.

Grant, George. *Technology and Justice.* Toronto: House of Anansi, 1986.

Hawking, Stephen. *A Brief History of Time: From the Big Bang to Black Holes.* New York: Bantam Books, 1988.

Hurley, Kathleen, and Theodorre Donson. *My Best Self: Using the Enneagram To Free the Soul.* San Francisco: Harper San Francisco, 1993.

Jack, Homer. *WCRP: A History of the World Conference on Religion and Peace.* New York: World Conference on Religion and Peace, 1993.

John Paul II, *Faith and Reason,* encyclical letter. Ottawa: CCCB Publication Service, 1998.

Kaku, Michio. *Visions: How Science Will Revolutionize the 21st Century.* New York: Doubleday, 1997.

Kovats, Alexandra. "A Cosmic Dance: The Cosmic Principles of Differentiation, Autopoeisis and Communion, and Their Implications for an Ecological Spirituality." Unpublished Doctoral Dissertation, 1997.

McFague, Sallie. *The Body of God: An Ecological Theology.* Minneapolis: Augsburg Fortress, 1993.

_____. *Super, Natural Christians: How We Should Love Nature.* Minneapolis: Fortress Press, 1997.

O'Murchu, Diarmuid. *Quantum Theology: Spiritual Implications of the New Physics.* New York: Crossroad, 1997.

Poupard, Paul Cardinal. *Après Galilee: Science et foi, nouveau dialogue.* Paris: Desclee de Brouwer, 1994.

Rifkin, Jeremy. *The Biotech Century: Harnessing the Gene and Remaking the World.* New York: Tarcher/Putnam, 1998.

Riso, Don Richard, and Russ Hudson. *Personality Types: Using the Enneagram for Self-Discovery.* Revised edition, New York: Houghton Mifflin, 1996.

Silver, Lee. *Remaking Eden.* Toronto: Hearst Book Group of Canada, 1998.

Suzuki, David, with Amanda McConnell. *The Sacred Balance: Rediscovering Our Place in Nature.* Vancouver: Douglas & McIntyre, 1997.

Swimme, Brian. *Canticle to the Cosmos.* Boulder, CO: Sounds True Audio, 1995. (Video and Audio Series)

_____. *The Hidden Heart of the Cosmos: Science, Religion and Cosmology.* Mill Valley, CA: Video Centre for the Story of the Universe, 1996.

Swimme, Brian, and Thomas Berry. *The Universe Story: From the Primordial Flaring Forth to the Ecozoic Era -- A Celebration of the Unfolding of the Cosmos.* San Francisco: Harper and Row, 1992.

_____. *The Universe Story.* San Francisco: Harper and Row, 1992.

Turok, Neil, ed. *Critical Dialogues in Cosmology.* Princeton: World Scientific Publishing Company, 1996. (June 24-26)

Wheatley, Margaret J. *Leadership and the New Science: Learning about Organization from an Orderly Universe.* San Francisco: Berrett-Koehler, 1994.

Wilber, Ken.. *Quantum Questions: Mystical Writings of the World's Great Physicists.* London/Boston: Shambhala, 1985.

_____. *A Brief History of Everything.* London/Boston: Shambhala, 1996.

_____. *The Marriage of Sense and Soul: Integrating Science and Religion.* New York: Random House, 1998.

Chapter 4: "All My Relations"

Alexander, Anne. *The Antigonish Movement: Moses Coady and Adult Education Today.* Toronto: Thompson Educational Publishing, Inc., 1997.

Beaudin, Michel. *Le pouvoir de l'argent et le développement solidaire.* Edited by Yvonne Bergeron and Guy Paiment. Quebec: Fides, 1997.

Cobb, John. *Sustaining the Common Good: A Christian Perspective on the Global Economy.* Cleveland: Pilgrim Press, 1994.

Daly, Herman E. *Beyond Growth: The Economics of Sustainable Development.* Boston: Beacon Press, 1996.

de Chardin, Pierre Teilhard. *The Phenomenon Of Man*. New York: Harper & Bros., 1959.

De Roo, Remi J. *Cries of Victims, Voice of God*. Ottawa: Novalis, 1986.

_____. *A cause de l'evangile: Un eveque parle de justice sociale*. Ottawa: Novalis, 1988.

Dorr, Donal. *The Social Justice Agenda: Justice, Ecology, Power and Church*. Maryknoll, NY: Orbis, 1991.

_____. *Option for the Poor: Catholic Social Teaching*. Revised edition, Dublin: Gill and Macmillan, 1992.

Durning, Alan. *How Much is Enough? The Consumer Society and the Future of the Earth*. New York: Norton, 1992.

Fox, Matthew. *The Reinvention Of Work: A New Vision Of Livelihood*. San Francisco: Harper San Francisco, 1995.

Goudzwaard, Bob, and Harry de Lange. *Beyond Poverty and Affluence: Towards a Canadian Economy of Care*. Toronto: University of Toronto Press, 1995.

Gutiérrez, Gustavo. *We Drink from Our Own Wells: A Spiritual Journey of a People*. Translated by Matthew J. O'Connell. Maryknoll, NY: Orbis, 1984.

Haq, Mahbub ul. "New Imperatives for the Human Society." 1994 Barbara Ward Lecture. Mexico City: Society for International Development, SID.

Hill, James H. "Dr. Yes." *The New Yorker*, August 25 & September 1, 1997.

John Paul II. *Centesimus Annus:The Social Teaching of the Church*. Sherbrooke, Que.: Editions Paulines, 1991.

Korten, David C. *When Corporations Rule the World*. West Hartford: Kumarian, 1995.

Kung, Hans. *Global Responsibility: In Search of a New World Ethic*. New York: Continuum, 1993.

Lind, Christopher, and Joe Mihevc. *Coalitions for Justice*. Ottawa: Novalis, 1994.

Mallea, Paula. *Aboriginal Law: Apartheid in Canada?* Brandon, Man.: Bearpaw Publishing, 1994.

Maracle, Lee. *Raven Song*. Vancouver: LPC In Book, 1992.

_____. *I Am Woman: A Native Perspective on Sociology and Feminism.* Vancouver: LPC In Book, 1996.

Rahner, Karl. *Christian in the Market Place.* New York: Sheed & Ward, 1966.

Reich, Robert. *The Work of Nations: Preparing Ourselves for 21st Century Capitalism.* New York: Random House, 1992.

Rifkin, Jeremy. *The End of Work.* New York: Tarcher/Putnam, 1995.

Roche, Douglas. *The Ultimate Evil: The Fight to Ban Nuclear Weapons.* Toronto: Lorimer & Co., 1997.

Ryan, William F. *Culture, Spirituality and Economic Development.* Ottawa: International Development Research Centre, 1995.

Saul, John Ralston. *Voltaire's Bastards: The Dictatorship of Reason in the West.* Toronto: Simon & Schuster, 1993.

_____. *The Unconscious Civilization.* Toronto: Simon & Schuster Trade, 1996.

Sheridan, Edward F., ed. *Do Justice: The Social Teaching of the Canadian Catholic Bishops, 1945-1986.* Sherbrooke, Que.: Editions Pauline; Toronto: Jesuit Centre for Social Faith and Justice, 1987.

_____. *Love Kindness: The Social Teaching of the Canadian Catholic Bishops, 1945-1986.* Montreal: Editions Paulines; Toronto: Jesuit Centre for Social Faith and Justice, 1991.

Chapter 5: Created Man and Woman

Berger, Peter. *The Social Construction Of Reality.* New York: Doubleday, 1967.

Chittister, Joan D. *Heart of Flesh: A Feminist Spirituality for Women and Men.* Grand Rapids, Mich.: Eerdmans; Ottawa: Novalis, 1998.

John Paul II. *Theology of the Body: Human Love in the Divine Plan.* Boston: St. Paul Editions, 1997.

McKeen, Jock, and Bennet Wong. *The Relationship Garden.* Gabriola Island, BC: PD Publishing, 1996.

Moore, Brian. *The Luck Of Ginger Coffey.* Toronto: McClelland & Stewart, 1972.

Pagels, Elaine. *Adam, Eve and the Serpent.* New York: Vintage Books, 1989.

Ruether, Rosemary. *Gaia and God: An Ecofeminist Theology on Earth Healing.* San Francisco: Harper San Francisco, 1992.

Spretnak, Charlene. *States Of Grace: Spiritual Grounding in the Post-Modern Age.* San Francisco: Harper San Francisco, 1992.

Winter, Miriam Therese. *Woman Witness: Women of the Hebrew Scriptures,* Part 2. New York: Crossroad, 1992.

_____. *Woman Word: Women of the New Testament.* New York: Crossroad, 1992.

_____. *Woman Wisdom: A Feminist Lectionary and Psalter - Women of the Hebrew Scriptures,* Part 1. New York: Crossroad, 1993.

Chapter 6: Intimacy and Family

Kaiser, Robert B. *The Politics of Sex and Religion.* Kansas City: Leaven Press, 1985.

_____. *The Encyclical that Never Was.* London: Sheed and Ward, 1987.

McClory, Robert. *The Turning Point.* Crossroad: New York, 1995.

Parenteau-Carreau, Suzanne. *Planning Your Family the S-T Way.* Ottawa: SERENA-Canada, 1987.

_____. *Love and Life: Fertility and Conception Prevention.* Fourth Edition, Ottawa: SERENA-Canada, 1989.

Paul VI. *On Human Life: Encyclical letter* Humanae Vitae. In *Vatican Council II,* Austin Flannery, ed. Northport: Costello, 1988. Vol. 2, 397-416.

Plenary Assembly of Canadian Catholic Bishops. "Statement on the Encyclical *Humanae Vitae,* 27 September 1968." *Love Kindness,* Edward F. Sheridan, ed. Ottawa: CCCB, 1991, 142-146. See also "Statement on Family Life and Related Matters," *Love Kindness,* 154-155.

Satir, Virginia, John Banmen, Jane Gerber, and Maria Gomori. *The Satir Model: Family Therapy and Beyond.* Palo Alto, CA: Science and Behavior Books, Inc., 1991.

Chapter 7: The Holy Spirit

Congar, Yves. *I Believe in the Holy Spirit.* New York: Crossroad, 1997.

Dunn, James D. G. *The Christ and the Spirit.* Vol. 1: Christology. Grand Rapids, Mich.: Eerdmans, 1998.

Hanh, Thich Nhat. *Being Peace.* Berkeley: Parallax Press, 1996.

Kavanagh, Aiden. *The Shape of Baptism: The Rite of Christian Initiation.* New York: Pueblo Publishing, 1978.

Lash, Nicholas. *Believing Three Ways in One God: A Reading of the Apostles' Creed.* London: SCM Ltd., 1992.

Moltmann, Jurgen. *The Church in the Power of the Spirit.* Translated by Margaret Kohl. London: SCM Press, 1977.

_____. *The Source Of Life: The Holy Spirit and the Theology of Life.* London, SCM Press, 1997.

Montessori, Maria. *The Discovery of the Child.* New York: Ballantine, 1972.

_____. *The Secret of Childhood.* New York: Ballantine, 1972.

Osborne, Kenan. *The Christian Sacraments of Initiation: Baptism, Confirmation, Eucharist.* New York/Mahwah: Paulist Press, 1987.

Rite of Christian Initiation of Adults. Ottawa: CCCB Publication Service, 1987.

Sacred Congregation for Divine Worship. *General Introduction to Christian Initiation.* In *Vatican Council II.* Austin Flannery, ed. Northport: Costello Publishing, 1988. Vol. 2, 22-28, 29-34.

Searle, Mark. *Christening, the Making of Christians.* Essex: Devin Mayhew Ltd., 1977.

World Council of Churches. *Baptism, Eucharist and Ministry.* Geneva: WCC, 1982.

Chapter 8: All Are Called to Holiness

Au, Wilkie. *By Way of the Heart: Towards a Holistic Christian Spirituality.* Mahwah, NJ: Paulist Press, 1989.

Caltagirone, Carmen L. *Friendship as Sacrament*. New York: Alba House, 1988.

Carmody, John. *Toward a Male Spirituality*. Mystic, CT: Twenty-Third Publications.

Chittister, Joan D. *A Passion For Life*. Maryknoll, NY: Orbis, 1996.

Cobb, Jennifer. *Cybergrace: The Search for God in the Digital World*. New York: Crown, 1998.

Conlon, James. *Ponderings from the Precipice: Soul Work for a New Millennium*. Leavenworth, Kansas: Forest of Peace, 1998.

Conn, Joan Wolski. *Spirituality and Personal Maturity*. Mahwah, NJ: Paulist Press, 1989.

Downey, Michael, ed. *New Dictionary of Catholic Spirituality*. Collegeville: Liturgical Press, 1993.

Drewermann, Eugene. *Fonctionnaires de Dieu*. Paris: Editions Albin Michel, 1993.

Fumoleau, René. *The Secret*. Ottawa: Novalis, 1997.

Jager, Willigis. *Search for the Meaning of Life: Essays and Reflections on the Mystical Experience*. Ligouri, MO: Triumph Books, 1995.

Johnson, Elizabeth A. *Friends of God and Prophets: A Feminist Theological Reading of the Communion of Saints*. New York: Continuum, 1998.

Keating, Thomas. *Open Mind Open Heart: The Contemplative Dimension of the Gospel*. New York: Continuum, 1998.

Nouwen, Henri J. M. *Reaching Out: The Three Movements of the Spiritual Life*. New York: Doubleday, 1975.

_____. *The Return of the Prodigal Son: A Story of Homecoming*. New York: Doubleday Image, 1992.

O'Murchu, Diarmuid. *Reclaiming Spirituality: A New Spiritual Framework for Today's World*. New York: Crossroad, 1997.

Rahner, Karl. *On Prayer*. Collegeville: Liturgical Press, 1993.

Raya, Joseph M. *The Face of God: An Introduction to Eastern Spirituality*. Denville, NJ: Dimension Books, 1976.

Wilber, Ken. *No Boundary: Eastern and Western Approaches to Personal Growth*. Boston/London: Shambhala, 1985.

Chapter 9: Together We Remember Who We Are

Cabie, Robert. *History of the Mass.* Translated by Lawrence J. Johnson. Washington, DC: The Pastoral Press, 1992.

Deiss, Lucien. *The Mass.* Collegeville: Liturgical Press, 1989.

Foley, Edward. *From Age to Age: How Christians Celebrated the Eucharist.* Chicago: Liturgical Training Publications, 1991.

Guzie, Tad. *The Book of Sacramental Basics.* New York: Paulist Press, 1981.

Hellwig, Monika. *The Meaning of Sacraments.* Dayton: Pflaum-Standard, 1972.

_____. *The Eucharist and the Hunger of the World.* New York: Paulist Press, 1976.

Heschel, Joshua Abraham. *The Sabbath.* New York: The Noonday Press, 1951.

Stern, David H. *Restoring the Jewishness of the Gospel: A Message for Christians.* Jerusalem/Clarksville, MD: Jewish New Testament Publications, 1990.

_____. *Commentary on the New Testament.* Jerusalem/Clarksville, MD: Jewish New Testament Publications, 1990.

Strassfeld, Michael. *The Jewish Holidays: A Guide and Commentary.* New York: Harper & Row, 1985.

Tillard, J. M. R. *The Eucharist: Pasch of God's People.* New York: Alba House, 1967.

Chapter 10: Gifts Come before Laws

Brady, Patricia. *Has Anything Really Changed? A Study: The Diocese of Victoria since Vatican II.* Victoria, BC: Wood Lake Books Inc., 1986.

Brown, Raymond. *The Churches the Apostles Left Behind.* New York: Paulist Press, 1984.

Brown, Raymond, Karl Donfried, and John Reuman, eds. *Peter in the New Testament.* Minneapolis: Augsburg Publishing, 1973.

Congar, Yves. *Lay People in the Church: A Study for a Theology of Laity.* Westminster, MD: Newman Press, 1967.

Gervais, Pearl, and Grant Maxwell, eds. *Forward in the Spirit: Challenge of the People's Synod.* Victoria, BC: Diocese of Victoria, 1991.

Hillman, Eugene. *Toward an African Christianity, Inculturation Applied.* New York/Mahweh: Paulist Press, 1993.

Hughes, John Jay. *Pontiffs: Popes Who Shaped History.* Huntingdon, IA: Our Sunday Visitor Publications, 1994.

John Paul II. Christifideles Laici: *Vocation and Mission of the Lay Faithful.* Post-Synodal Apostolic Exhortation. Sherbrooke, Que.: Editions Paulines, 1989.

MacEoin, Gary, ed. *The Papacy and the People of God.* Maryknoll, NY: Orbis, 1998.

Mesters, Carlos. *Defenseless Flower: A New Reading of the Bible.* Translated by Francis McDonagh. Maryknoll, NY: Orbis, 1989.

Peelman, Achiel. *Christ Is a Native American.* Ottawa: Novalis, 1995.

Pelton, Robert S., ed. *Small Christian Communities: Imagining Future Church.* Notre Dame, IN: University of Notre Dame Press, 1997.

Tillard, J. M. R. *The Bishop of Rome.* Wilmington, DE: Michael Glazier Inc., 1983.

_____. "The Mission of the Bishop of Rome: What is Essential? What is Expected?" *Ecumenical Trends,* January 1998, 1-10.

Chapter 11: The Reach of the Spirit

Berrin, Susan. *Celebrating the New Moon: A Rosh Chodesh Anthology.* Northvale, NJ: Jason Aronson, 1996.

Botsis, Peter A. *What is Orthodoxy?* Athens/Meteora: Monastery of Varlaam, 1997.

Congar, Yves. *Diversity and Communion.* Mystic, CT: Twenty-Third Publications, 1985.

Dessaux, Jacques. *Twenty Centuries of Ecumenism.* New York/Ramsey, NJ: Paulist Press, 1984.

Fries, H., and Karl Rahner. *Unity of the Churches, an Actual Possibility.* Philadelphia: Fortress Press, 1985.

John Paul II. *Christian Unity:* Encyclical Letter *Ut Unum Sint.* Sherbrooke, Que.: Mediaspaul, 1995.

The Ecumenical Dimension in the Formation of Those Engaged in Pastoral Work. Vatican City: Pontifical Council for the Promotion of Christian Unity, 1998.

Ware, Timothy. *The Orthodox Church.* New York: Penquin Books, 1983.